A Treasury

OF

AMERICAN SONG

A *Treasury*

OF

AMERICAN SONG

TEXT BY Olin Downes AND Elie Siegmeister

MUSIC ARRANGED BY ELIE SIEGMEISTER

THIRD EDITION Revised with a new Introduction

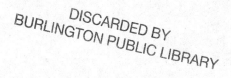
CHERRY LANE MUSIC CO., INC.
Port Chester, New York

Cherry Lane Music Co., Inc.
Port Chester, New York 10573
First Printing Revised Edition 1985

Library of Congress Cataloging in Publication Data

A treasury of American song.

Includes index
1. Folk music—United States.   2. Folk-songs, English—United States.
3. Ballads, English—United States.
I. Downes, Olin, 1886-1955.   II. Siegmeister, Elie, 1909-   arr.
III. Okun, Milton
M1629.T74 1985
ISBN 0-89524-152-8   84-759768

Printed in the United States
of America

Contents

CONTENTS

CONTENTS

CONTENTS

Preface To The Third Edition

MILLIONS OF QUARTER NOTES have flowed under the musical bridge since this book first appeared forty-five years ago. In those days, American song was still an outsider, not yet accepted as part of the great literature of world music. At most, an occasional concert singer would sometimes program one or two native songs (usually Negro spirituals) as a "light touch" at the end of an otherwise "serious" program of European *Lieder* and arias.

It is a sign of the maturing of American culture that in a mere two generations since this volume first appeared the songs springing up from our land-and-city-scapes, those songs that mirrored the populace, their everyday doings, passions, experiences and dreams, have entered the very fabric of our musical life. This has come about in three ways: First, the songs themselves continue to be sung, not only in field and farm, but also in city apartments, schoolrooms, on radio and TV, in concert halls, theaters, and even in an American opera or two. Second, the old-style ballads, blues and vaudeville tunes have continued to evolve in new and ever-changing forms—hillbilly, rhythm-and-blues, country music, gospel songs, rock and theater music, and labor and protest songs of the recent past. And third, American concert composers have continued the pioneering work of Charles Ives and George Gershwin in bridging the gap between "popular" and "serious" styles, Ives in his songs and symphonies, Gershwin in his pop tunes and the masterly *Porgy And Bess*.

Since 1940, American songs have enriched the texture and fiber of some of our finest symphonic music, with Copland (*Appalachian Spring*), Thomson (*Louisiana Story*), Gould (*Spirituals for Orchestra*), Floyd (the opera *Susannah*), Foss (*American Cantata*), Kay (*Southern Harmony*), Colgrass (*Best Wishes, USA*) and many others. American song is a broad stream that, flowing out of the past, nourishes the present, and will no doubt form part of the rich future of American music as a whole.

After more than half a lifetime of labors in the musical vineyard, I am very happy that this book, which has played a seminal role in my own work and possibly that of other American musicians as well, is appearing before the public once more. Olin Downes, had he lived, would likewise have been proud to see our book brought to life again. I hope that it may continue, as in the past, to bring pleasure and pride in our rich heritage to young musicians and just plain people of today who may wish to get a true picture of what this country is all about.

E.S. - August 1984

Introduction
1940 Edition

SAID WHITMAN: "I am multitudes." The songs in this Treasury are those of multitudes and generations who have made America. They have been selected from an overwhelmingly rich store of material with a view to providing informal entertainment. But there is more than that in the matter. If ever there was a time in the history of the nation that our people should know themselves and renew faith in the purposes and traditions which are part of us, that time is now. This faith and these accretions of the national experience are contained in the most characteristic of our songs. They come directly and without intellectual corruption from the people — those, in the homely phrase of Abraham Lincoln, whom God must have loved since He made so many of them! Some of these songs are noble and some comical. Some carry the fragrance and nostalgia of ancestral memory, others are alert, and a-quiver with the audacity and buoyancy of a youthful people. Or they are flippant, waggish, sentimental, capering to the rhythms of the juke-box and the nervous pace of city streets. And some have the cosmic beat of seas and tides, and properly pertain to the culture which produced a Melville and a Whitman. All of them, from far or near, from yesterday or the immemorial ages behind us, are part of the American adventure and the sweep of the national epic.

Yet it has been said that America has no songs; at least few to be identified with us as a people, and still fewer upon which a national musical culture could be founded.

This doctrine, as ill-informed as it is superficial and supercilious, stems from what has been the esthetically narrow and pedantic nature of our higher education, from social and intellectual snobbery, and an unsound attitude toward our native culture on the part of many a professed lover and patron of "good" music. The arenas of prestige, where music was concerned, have been the opera house, the concert hall, the conservatory, and the salon, safe for an unenlightened dillettantism. The notion, advanced by a majority of foreign-born artists and teachers, that there is no such thing as American music has been parroted through the length and breadth of the land, especially by individuals hardly capable of recognizing such a racy and original folk-tune as "Dixie" if they met it walking down the street, and who, even then, would not acknowledge its acquaintance unless the introduction were sponsored by an unquestioied musical authority, preferably a European. These people, who have had too much to do with our culture, would be the last to comprehend the remark of Debussy, that there is one music, which may be present in a waltz or a symphony.

All this time, of course, there was burgeoning, under the surface of officially recognized art, a whole song literature generated by the life of the nation. Throughout America's history, and all the adventures of her peoples, song was being born, not of luxury or cultivated leisure, but from the urgencies of living, from the common tasks and experiences of a nation taking shape in a new land.

Song gave men a common bond in a land where, as late as 1800, the white population over the whole Atlantic seaboard numbered less than the present population of Greater New York; in areas where for long there was only one person for every ten square miles; in communities and on frontiers where a babel of tongues and races, and every rank and type of citizen, were thrown together in the welding of the nation. Under these circumstances, ancestral songs were remembered, new songs were improvised, some fresh-minted, others variants of strains dimly recalled, to serve the expressive needs of farmers, woodsmen, sailors, mechanics, lumberjacks, cowboys, canal-men, those who laid the rails and rode the iron horse. Such melodies became the language alike of the educated and the illiterate, the aristocrat and the commoner. The song was part of the act and the event — of worshipping God, fighting battles, playing games, putting children to sleep, lighting a black wilderness. How could men have marched in the wars, sailed the ships, or laid the rails if the song had not functioned? The New England sea captains never would have hired and paid the chantey men for the sake of esthetic enjoyment. The straw bosses leading Irish laborers on the Union Pacific, or Negro construction gangs on the Baltimore and Ohio, knew the value of a leader whose songs were always worth extra dollars. The songs spread the news and carried the political campaign, made local history, kept flocks together, enlivened a drinking bout, or released emotions of aspiration or revolt or despair.

Do not think that the songs that came out of this turmoil, this epic, this babel of sounds and tongues were all great or artistic. Far from it. These songs have no pride of authorship, no smug polish or conceit of style. They are not belles-lettres, and they do not represent the classical education. They were not written by people trying to be artists. The song served the turn of the moment, or the crisis of the heart. For the song begins where the event stops. One consults the written record for facts which can or cannot be made to speak the spirit of a community or epoch. The songs *are* the spirit of the community or epoch, and as such may constitute the most revealing of our records.

The songs in this collection have been grouped in rough historical and geographical sequence, but without stricter classification. Any more formal design would have been out of keeping with the environment and history that produced them. Had this been a collection made from the folklore of an older country, or a more stratified society, a more precise order might have been attempted. But it is no more possible to pigeonhole the songs of the

American people than it is to discover academic rule in the development of our society or regimentation in the nation's experience.

What shall we call these songs? Have they a generic title?

"Folk-song"? To the modern mind the word may savor of the past, of that which is naïve, archaic, and socially stratified. "Popular song" has a misleading connotation. "American song" is safe though not definitive. What—come down to it—is a folk-song?

The purists distinguish between a so-called "true" folk-song and all other songs that pertain to a nation's melodic literature. They designate a folk-song as a melody of anonymous authorship orally passed from person to person and adopted by a community or nation. But this turns out to be a definition too narrow for practical use. There are many folk-songs of identified authorship which have been welcomed just as warmly as those of unknown origin. In the last analysis the folk-song is the song that a people cherishes and sings. Its ancestral or geographical origins may be dubious. For the seeds of song are flung on the winds to uncounted destinations. If the seed falls on propitious soil, it flourishes. It seldom fails eventually to cross with neighboring species and to produce new growths. No nation in the world can point to an unadulterated musical ancestry, any more than it can point to a blood stream exclusively its own. If the segregation of community from community and nation from nation were a tenable truth, instead of a most destructive theory, we should have a different proposition. But all national music is an amalgam of racial strands and historical processes consequent upon wars, migrations, trade, and other forms of interpenetration. And the richer and more characteristic the folk strains of a people, the more varied and colorful the music is likely to be. Thus in the music of Russia we discern such elements as the Byzantine chant, the Tartar influence, and other melodic currents from Orient and Occident. In Spain the Moorish arabesque is prominent in architecture and music. What shall we say of such a specifically German form as the Lutheran chorale, with its appropriations from folk-songs and many other sources, including the Latin Gregorian chant—that cantillation which, in turn, leans heavily over a stretch of hundreds and thousands of years upon the already ancient chants of the Jewish synagogue! These instances, which could be multiplied in the folk music of every people on earth, are sufficient answer to those who insist that a nation's music must be of ancestral origin and indigenous to the soil, and who demand references and pedigrees before they will acknowledge a folk-song's title to citizenship.

I have referred to the word's social connotation, which is that of society as stratified in the older countries of Europe. There the folk-song was essentially the song of the peasant and the illiterate — in other words, of simple untutored "folk." It is true that the music of the illiterates and the music of educated composers came closer together as society itself became more democratic in its institutions. The days are long past when there was one music for church and court, and another music for the common people. With every great social revolution, such as the French and American revolutions that ushered in the nineteenth century, and the Civil War, accompanied by the freeing of the slaves in America and followed by the freeing of the serfs in Russia, so-called "folk music" and so-called "art music" came nearer together. But it is not until the founding of the American nation, wherein classes, types, and races mingled in a great polyglot, that we perceive the genuine diffusion of democratic essence, not only in our society, but in the body of our national music.

It is not too much to say that the literature of America's popular song is indeed an unparalleled literature of democracy. It has been so through the whole history of the nation, as will be seen in succeeding pages. There are the old Puritan songs of worship, in their original forms predating Bach and Luther. There are the fierce, satirical songs of the Revolutionary period; the sea songs of sailors in Yankee clipper days; the songs of pioneers crossing the Alleghenies and frontier settlements of the Middle West; of the forty-niners climbing the Rockies or rounding Cape Horn; the marching songs of those who followed John Brown's body; the songs of the Negro slaves and of the cowboys who rode the plains; of the dives and the gambling places, and the labor meetings in union halls; of the dust-bowl refugees—that is to say, the "Okies," who, on their weary trek, not ten years ago, sang a new version of the exquisite English folk-song "Barbara Allen," which Samuel Pepys heard and infinitely enjoyed as sung by his friend the actress Mrs. Knipp in the year 1666 — one of the many folk-songs which weave like a golden thread through the rich and tangled tapestry of the nation's experience.

There is inevitably much confusion between the songs migrated here and those which have sprung directly from local sources. Some notable errors and corrections have recently been made in this field by both American and European investigators. When Cecil Sharp made his memorable visit to the Appalachian mountain regions more than a decade ago, he believed that he had found in their isolated communities a treasure trove of unadulterated English song — songs which had vanished centuries previous in England. He did indeed unearth a store of old British melody in a singularly fresh state of preservation. But Mr. Siegmeister has called my attention to such mountain songs as "Ground Hog," "Kentucky Moonshiner," "John Hardy," "Come All You Kansas Girls," which he characterizes as being "as American as corn pone, chewing tobacco, or Boston baked beans." Mistakenly, as it appears, Sharp included these latter as English songs.

On the other hand, a British melody long attributed by hearsay to the Negro—one of the liveliest, wittiest, we might even say "Yankee-est" of the fiddle tunes, "Zip Coon" or "Turkey in the Straw"—is shown by recent research to be in all probability a derivation from an Irish harvesting song of antiquity, "The Old Rose Tree." It is the tune of tunes for the barn dances and break-downs. David Guion, who has made an uncommonly ingenious and effective piano arrangement of it, calls it the "cowboy's national hymn." Once himself a cowboy, he ought to know.

Many new ballads appeared at the time of the opening of the West. Cowboy songs were often derivative, others are justly famed for their originality and their reflection of mood and scene. "The Old Chisholm Trail" is apparently indigenous. The man on the plains knew solitude, and spaces, and death. The words of "Bury me not on the Lone Prairee" are an avatar of the verse of a sea ballad which voiced a similar apprehension of interment in the deep. From a dozen versions of this haunting song, Mr. Siegmeister has chosen one. He could have quoted a hundred. Where do these melodies come from? Who can claim original authorship?

Like all other living languages, folk-song is constantly changing, welling up, as it does from an eternal spring, and undergoing Protean transformations.

An item of this Treasury is the broadside ballad "Captain Kidd," one of the first "bad men" songs to appear on this side of the water soon after the hanging of that gentleman of fortune in London at the beginning of the eighteenth century. Look farther in the volume and you will find a reincarnation of the same tune, altered in pace and rhythmic emphasis, with archaic harmony which admirably fits the quaint pastoral verse with its exquisite picture of God in nature. Another use, indeed, for the old pirate's air, plainly designated in Walker's "Southern Harmony, and Musical Companion," by its rascally title. Incidentally, the choral setting of Walker is not of the easiest to sing, which is testimony to the work of the old singing schools taught by itinerant leaders who went the circuit and trained their weekly classes to the point where they could undertake such a harmonization as the one which Mr. Siegmeister has transferred to his piano accompaniment. How little we of today can know of the earnestness with which those meetings were attended, where they sang without the support of any instrument save the tuning fork—instruments, even the organ, being re-

garded till well into the last century with suspicion, if not abhorrence, by the die-hards of certain sects. My mother remembered well one of these singing schools in Tuckerton, New Jersey, when as a girl she was taught by the circuit leader Will Bentley to "sing alto"; and Isaac Styles, sitting one Sunday in the Amen Pew, rose and left the church at the first sound of the harmonium which my grandmother—arrant revolutionist!—had purchased with the accumulated proceeds of raspberry festivals!

Nor was the part played by the singing schools confined to the interpretative field. A whole important division of our folk music comes from the hymns composed by traveling deacons or singing masters for their classes and congregations—usually anonymous composers whose creations were identified solely by the name of some small village or township where they were produced. The "Putney Hymn" is one of these creations. The profound part that religion played in the daily lives of our forefathers is mirrored unforgettably in this phase of our national song. And if you want to sense the reality of the "old-time religion," listen to the voice of the repentant Baptist minister in the Kentucky hills who expects to die and improvises his moving supplication to his Maker, "Oh, Death"; or to the hymn, perhaps a century older, of the Moravian, Count Zinzendorf, whose song gave Bethlehem, Pennsylvania, present city of steel mills and the Bach Festival, its name; when on a Christmas Eve in the eighteenth century he led his flock to the communal house which sheltered men and beasts alike, and standing, as if before the manger, improvised the chorale beginning: "*Not* Jerusalem, but Bethlehem."

And there are the wonderful songs which echo the impersonality and the mystery of nature. Here river and plain, forest and ocean, speak. When the solitary call of the Mississippi roustabout, "I'm G'wine to Alabamy, Oh," falls upon the ear, it carries the overwhelming sense of the majesty of the great river, the Father of Waters, and the unanswered question of the human lives that have passed their moment on his stream and then vanished as a drop of the current that wends forever to the sea. Or a man pulls on a rope, or works the capstan bar, the while bawling out his complaint of his miserable "dollar and a half a day," and so making a music as grand and cosmic, as eerie and spacious as the ocean waste—the "Lowlands" song—perhaps the one melody in existence that measures to the Homeric line of Melville in the peroration of "Moby Dick": "and the great grey shroud of the sea that rolled on as it had rolled five thousand years ago." An American composer, not so long ago, dared attempt a musical setting of Melville's story. He failed, as nearly any composer would be certain to do. If, for his orchestral finale, he had simply quoted that melody, he could have gone far toward saving the day.

But we may admit that of all the phenomena of folk-song in our midst none seems to partake so completely of the nature of the miraculous as the Negro spiritual. The attempt to explain this product as merely a Negro adaptation of the hymns of the whites is a grudging acknowledgment which does not explain at all. Few if any white hymns have their melodic poignancy or richness of color, and individuality of design. In preceding paragraphs processes by which melodies are gradually transformed in the crucible of a people's consciousness, usually over a long period of time, have been mentioned. Here is a music which has sprung up and reached a mysterious perfection, comparatively speaking, in a night. Once, to a question of mine concerning the breeding of plants, the naturalist Luther Burbank replied that he could combine very distant species by slowly breeding them toward each other, gradually developing in each of them certain common characteristics, and at last establishing the new form. Even when the new plant-form was established it had to be fixed for at least fifteen generations before it could be considered a permanent stock. Here is a unique and wholly unprecedented growth of folk melody, consequent upon the proximity of two races as opposite as they well could be in physique, tradition, circumstances, and with the strongest of social and racial barriers between them. And

out of these apparently inimical conditions the glorious song comes to flower.

I cannot dilate here upon the sheer poetry of texts improvised from Biblical suggestions, and the beauty of the language in which there is no single dry or ugly sound. The race which created the thunderous "Go Down, Moses," or "Deep River," or "Swing Low, Sweet Chariot," with its mystical swing upwards on the second line: "Comin' for to carry me home"—those "whispers of heavenly death"—that thought of the home in the sky has injected a most potent influence into the nation's music. Needless to say, not all the Negro spirituals are on the same serious and exalted plane. Many of them have the most amusing rhythms and descriptive effects, and are exuberantly gay. With their authors, religion is such a reality that they find everything in it, from poetical myth to orgiastic rejoicing, childlike joy. And by no means are all Negro songs spirituals, as any glance at their literature and their by-products in various forms of contemporaneous musical expression will immediately show. What is invaluable to art, and past emulation by another race, is the truthfulness and spontaneity of their musical utterances. The greatest of American poets once said that he would permit no conventions to come between him and the truth; that he would seek to reflect in his poems the careless and unimpeachable rectitude of the animals and plants—the truth of nature. This uninhibited rectitude is present, inimitably, in Negro song. Its range of subject matter is unlimited. For these people make song of anything—any sight or sound, event, personality, movement or gesture, whether of the dance or the breathing and heaving of the convict laborers on the Georgia roads. And this new freedom has had an extremely beneficial and leavening effect upon American music, and indeed upon modern music everywhere. To our musicians, composers and performers, as to the plain man in the street, it has brought creative liberation and release. Indeed, it is hardly stretching the point to say that if the white American, after oppressing the black one, gave him back freedom and citizenship in certain and varying degrees, the Negro has reciprocated by freeing the white man's art from a long period of regimentation and domination by foreign tradition.

I have spoken thus far of certain folk-songs of anonymous origin. No greater tribute to artistic genius could be rendered than to remark that by the side of these we can place certain songs of identified authorship, by composers simple and great enough to speak with native eloquence for their fellow creatures and strike immortally the universal note. No doubt the greatest of these in the literature of America—great despite weaknesses and manifest inequalities of his contributions—was Stephen Foster. The songs of this most touching lyrical poet breathe the sentiment of beloved scenes when American life was still, in the main, a rural existence, and when we were not as a nation sophisticated and debunked. The best Foster songs forever enshrine these things. His genius mated poetry and music. The quality of his inspiration, at its highest, completely transcended his technical limitations and gave the world certain matchless lyrical outpourings which speak alike to the lowly and the great, and have traversed the world and can never die. The folk quality of his inspiration is manifest in the character of the songs and their reception by the people. Indeed, Foster would be fairly a folk composer if only for the fact that Christy and others bought or purloined his creations and kept the true authorship of them a secret as long as possible. But the songs needed no signature.

Nor would that reckless, skirling song of the American spirit, Dan Emmett's "Dixie"! As Foster's songs are essentially songs of a dreamer and a homeland, so is Emmett's the music of the wanderer and the debonair challenger of the unknown. It is the laughing, high-spirited, nervous-paced song that only an American could conceive. It is the glorious song that Dan Emmett, the blacksmith's son, the typesetter, the fife and drum boy in the Civil War, was asked to write for the walk-around of next Monday's show. So he sat down with a bit of paper and whittled out that glorious air as naturally as a Yankee farmer whittles a piece of wood among his cronies in the grocery store. It is the tune which tells us anew that whereas an Englishman enters a house as if he owned it, the American enters as if he doesn't care who in hell owns it. The song went around the world like wild fire, and the finest tribute that could be paid Dan Emmett when he died was extended him. He was buried in his minstrel clothes, and "Dixie" was played as he was lowered into the grave. . . .

I shall not soon forget my impatience, one night in 1932, in Tiflis, when, having sought sedulously for days and nights to discover some real Caucasian music, I induced the leader of a native orchestra to play some local dances and airs, only to have him break off after a few perfectly fascinating tunes, and launch with most mistaken zeal into an out-of-date sample of jazz, palpably bearing what we could call a fly-specked label of Tin Pan Alley, U. S. A. I jumped up and left the place, only to be pursued by an orchestra player who could speak a little English, and to hear myself entreated, through this translator, to send back to his director, when I returned home, a few fox trots, intensely craved by the Caucasian public, from dear old Broadway! That the gentleman was thus willing, more than willing, to exchange his birthright for foreign pottage; that, in so doing, he was emulating precisely the attitude of genuflection in the presence of imported goods that I deplore in my own countrymen, is for present purposes beside the mark. The case is cited merely to point out the astonishing vitality and allure of our popular dance music, permeated with Negroid elements, as demonstrated in a community not of worldlings or enlightened internationalists, but of simple and relatively untutored folk in a far distant land. As for the eagerness and interest shown in this American manifestation by the leading composers of Europe—Debussy and Ravel, Hindemith and Stravinsky, et al.— it speaks for itself, and supplies a highly suggestive commentary on the state of our music, and theirs. The freshness of the idiom did not suffice to breathe creative life into artistic expressions of a culture that was weary and decadent, nearly defunct, whereas in America, first by our professional jazz composers, secondly by creators of individual rank, from Henry F. Gilbert and John Alden Carpenter to George Gershwin of the "Rhapsody in Blue" and other scores in the same direction, the rhythmic and harmonic attributes of jazz enabled them to build structures of their own, on the basis of the native product. Once and for all, despite structural weaknesses and a limited technique, George Gershwin put to rout, with the twist, the color, and the rhythmical novelty of the opening theme of the famous "Rhapsody," the often repeated contention that a jazz tune could·never escape monotony of rhythm and conventionality of pattern and style. He opened the door to the possibility of developments of jazz motives, in ways that had not been indicated before, and in so doing furnishes a striking demonstration of the process at work in our musical culture which is progressing in an ascending spiral from the ground up, and not, if one may so put it, from the ceiling down.

The principles of this growth are manifested by the varieties of folk-song as they have been designated by specialists in the field. There are three phases through which the folk-song principle manifests itself, just as there are three corresponding phases through which the musical culture of a nation passes, in its evolution from that of a folk art to the most individual and highly specialized manifestation.

In the case of the folk-song: (1) The oldest songs, of unknown authorship, which have become traditional with the community. (2) The folk-song, by an identified composer, which finds the same acceptance and fulfills the same mission as the one of anonymous origin. And finally, (3) what some call the "composed" folk-song—that is, the song written with deliberate intent in the folk spirit and style, by the sophisticated composer. "Barbara Allen," "Hangsaman," or any one of the great Negro spirituals is an example of the first type; "Dixie" or "My Old Kentucky Home," of the second; and, let us say, "Ol' Man River," a

song consciously in the folk vein, and already a part of our musical folklore, from Jerome Kern's "Showboat," is a third. It will be seen how the individuality of the purposeful composer gradually emerges in this ascending spiral of artistic development.

In the broader process of the evolution of a nation's musical culture, there occur three parallel stages. The first is the escape from the domination of foreign influence by the cultivation of folk music, songs in simple forms of the native land. The second phase is the one in which folk melodies are used as basic thematic material and points of departure for development by individual composers of advanced craftsmanship. Such composers as Dvorák, Grieg, Smetana, Rimsky-Korsakov employ folk motives of their people in this way, and whole schools of national composition have arisen on this basis. A third evolutionary stage is reached when, in the hands of such masters and individualists as Wagner or Sibelius, the melodic insignia of race and nation disappear, to be transformed and sublimated in a way which is a distillation of the popular expressions, in forms of highly developed art.

Glinka, the founder of the Russian national school, had this evolution in mind when he said that it was really the people who composed, while the individual composer only arranged what they had already created. He was defining the great truth that no individual is an entity separate from his fellows or apart from his time, environment, and ancestral background; and that the most highly individualized art, if sincere and inspired, is but a fulfillment of the thought and vision of the race. There are, of course, those who completely contradict such a theory. They claim that it is men, and not man, who make history and create new worlds; that art in its greatest aspects is not a national but an international expression; that localism means provincialism and a sterile isolation from which nothing of broad meaning or universal significance can arise. So far as one observer can discern, real art never grew that way. Science, in very essence impersonal, which often employs a terminology not even that of a living tongue for purposes of definition and standardization, deals with absolutes and formulæ of international application.

But art is the most local and personal expression that humanity knows. It must always be the mirror of individual experience—the world as the artist sees it. Nothing else will suffice for his—and our—creative need.

In the past twenty-five years, art music in America has developed in a most impressive manner, and this with a rapidity and distribution probably unparalleled in a like period of time in the history of any other nation. This is extremely impressive, but much more impressive if we properly understand its profound significance is the growth of our native and untutored art and the part that the spirit of our nation plays in it. It is good that this process is gradual and real in the life of our people. I deem it more fortunate than otherwise that the average American still deprecates his knowledge of art and protests that it is something rather beyond him and his experience. It is good that he will not deceive himself in these matters, that as a class he refuses to read a book or gaze at a picture or listen to an opera or symphony which does not say something to him. He tells you that he doesn't understand Schönberg and Stravinsky very well, and that for his enjoyment he's mainly obliged to fall back on the songs that he hears on the street and in the theaters, or the older melodies that he learned from his father and mother.

He is absorbing his music from the ground up and not the other way around. He is not being instructed in art for purposes of class education or snobbish, sterile, superficial culture. Only today, through the development of orchestras and machines of transmission, is he becoming aware that the great foreign composers, whom he has held in such awe, also wrote for him and for their fellow men in terms of a highly developed utterance which nevertheless had its true roots, just as he has his, in the common speech, the common thought, the common life and experience.

A hundred years ago Emerson cried out against American minds which still occupied themselves, to the exclusion of their own intellectual possessions, with "the sere remains of foreign harvests." He wanted a national and a democratic literature. He said: "I ask not for the great, the remote, the romantic; what is doing in Italy or Arabia; what is Greek art, or Provençal minstrelsy; I embrace the common; I explore and sit at the feet of the familiar, the low."

Thus the poet and philosopher. Listen in turn to the words of an American composer, the late Henry F. Gilbert: "As the spirit of the composer is truly great, it will be found to have drawn its deepest inspiration from that spirit of the folk which gave birth to the folk songs, and to bear a deep and fundamental relation to the latter . . . for it is the function of genius to contribute to that folk-spirit from which it sprang, that the folk may ever rise to new horizons of power and beauty." We must follow that course.   O. D.

About the Music

In their native environment, folk songs are sometimes sung to guitar or banjo accompaniment, but far more often, without any harmony whatsoever. In such cases, the physical surroundings, the setting of the scene—whether it be railroad embankment, riverside shack, or mountain still—seem to complete the picture and make any other background unnecessary. But when lifted out of their natural setting and placed in the (to them) strange and bare atmosphere of the printed page, the simple melodies are often ill at ease. In composing the settings for these songs, I have preserved the tunes intact, while adding a harmonic background in the piano intended to suggest the color originally provided by the physical background.

I have tried to compose settings that would fit the special environment in which each song arose. I have used as a guide historical and human clues arising out of the texts rather than any abstract musical rules. But often it was the tunes themselves that dictated the type of harmonization.

In the case of composed songs by Billings, Law, Emmett, Foster, Work, and others, I often found the original arrangements for one reason or another unfitted to the purposes of this book. Wherever possible I have adapted the choral or piano harmonies of the original setting, but I have not hesitated to compose entirely new arrangements when I felt they were needed.

For instance, the "Battle Hymn of the Republic" (John Brown's Body) as it is generally arranged in the traditional four part text-book harmony gives more the feeling of a Sunday school hymn tune than the militant song that men chanted while marching into battle. In my setting I have tried to catch the feeling of trumpets and drums, of raucous voices rising above the sounds of war.

In setting "Heave Away," I felt it should have the unfettered quality of strong men hard at work; in "Gwine to Alabamy" I thought of far-away, primitive voices floating over a wide river. In "Ground-hog" I heard the scrape of a lively fiddle; in "Oh Susannah," the rasping twang of banjos at a minstrel show; in "Alabado" the medieval seclusion of an old mission.

In some cases the harmonies may sound unconventional—there I have made them so because the songs themselves have come out of lives that have been strange and unconventional. Most of the songs in this book do not come out of the studio, the salon, the concert hall where the traditions of smooth, pleasant, euphonious musical style originated. The convict on a rock pile, the cowboy yelling at his herd, the farmer at a Saturday night barn dance, think little and care less about beautiful tone quality, blended harmonic colors, smooth phrasing—all those esthetic qualities that city people have come to expect from "good music." I have not tried to "civilize" the melodies that have come up out of the soil by dressing them up in polite, well-behaved harmonies. Where I heard the melodies raucous I made the accompaniment equally so; where they are lyrical and sentimental, I have let the piano be so, too.

Of course, these harmonies are made as I felt them. Others will feel otherwise. They are welcome, and urged, to "roll their own." The same applies to all the indications of tempo, rhythm, dynamics, etc. They are intended as guides, and should be (and I have no doubt, will be) constantly disregarded by those who hear and see the songs differently. Folk music is flexible that way. Sung fast or slow, high or low, loud or soft, with sweet voices or way off pitch, it still manages to survive.

As to the melodies themselves: they are in all cases given exactly as I heard them sung or found them recorded, except in those cases where there were grossly obvious mistakes in notation. In some cases an obviously faulty barring has been rearranged,* in others, complex notation simplified.† In a few cases, the time values of an entire piece have been halved, ‡ as the old notation when played by pianists of average ability gave a far slower reading than the real tempo of the piece, as played and sung today, calls for. In one case ("David's Lamentation") the original time values have been doubled for the opposite reason.

However, it must be borne in mind that notations of folk music on paper can be only approximations at best. Those who have heard two folk singers sing the same song, or even have heard the same singer do the same number twice, know that there is not, and cannot be, any fixed or final version of any folk song, for the reason that this music by its very nature is ever varying, changing, growing. Unlike the composer, who sets his musical thoughts down on paper, thereby fixing the relationship of its tones and rhythms forevermore, the folk singer is constantly and instinctively adding to the songs he sings, embellishing them, changing them as his mood and memory dictate. In some singers the element of reproductive memory is strongest; in others personality and imagination play a larger role and from these we are apt to get so much unconscious variation and conscious improvisation that it is often a question whether their versions of old songs are really the old songs or something entirely new.

Songs keep on being born and disappearing with the seasons. Some melodies preserve their vitality over long periods of time, and the his-

tory of the various verses which are set to them is almost the history of a people.* Others flare up for a time, answering to the need of a moment, and vanish; among these may be some very beautiful and valuable ones.† Others disappear when the type of life or activity which called them into being and with which they are associated, dies out. ‡

At any rate, the selection of one version of a song rather than another can only be made on the basis of following one's musical instinct. And that, for better or worse, is what I have done.

The same holds true regarding the selection of verses accompanying many of the songs. Many folk songs have fluid texts: words which vary with almost every performance, or whole verses which come in or go out with the greatest of ease. Words of one song are often found tacked on to an entirely different tune. Sometimes roving verses or "floaters" are found which turn up in several different songs, often when you least expect them. Some songs have almost endless verses, for use on varying occasions (the record being held apparently by "Skip to My Lou" of which 160 verses are said to have been recorded). It is obviously impossible to print all the verses of all the songs. As in the case of the tunes, selection has been made on the basis of singability, value as Americana, variety and broad human appeal.

There is another reason why any written recording of our traditional music is always less than satisfying. That is because the true folk singer knows little and cares less about 4/4 time or do-re-mi-fa-sol. He often sings in a scale that is neither major nor minor, nor any other that can be played on the piano. Instead of singing whole or half tones, he often hits in between them, and the sliding pitches, the sudden catches, quirks and scoops in the voice, the characteristic intonations, form al-

---

* As in "The Dying Californian."
† The original notation of "John Hardy" contained double sharps!
‡ As in "Old Joe Clarke."

* I.e. "Yankee Doodle," "John Brown's Body."
† The runaway slave song, "Link O'Day," for example.
‡ The sea shanties, which passed from the status of active, functional music to that of entertainment and even of concert songs, when the old time sailing boats operated by manual labor gave way to the steamboat.

most the essence of folk style. These our common system of notation is utterly inadequate to express.

However it is the one we must rely on, if the music is to be read and played. We offer it therefore with one suggestion: when you sing the songs here presented, do not hesitate to "worry," embroider, or embellish the notes you see recorded, let the spirit move you!

E. S.

ACKNOWLEDGMENT

Completion of this volume would not have been possible without the advice and assistance of Hannah Siegmeister and Lou Cooper. To them warmest thanks! And, of course, as in all anthologies, there are the many publishers, song-collectors, composers, and copyright-holders to whom we are deeply indebted for permission to reprint published and unpublished material.

E. S.

Plymouth Rock to Bunker Hill

[PILGRIM, COLONIAL SONGS, EARLY BALLADS]

FOR A LONG TIME it has been customary to look upon the first hundred and fifty years of white settlement on this continent as a period of complete cultural barrenness. Our forefathers—so the conventional story goes—were a dour, hard-working, God-fearing lot, who veered away from art and pleasure as devilish, and whose entire musical experience lay in the singing of a few dreary hymn tunes on Sundays, in between stretches of interminable sermons breathing repentance and hellfire.

Like all popular traditions, this one has a large element of truth. Early Plymouth and Salem were certainly no Viennas. There were no operas, no concerts, no chamber music in the homes. But modern scholarship has revealed the fact that the non-musicality of our early ancestors has been greatly exaggerated. The Pilgrim Fathers considered music so important that, while refugees in Holland and only several hundred strong, they brought out a special Psalm-book of their own.

Sung in Plymouth, many of these psalms were of rare musical beauty, and were sung in lively and sparkling rhythms, with robust, hearty accents. As Carleton Sprague Smith has pointed out, psalm-singing was not only an act of worship, but "the favorite pastime at social gatherings" as well. Complex, madrigal-like versions of the psalms—for whose performance a high degree of musical skill was required—were sung in some early New England homes.

The period of earliest English colonization—the first decades of the seventeenth century—was the height of the great musical Renaissance in the mother country. It was the time of Byrd, Gibbons and Morley, when every Gentleman was an amateur musician, expected to be able to sing madrigals at sight. No doubt the Cavaliers who settled Virginia and the South brought with them this high musicality, for it was in the South that, some time later, the first recorded performance of an opera took place, the first musical society was founded, the first regular playhouse established.*

Meanwhile, both in New England and in the South, the practice of ballad-singing was being actively pursued and folk song culture was in a flourishing state, as the repeated fulminations of the clergy against it inform us. As early as 1625, John Cotton inveighed against "lascivious dancing to wanton ditties, and amorous gestures and wanton dalliances." An early Plymouth court register recorded that one Mercy Tubbs "was to answer for mixed dancing." Almost a century later, Cotton Mather was still thundering from the pulpit against the "foolish songs and ballads" which "hawkers and peddlers carry into all parts of the country." These songs were apparently so attractive and popular that other New England preachers, adopting a different technique from Mather's, set up music committees in their congregations to gather the more appealing profane melodies to be fitted out with holy words and used as hymns—thus reviving the earlier practice of Martin Luther, who had said, "Why should the Devil have all the good tunes?"

Many of these popular ballads brought over by the early colonists from Europe recorded news events of the day. One of these related in song the story of the famous pirate Captain Kidd. Others dealt at length and in great detail with the loves and intrigues of noble lords and ladies. Singing the long narrative ballads was one of the few available forms of entertainment and pastime, and it provided not only "heart interest," but often was the only

*According to John Tasker Howard in "Our American Music."

means of passing on historical and other information. Songs also served for dancing, playing games, courting, spreading news, political comment, satire, scandal and what not.

While the circulation of these ballads was not as immediate as the popularization of songs today by radio, they were spread very widely throughout the thirteen colonies. Printed on sheets known as broadsides, in editions of many thousands, they were sold by peddlers in both town and country, at the democratic price of one penny. Collections of these ballads were imported to Boston in the 1680's, indicating that there must have been a large demand for them even before that date.

The appeal of these ballads in their day must have been as great as that of our own popular song hits. But unlike ours, they did not fade out with the passing season; they have been handed down by word of mouth for more than three hundred years, and are still found today in separated places such as Vermont, Florida, Michigan, Virginia and Texas. Their historical importance lies in the fact that they reveal a love of excitement and gaiety and a passion for romance not ordinarily associated with our early colonial forefathers. Their nature, too, shows that they were popular among the common people, where, perhaps, the strictures and restraints of a highly moral life were not so stern as among the righteous of the better classes. True, many of these ballads were originally brought over from Europe, but they have been so radically changed in the course of their transit from mouth to mouth that they have become thoroughly American in intonation and may be regarded as an integral part of our national culture.

Some of the earliest broadside ballads printed in this country can be identified as the work of known authors. Among these were two written in 1718 by a nine-year-old boy, Benjamin Franklin. Later he told of it: ". . . my brother . . . put me on composing occasional ballads. One was called the *Lighthouse Tragedy* . . . and the other was a sailor's song, on the taking of Teach (or Blackbeard) the pirate. They were wretched stuff, in the Grub Street ballad style; and when they were printed he sent me about the town to sell them. The first sold wonderfully, the event being recent, having made a great noise." *

However, we have no record of contemporary composers of the tunes, if any. The first record of any original music written in this country comes from another source. This was the settlement of German mystics in the then wilderness of eastern Pennsylvania. One of their number, Johannus Kelpius, wrote the words and music of a series of hymns, called by the lugubrious title of "The Colloquium of the Soul with Itself" in 1697. Some forty years later, however, the first highly organized musical culture took root in America with the founding of the town of Bethlehem, Pennsylvania, by Moravian refugees from Switzerland and Germany. Although occupied with the most arduous tasks of clearing the wilderness and settling it, these early Americans found time every day for a *Singstunde*—an hour of communal singing.

Skilled musicians instructed the people in the art of choral singing, and formed them into such unusual instrumental ensembles as trombone quartets. Bethlehem was the first truly musical community in the United States, for it is recorded that the people worshipped, worked and played to music. In 1787, when New England divines were still debating whether or not congregational singing was fitting in the house of God, a little girl wrote, from her boarding school in Bethlehem: "I play the guitar twice a day; am taught the spinet and forte piano, and sometimes I play the organ." †

Early Bethlehem composers were the first to write music in the larger forms of cantata, string quartet, sonata, etc., in this country. But to this community music was not only entertainment or religion, it was a practical help in daily life. The constant fear of the early settlers was from attack and massacre by the In-

* Franklin: "Autobiography."

† Quoted by John Tasker Howard: "Our American Music."

24

dians. One Christmas Eve in the 1740's the story goes that news was brought to the settlement that a band of Indians had surrounded and was planning to attack and annihilate the colonists. With the ingenuity of pioneers, the people decided to send their trombone choir into the loft of the meeting house to play hymns, believing the unusual sounds would impress the superstitious Indians. The four trombonists played through the holy night, and at dawn the savages had vanished. They thought the awesome harmonies were the warning voice of some great deity.

Whether or not the story is true, it can stand as a symbol of the place of music in the big job of building America.

E. S.

WHO IS THE MAN?

Arrangement by Elie Siegmeister

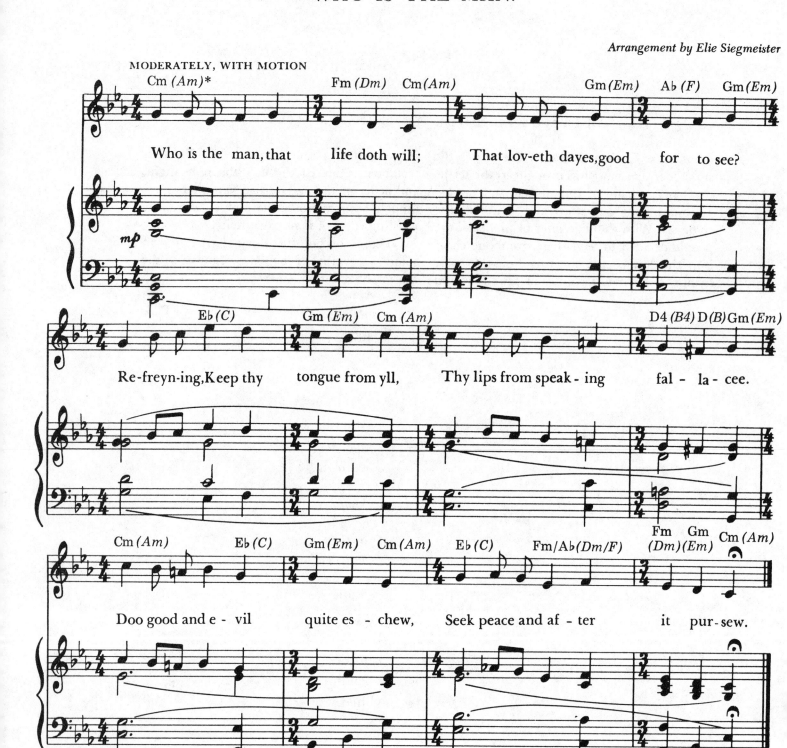

MODERATELY, WITH MOTION

Who is the man, that life doth will; That lov-eth dayes, good for to see?

Re-freyn-ing, Keep thy tongue from yll, Thy lips from speak - ing fal - la - cee.

Doo good and e - vil quite es - chew, Seek peace and af - ter it pur-sew.

2

In all time bless the LORD will I
His praise within my mouth, alway.
My soul shall in the LORD glory;
The meek shall heare, and joy shall they.
O magnifie the LORD with me
His name together extoll we.

3

I sought JAH (Jehovah) and he me answered;
And from my fears all, rid me free.
To Him they looked and flowed;
And ashamed let not their faces bee.
JAH heard when this poor man did call:
And saved him from his troubles all.

* Chord symbols in italics for guitar with capo across 3rd fret.

4

Jehovah's angel camp doth lay,
'bout them that fear him; and frees them.
Taste ye and see that good is JAH:
O bless man, that hopes in him.
Fear ye Jehovah, saints of His:
For to his fearers, want none is.

Evil shall cause the wicked die:
And haters of the just man, they
Shall be condemned as guilty.
His servants soul, redeem doth JAH:
And they shall not be judged unjust,
All that in him for safety trust.

WHO IS THE MAN?

THIS GRAND old tune came to America across continents, seas and centuries. It sounded through the trials and portents of the fateful Pilgrim voyage of 1620, and may well have rung across the waters of Plymouth harbor during the service conducted on the Mayflower by Elder Brewster on the cold Sunday in December, when a landing could not be made, and the faithful "cried out unto the Lord and He heard their voyce and looked upon their adversitie." For "Who is the Man?" was one of the hymns of the Ainsworth Psalter, the only book of printed music which the Pilgrims brought with them to America. Longfellow, in "The Courtship of Miles Standish," sees to it that John Alden, bearing the Captain's message, finds Priscilla with the volume on her knees.

Open wide on her lap lay the well-worn psalm-book of Ainsworth
Printed in Amsterdam, the words and the music together,
Rough-hewn, angular notes, like stones in the wall of a churchyard,
Darkened and overhung by the running vine of the verses.

The melody of "Who is the man?" is an ancient European folk-song which served Luther in 1539 for his chorale version of the Lord's Prayer. J. S. Bach treated it in fully a dozen different ways and included it in the score of his "Passion according to St. John." The Ainsworth version of the tune dates from the time when music was written without bar-lines. These Mr. Siegmeister has supplied, indicating the rhythmic design in alternating 4-4 and 3-4 measures.

CONFESS JEHOVAH

Arrangement by Elie Siegmeister

LIVELY, JOYFUL

Con-fess Je-ho-vah thank-ful-ly. For He is good; for, His mer-cy

Con-tin-u-eth for-ev-er. To God of Gods con-fesse doe ye:

Be-cause, His boun-ti-ful mer-cie Con-tin-u-eth for-ev-er.

Un-to the Lord of Lords con-fess Be-cause His mer-ci-ful kind-ness

28

2

To Him that spread the earth more high
Than waters are: for His mercy
Continueth forever.
To Him that made great lights to bee:
Because His bountiful-mercie
Continueth forever.
The sun to have the soveraigntie
By day: for His benigne-mercie
Continueth forever.
The moon and starrs for soveraigntie
By night: for His benigne-mercie
Continueth forever.

3

To Him that with their firstborn-race
Smote Egypt: for His bounteous grace
Continueth forever.
And Israel bring forth did Hee
From mids of them: for, His mercie
Continueth forever.
With strong hand, and arm stretched-high:
Because His bountiful-mercie
Continueth forever.
To Him that parted the Red Sea
In parts: because, His kind-mercie
Continueth forever.

4

And caused Israel through to passe
Amids it: for, His bounteous grace
Continueth forever.
And threw Pharoh and his armie
In the Red Sea: for His mercie
Continueth forever.
To Him that in the wilderness
Did lead his folk: for His kindness
Continueth forever.
To Him, that kings of greatness-high
Did smite: for, His benigne-mercie
Continueth forever.

NOT ALL or even the greater number of the Puritan hymns were sung lugubriously. In most cases they were intoned with emphasis and vigor. And look at this tune, also from the Ainsworth Psalter. A lively tune, if no worse! A tune in which the godly might sniff brimstone, and mutter of "Geneva jigs." Even is it rumored that some of these psalm-tunes found their way out the church door, and could be heard echoing from taverns, to the accompaniment of unseemly mirth and the guzzling of strong waters. This melody had more than one association. It was known to the early Lutherans as a "Strassbourg tune," and in their French version became a war-song of the Huguenots. Chanted thus in camp and battlefield it earned the title in a later century of the "Huguenot Marseillaise." Though the text sits clumsily upon it, the two-fisted energy and forthrightness of the music may well have sustained the faithful through the trials and vicissitudes of life in the new land. Of such are the adventures of a folk-song!

ROSA

THIS SONG comes from the Dutch colony of New Amsterdam, where they were a little less afraid of merriment than in the colonies further north. In this locality, and very early, was to be found a diverse selection not only of hymns but of popular songs, ballads, dances, and children's games from the old world. The simplicity and innocence of the melody is that of an earlier time and perhaps a simpler and happier people than our own—today.

3

Rosa, let us get married, married, married.
Rosa, let us get married, O Rosa sweet!
Rosa with her hat of flowers
Has little wealth but happy hours,
And dances sweetly.
Rosa, let us get married, married, married.
Rosa, let us get married, O Rosa sweet!

3

Rosa, willen wy trowen? Trouwt Rosa, trouwt Rosa.
Rosa, willen wy trowen? Trouwt Rosa, zoet!
Rosa med haer bloemenhoed—
Zy had de geld, maer weining good;
Danst Rosa zoet!
Rosa, willen wy trowen? Trouwt Rosa, trouwt Rosa.
Rosa, willen wy trowen? Trouwt Rosa, zoet!

ROSA

Arrangement by Elie Siegmeister

2

Rosa, will you be mine now, mine now, mine now?
Rosa, will you be mine now, O Rosa sweet!
Rosa with her hat of flowers
Has little wealth but happy hours,
And dances sweetly.
Rosa, will you be mine now, mine now, mine now?
Rosa, will you be mine now, O Rosa sweet!

2

Rosa, willen wy minnen? Mint Rosa, mint Rosa.
Rosa, willen wy minnen? Mint Rosa, zoet!
Rosa med haer bloemenhoed—
Zy had de geld, maer weining good;
Danst Rosa zoet!
Rosa, willen wy minnen? Mint Rosa, mint Rosa.
Rosa, willen wy minnen? Mint Rosa, zoet!

LOWLY BETHLEHEM

Words by Count Zinzendorf
Music traditional
Arrangement by Elie Siegmeister

CALM AND FLOWING

Not Je - ru - sa - lem low - ly Beth - le - hem, 'Twas that gave us Christ to
Nicht Je - ru - sa - lem, son - dern Beth - le - hem Hat be - scher - et was uns

save us. Not Je - ru - sa - lem fa - vored Beth - le - hem, Ho - nored
nähr - et; nicht Je - ru - sa - lem, werth - es Beth - le - hem. Du bist

is that name. Thence came Je - sus to re - lease us, Fa - vored Beth - le - hem.
an - ge - nehm Aus dir kom - met was uns from - met, werth - es Beth - le - hem.

THIS SONG has a remarkable story. It is said to have been improvised on Christmas Eve, December 24, 1741, on a momentous occasion when the neighbors had gathered from miles around to celebrate their holiday in the first house that the Moravians had built in the town now known as Bethlehem, Pennsylvania. This house, in its humble way, served almost the mission of the medieval cathedrals of Europe. It was a house adapted to purposes of worship as well as shelter and defense against foes for man and beast. People lived in one part of it, and their animals in another. The question had arisen and was being hotly debated as to whether the town—which now has fame as the site of the steel industry on one hand and the Moravian church where the famous annual Bach festivals are held on the other—should be named Jerusalem or Bethlehem. The story goes that in the midst of the service the leader of the community, Count Zinzendorf, who had a remarkable gift of extemporization, arose, and leading his followers to where the cattle were kept, improvised the melody and the words which begin "Not Jerusalem—lowly Bethlehem, 'twas that gave us Christ to save us." And the narrative goes on to assert that the gathering was so profoundly moved that the name of Bethlehem was decided upon that night. This is believed to be one of hundreds of melodies composed in the spirit and style of the German chorale that were created by the German-Moravians who settled early in this country.

BARBARA ALLEN

Arrangement by Elie Siegmeister

'Twas in the mer - ry__ month of May,___ When all gay flo - wers were__ bloom-ing, Sweet Wil - liam on his__ death bed lay For the love of Bar - b'ra__ Al -len.

2

He sent a servant to the town
Where Barbara, she was dwellin'.
"My master's sick and sends for you
If your name be Barb'ra Allen."

3

So slowly, slowly she got up,
And slowly went unto him,
And all she said when she got there:
"Young man, I think you're dyin'."

4

"Yes, I am sick and low indeed
And death is on me dwellin';
No better, no better will I ever be
If I don't get Barb'ra Allen."

5

"Sir, do you remember the other night
In a gathering over yonder
You gave your gifts to all around,
And slighted Barb'ra Allen?"

6

"Now you are sick and low indeed,
And death is in your dwellin';
No better, no better will you be
for you'll not get Barb'ra Allen."

7

He turned his face unto the wall,
While death was creeping o'er him;
He bid his friends adieu, and said:
"Be kind to Barb'ra Allen."

8

She hadn't got more than a mile from the place
Till she heard the death-bells ringing—
A ring and knock at ev'ry door,
Crying, "Woe to Barb'ra Allen."

9

She looked to the east, she looked to the west,
She saw the corpse a-coming.
"Set the lowly corpse down here
And let me look upon him."

10

"Go dig my grave both wide and deep,
Oh, dig it deep and narrow
Sweet William died for me in love
I'll die for him in sorrow."

11

Sweet William was buried in the high churchyard,
And Barbara buried by him,
And out of his grave grew a blood red rose
And out of her's a briar.

12

They grew and grew to the steeple top
Till they could grow no higher;
They lapped and tied in a true love knot—
The rose around the briar.

BARBARA ALLEN

IT WAS an embarrassing problem to make a final choice for this volume
of the innumerable versions to be found in America of the exquisite song
about the love and cruelty and the tragic fate of Sweet William and
Barbara Allen. The melody, which is that of an old Scottish folk song, is
one of the greatest treasures of the folk lore of Britain.

Pepys heard it from the lips of Mrs. Knipp, the actress, in 1666. "In
perfect pleasure I was to hear her sing, and especially her little Scotch
song of Barbary Allen." Goldsmith was "sung into tears" by it. It is no
wonder that the song has haunted the memory of men wherever the
descendants of the British people went in America. "Barbara Allen"
was found in the Kentucky mountains by Cecil Sharp. Helen Harkness
Flanders and George Brown have found many variants in Vermont and
other of the New England states. Innumerable forms of the melody are
to be heard today in Mississippi, Georgia, and Nebraska. Ninety-eight
versions have been taken down from the lips of untutored singers in
Virginia alone. The ballad has even been assimilated with characteristic
alterations of text and tune by the American Negro. The "Okies" had a
mournful version of their own which they sang in their trek from the
dust-bowl.

Like the early Puritan melodies of this collection, this one bears witness to its age, by its "pentatonic" or five-tone scale, which omits the
F sharp and the C from its gamut, and also by the rhythmical freedom
of the meter, which clings so closely to the lilt of the words of the old
ballad.

TOM BOLYNN

Arrangement by Elie Siegmeister

Tom Bo-lynn was a Scotch-man born, His shoes worn out, his stock-ings torn, His shirt was rag-ged, his Spenc-er thin, "This is my best suit," said Tom Bo-lynn.

Tom Bo-lynn, Tom Bo-lynn, Tom Bo-lynn, Hi-ho!

Tom Bolynn had no breeches to wear,
He bought a sheepskin to make him a pair,
The flesh side out, the fur side in,
"They are charming and cool," said Tom Bolynn.
    CHORUS: Tom Bolynn, etc.

3

Tom and his wife and his wife's mother
Got into one bed together;
The weather was cold, the sheets were thin,
"I'll sleep in the middle," said Tom Bolynn.
    CHORUS: Tom Bolynn, etc.

4

But his wife's mother said the very next day,
"You'll have to get another place to stay.
I can't lie awake and hear you snore.
You can't stay in my house any more."
    CHORUS: Tom Bolynn, etc.

5

Tom got into a hollow tree,
And very contented seemed to be,
The wind did blow and the rain beat in,
"This is better than home," said Tom Bolynn.
    CHORUS: Tom Bolynn, etc.

TOM BOLYNN

A TART, racy tune, imported at an early date along with Scotch worsted and whiskey, and man's eternal revolt against mothers-in-law.

SPRINGFIELD MOUNTAIN

Arrangement by Elie Siegmeister

On Spring - field Moun - tain there did dwell A love - ly youth, I

knowed him well.— Too roo dee nay, Too roo dee noo, Too roo dee nay, Too roo dee noo.

2

This lovely youth one day did go
Down to the meadow for to mow-i-ow.

CHORUS: Too roo, *etc.*

3

He had scarce mowed quite round the field
When a pisen sarpint bit his hee-i-eel.

CHORUS: Too roo, *etc.*

4

They took him home to Molly dear
Which made her feel so very quee-i-eer.

CHORUS: Too roo, *etc.*

5

Now Molly had two ruby lips
With which the pisen she did si-eye-ip.

CHORUS: Too roo, *etc.*

6

Now Molly had a rotting tooth
And so the pisen killed them be-i-oth.

CHORUS: Too roo, *etc.*

PROBABLY the first original American ballad, of which four distinct types are now known. The story is conceded to be a true one, although it is claimed by different localities, where different names of the protagonists are given. According to the present version the victim was Lieutenant Thomas Merrick, bitten by a rattlesnake on Springfield Mountain, August 7, 1761, and dying within three hours, being at the time twenty-two years, two months, and three days old and on the point of marriage. This ballad has been sung to various melodies, among them "Old Hundred," and in 1840 and after on the stage, to the tune of the Scotch jig "Merrily danced the baker's wife." In its first form the song, identified as the creation of Nathan Torrey, was a sincere lament for the departed. It was widely adopted and, as we have seen, variously handled as a folk song. Reaching the vaudeville stage it was parodied with highly exaggerated and melodramatic details. By this time it was not only the hero but also the sweetheart who met a horrible end. Then the vaudeville parody returned in some way to the populace, was again passed from lip to lip, and in this comic version is found today all over the United States.

The grace notes and slides in the score are meant to indicate approximately the slides and scoops employed by genuine folk singers.

A recent visit to Springfield, Massachusetts, revealed the information that the grave of Thomas Merrick, original hero of the ballad, is still to be seen some fourteen miles from that city.

CAPTAIN KIDD

Arrangement by Elie Siegmeister

Oh! my parents taught me well, as I sailed, as I sailed,
Oh, my parents taught me well, as I sailed,
My parents taught me well to shun the gates of hell,
But against them I rebelled, as I sailed, as I sailed,
But against them I rebelled, as I sailed.

3

Oh! I murdered William Moore, as I sailed, as I sailed,
Oh, I murdered William Moore, as I sailed,
I murdered William Moore and left him in his gore,
Not many leagues from shore, as I sailed, as I sailed,
Not many leagues from shore, as I sailed.

4

And being cruel still, as I sailed, as I sailed,
And being cruel still, as I sailed,
And being cruel still, my gunner I did kill,
And his precious blood did spill, as I sailed, as I sailed,
And his precious blood did spill, as I sailed.

5

Oh! I steered from sound to sound, as I sailed, as I sailed,
Oh, I steered from sound to sound, as I sailed,
I steered from sound to sound, and many ships I found,
And most of them I burned, as I sailed, as I sailed,
And most of them I burned, as I sailed.

6

Oh! I'd ninety bars of gold, as I sailed, as I sailed,
Oh, I'd ninety bars of gold, as I sailed,
I'd ninety bars of gold, and dollars manifold,
With riches uncontrolled, as I sailed, as I sailed,
With riches uncontrolled, as I sailed.

7

Then fourteen ships I saw, as I sailed, as I sailed,
Then fourteen ships I saw, as I sailed,
Then fourteen ships I saw, and brave men they were,
Ah! they were too much for me, as I sailed, as I sailed,
Ah! they were too much for me, as I sailed.

8

Oh! to Newgate I am cast, and must die, and must die,
Oh, to Newgate I am cast, and must die,
To Newgate I am cast, with a sad and heavy heart,
To receive my just desert, I must die, I must die,
To receive my just desert, I must die.

9

Oh! Take warning now by me, for I must die, I must die,
Oh, take warning now by me, for I must die,
Take warning now by me, and shun bad company,
Lest you come to hell with me, for I must die, I must die,
Lest you come to hell with me, for I must die.

CAPTAIN KIDD

THIS IS one of the earliest of our bad men ballads. It originated at the time of William Kidd's trial and hanging for "murther and piracy" in 1701 in London. He it was who first captained an expedition to fight the pirates, then turned the tables and became one of the worst of them. He was quickly famous for terrible deeds, the news of which was spread via the grape-vine telegraph of the narrative ballad. Note the high moral tone and the gusto with which the hoister of the black flag relates his misdeeds and enjoins others to take warning from his fate. This rollicking ditty became very popular and is still to be heard in New England. It comes from a time when pirates might hang from the yard-arm or under more favoring circumstances land and "swagger the streets with impunity," for "the spending of the money they brought and the cheapness of the captured goods they sold brought them a following among rich and poor." (James Truslow Adams: "Provincial Society.") And they still hunt Kidd's treasure.

LOCKS AND BOLTS

Arrangement by Elie Siegmeister

SLOWLY, WITH TENDERNESS

Young men and maids, pray tell your age, I'll tell you of a sweet one.— She is the darl - ing of my heart, She is the most com - plete one.— Me and my love lay down one night. All on a bed to - ge - ther;— When I woke up, my love was gone, I was

forced to lie with - out her.____

2

Her yellow hair, like strands of gold,
Came rolling down my pillow.
She's the little one I love so well,
She's like the weeping willow.
"You've caused your parents to owe me a grudge
And treat me most unkindly,
Because you're of some high degree
And me so poor and needy."

3

I went into her uncle's house
Enquiring for my darling
The answer was: "She is not here,
I've no such in my keeping."
Her voice came from the roof above
Came straightway to the window,
"O love, O love, it's I'd be yours,
But locks and bolts doth hinder."

4

O passion flew, my sword I drew,
All in that room I entered,
O passion flew, my sword I drew,
All in that room I entered,
I took my sword in my right hand
All in that room I entered.
Come all young men that love like me
Fight on and take another.

5

Her uncle and three other men
Straightway after me did follow
Saying: "Leave this room, you villain, you,
Or in your heart's blood you shall wallow."
The blood was shed from every side
Till I got her from them.
And all young men who get such wives
Should fight till you overcome them.

LOCKS AND BOLTS

HERE IS a ballad of Colonial times, an old tale and an old tune which
had great popularity in our early settlements and indeed will live long
after these present settlers, as well as their ancestors, are gone. It has
been sung and orally transmitted these 300 years and more in our country and there may easily have been that many years behind the time of
its migration overseas.

The scale form, as will be seen, is precisely the same as that of "Barbara Allen," and there is a corresponding freedom in its rhythmical design, also, imperiously dictated by the rhythm of the poetical text. In all
probability, as with the foregoing song, this one too is of Scottish origin.

43

HANGSAMAN

Arrangement by Elie Siegmeister

LIVELY

Slack your rope, hangs - a - man, O, slack it for a - while; I

very legato   *simile*

think I see my fath - er* com - ing, Rid - ing man - y a mile. "O,

fath - er,* have you brought me gold? Or have you paid my fee? Or

have you come to see me hang - ing On the gal - lows tree?" "I

44

have not brought you gold;_____ I have not paid your fee,_____ But

I have come to see you hang - ing On the gal - lows tree."_____

*NOTE: *The second, third and fourth verses are the same as the first, except that the words "mother," "sister," "brother" respectively, are substituted for "father."*

5

Slack your rope, hangsaman,
O, slack it for a while;
I think I see my true-love coming,
Riding many a mile.
"O, true-love, have you brought me gold?
Or have you paid my fee?

Or have you come to see me hanging
On the gallows tree?"
"Yes, I have brought you gold;
Yes, I have paid your fee,
Nor have I come to see you hanging
On the gallows tree."

HANGSAMAN

ONE OF the oldest and youngest of the English ballads. Read Smith gives it a full five hundred years, beginning with a version called "Maid Freed from the Gallows." The original story was of a girl captured by pirates, about to be hanged, and ransomed by her lover. In America it is sung by whites and blacks, and is a favorite for children's game songs. They do not take too seriously the plight of the fair, who usually appeals in turn to father, mother, brother, and sister for ransom money to escape the hangman. In America some versions, particularly those of the Negro, tell the story the other way round: the man is in distress and his sweetheart comes to his aid with gold.

MY DAYS HAVE BEEN SO WONDROUS FREE

Words: Traditional
Music by Francis Hopkinson (1759)
Arrangement by Elie Siegmeister

IN 1788 Francis Hopkinson, poet, essayist, painter and man of society, Judge of the Admiralty of Pennsylvania and signer of the Declaration of Independence, sent a letter to his friend George Washington, in which he said, "However small the reputation may be that I shall derive from this work, I cannot, I believe, be refused the credit of being the first native of the United States who has produced a musical composition. If the attempt should not be too severely treated, others may be encouraged to venture on the path yet untrodden in America, and the arts in succession will take root and flourish amidst us."

Washington, replying, shrewdly avoided the responsibility of passing judgment on the songs dedicated to him, said, "My dear Sir: If you had any doubt about the reception your work would meet with or had the slightest reason to think that you should need any assistance to defend it, you have not acted in your usual good judgment in your choice of coadjutor for . . . I can neither sing one of the songs or raise a single note on any instrument to convince anybody. But I have one argument which will prevail with persons of true taste, at least in America. I can tell them that it is the production of Mr. Hopkinson. Your most obedient and humble servant, George Washington."

This at least proves the complete innocence of any musical pretensions on the part of the Father of his Country. Hopkinson's offering, written in 1759, is generally considered the first art song written by a native-born American. It is a salon song of the period, polished and melodious, with a pretty sentiment; suave and urbane as the tone of the above correspondence.

WHEN JESUS WEPT

[ROUND*]

Words and Music by William Billings
Arrangement by Elie Siegmeister

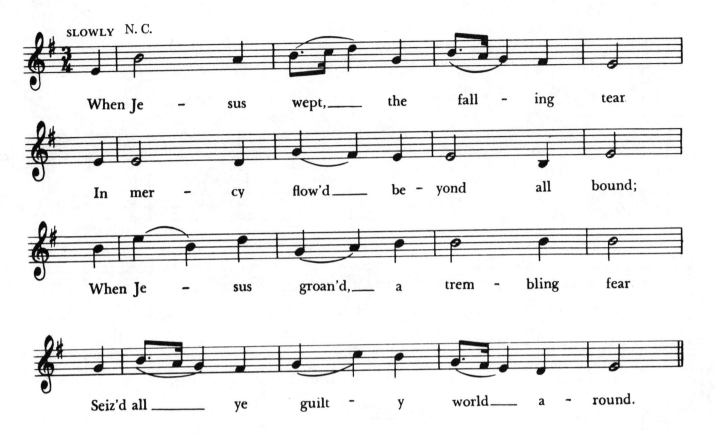

SLOWLY N.C.

When Je - sus wept,____ the fall - ing tear.

In mer - cy flow'd____ be - yond all bound;

When Je - sus groan'd,____ a trem - bling fear

Seiz'd all ____ ye guilt - y world____ a - round.

This round is to be sung by four voices. The first singer starts alone; when he reaches the second line, the second singer starts at the beginning (the first singer continuing). When the second singer reaches the second line, the third singer starts, and so on. Each singer sings the complete round through twice.

WHEN JESUS WEPT

WITH THIS eloquent setting in the form of a round of the sacred words, "When Jesus wept," there steps upon our scene one of the most rugged individualists in the history of American music—William Billings, of Boston. An artisan, self-taught in music, a flaming vortex of religious and patriotic feeling, he was as independent as they make 'em. One-eyed, with a game leg and arms of unequal length, his appearance was as exceptional as his personality. His stentorian voice could bellow his music with deafening ardor. He broke the peace of a Boston meeting house with his "fuguing tunes" which he roundly declared to be "more than twenty times as beautiful as the old slow tunes," and cited their effect upon "the audience, entertained and delighted, their minds surprisingly agitated and extremely fluctuated, sometimes declaring for one part and sometimes for another. . . . Oh ecstatic! Rush on, you sons of harmony!"

Billings was in the full sense of the word a man and artist of the people, whose music, after centuries of neglect, is coming back to public attention once more.

BRAVE WOLFE

Arrangement by Elie Siegmeister

MODERATELY, WITH VIGOR

Cheer up your hearts, young—— men, let— noth-ing—— fright you, Be

of a gal-lant—— mind, let— that de - light you.

Let— not your cour -age—— fail, till— af - ter tri - al, Nor

let your fan - cy—— move, at the first de - ni - al.

2

I went to see my love only to woo her,
I went to gain her love, not to undo her—
Whene'er I spoke a word, my tongue did quiver,
I could not speak my mind, while I was with her.

3

Love, here's a diamond ring, long time I've kept it,
'Tis for your sake alone, that I have kept it—
When you the posy read, think on the giver,
Madam, remember me, or I'm undone forever.

4

Brave Wolfe then took his leave of his dear jewel,
Most surely did she grieve, saying, "don't be cruel—"
Said he, " 'Tis for a space that I must leave you,
Yet love, where'er I go, I'll not forget you."

5

So then this gallant youth did cross the ocean,
To free America from her invasion—
He landed at Quebec with all his party,
The city to attack, both brave and hearty.

6

Brave Wolfe drew up his men in form so pretty,
On the plains of Abraham, before the city—
There, just before the town, the French did meet them,
With double numbers, they resolved to beat them.

7

When drawn up in a line, for death prepared,
While in each other's face their armies stared—
So pleasantly brave Wolfe and Montcalm talked,
So martially between their armies walked.

8

Each man then took his post at their retire,
So then these numerous hosts began to fire—
The cannon on each side did roar like thunder,
And youths in all their pride were torn asunder.

9

The drums did loudly beat, colors were flying,
The purple gore did stream, and men lay dying—
When shot from off his horse, fell this brave hero,
And we lament his loss in weeds of sorrow.

10

The French began to break their ranks and flying,
Brave Wolfe began to wake as he lay dying—
He lifted up his head while guns did rattle
And to his army said, "How goes the battle?"

11

His aid-de-camp replied, " 'Tis in our favor,
Quebec with all her pride, we soon shall have her,
She'll fall into our hands with all her treasure."
"O, then," brave Wolfe replied, "I die with pleasure."

THE CAPTURE of Quebec in June of 1759 by the British army, when
James Wolfe, mortally wounded in the hour of victory, met a dramatic
end, meant the conquest of Canada. The news went far and fast. It was
printed with the music on the sheet of one of the first original broadside
ballads of American origin that have come down to us. The archaic harmonization was suggested by the nature of the melody.

In Freedom We're Born

[REVOLUTIONARY SONGS, ODES, HYMNS]

IT WAS no coincidence that the first great outpouring of native song occurred at the time of the American Revolution. As long as the thirteen colonies looked to King George as their ruler and to England as their homeland, it was natural that their music should come from the country that nourished their social and economic life. But when the first feelings of American patriotism were born, after the arbitrary impositions and restrictions of the British Crown whipped up the resentment of the colonists to fever pitch, there came a surge of independent American song with it. The prejudice against all things British helped the new American composers and their works were greeted with intense enthusiasm.

The Sons of Liberty, organized in the 1760's to protest unjust and discriminatory taxation, found that satirical verses setting forth American grievances against the imperial crown, set to tunes of popular songs of the day, were an excellent means of furthering the cause of liberty. These works, printed on broadsides, and peddled and sung, at first surreptitiously, and then, as the struggle advanced, more and more openly, were the first American patriotic songs. The first of these, "The Liberty Song," written by John Dickinson, showed that in 1768 the Americans wanted, not independence, but freedom from unfair taxation—they were willing to pay, if they had a voice in allotting the share:

> *Our purses are ready. . . .*
> *Not as slaves, but as Freemen our money*
> *we'll give.*

The Tories, scorning such pretensions, responded with military force, and immediately after the Boston Massacre, warned the people in song:

> *You simple Bostonians, I'd have you beware,*
> *Of your Liberty Tree, I would have you take*
> *care,*
> *For if that we chance to return to this town,*
> *Your houses and stores will come tumbling*
> *down.*

And the patriots, thoroughly aroused, issued the bold call for "a capital chop"—independence—and gathered in meeting halls to sing:

> *There's no knowing where this oppression*
> *will stop.*
> *Some say, there's no cure but a capitol chop;*
> *And that I believe's each American's wish,*
> *Since you've drenched them with tea and de-*
> *prived 'em of fish.*

The leaders of the American cause well understood the power of song, and did not hesitate to take time off from other duties to create American songs. Thomas Paine, author of "Common Sense," wrote one on the "Liberty Tree" and followed it with "Bunker Hill." That tireless enthusiast, Samuel Adams, organized the people of Boston into clandestine singing societies for the express purpose of learning the exciting new songs. Francis Hopkinson lampooned the British generals in his "Battle of the Kegs." Music heartened the Americans in their fateful undertaking.

When the struggle for independence finally did break out, the songs began to come thick and fast. The capture of Burgoyne, the victory of Paul Jones, the death of Nathan Hale, the surrender of Cornwallis at Yorktown and a score of other events became music on Americans' lips. Ironically enough, most of these songs were sung to tunes of English origin.

At the same time there appeared a man of a striking, aggressive personality and fiery conviction, who was to invent new, characteristic

53

American tunes for these songs. He was William Billings, the Boston tanner's apprentice who had started his musical career scribbling tunes on cowhides with chalk, and had gone on to astound the good citizens of Boston with his strange and exciting "fuguing tunes." Billings was renowned as one of the very first composers of original hymn tunes. The people were so amazed that there was a man among them who set down music he had himself thought up that they crowded into his singing school classes, and those who could not squeeze into the room listened outside the door. Apparently religion was on the side of the patriots, for the composers' inclusion of a defiantly rebellious song, "Chester," in his first published collection of hymns (engraved in 1770, incidentally, by Paul Revere) was greeted with great enthusiasm. He again combined religion and patriotism in his "Lamentation Over Boston," a paraphrase of the Biblical psalm, "By the waters of Babylon we sat down and wept, as we remembered thee, Oh Jerusalem," which read, "By the rivers of Watertown, we sat down and wept, as we remembered thee, Oh Boston." Ragged continental soldiers were cheered when they sang Billings' melodies which assured them that God was on New England's side:

> We fear them [the British] not—we trust in
> God,
> New England's God forever reigns.

The energies released by the Revolution expended themselves not only in the development of popular patriotic songs, but were applied, too, to the development of musical life in general and religious music in particular. One characteristic feature of music in those days was the country singing school, also initiated by Billings. Thousands of our ancestors received their first notion of music through this early American institution. Its democratic purpose was outlined by Billings who vigorously opposed the old custom of having only the deacon read from notes, while the congregation slavishly droned back the tunes he had "lined out" to them. Said he: "As all now have books, and all can read, 'tis insulting to have the lines read in this way, for it is practically saying 'we men of letters, and you ignorant creatures.' "

The singing school was generally held under the guidance of an itinerant musician in the village tavern. "Those who attended were expected to bring their own candles. These were set on strips of board or inserted in an apple, turnip, or potato . . . To bring a tin or brass candlestick into the hall was scorned as a bit of aristocratic presumption." * Classes, often lasting three hours, were held for several weeks; young and old took part, beating time with the right hand while singing, and at the end of the period the town or village could boast a congregation that was able to read at least simple hymns in harmony by note. "Their voices were tremendous in power, issuing from ample chests and lungs, invigorated by hard labor and simple food, and unrestrained by dress. . . . It was no insignificant, tremulous voice, but grand, majestic and heart-stirring; and when applied to such tunes as *Old Hundred, Mear* and *Canterbury,* everything around seemed to tremble." †

So enthusiastic were these singing congregations that the teachers soon ran out of hymns, and took to writing new ones which were issued in collections published in a score of New England towns. As the number of tunes mounted, the composers, in order to distinguish them, named them after the towns or villages in which they were written. Thus we have the "Hartford Collection," the "Suffolk Harmony," the "Stoughton Collection," the "Putney Hymn" and hundreds of others.

The modern reader, examining these old hymn-books, will be taken aback at first. Not only will he find harmonies which sound empty, strange, dissonant; he will find among the hymns certain complex, contrapuntal compositions (the so-called "fuguing tunes" referred to previously) in which the voices seem

* W. A. Fisher: "Ye Olde New England Psalm-tunes."
† Nathan D. Gould, one of the last of the old singing-teachers, as quoted by Fisher, *ibid.*

to enter and drop out, cross and criss-cross in a most perplexing manner. A long, apparently rambling solo will break out of the mass of sound in a most irregular and surprising way. Again, here is the handiwork of that inveterate experimenter, Billings. Tired of the constant march of dreary four-voice harmony, he felt that if Americans could overthrow the British king, and do away with the traditions of the past, he could throw off the hand of musical tradition and create a new, more dramatic form. In a typical American statement, worthy of any young atonalist of today, he wrote:

"As I don't think myself confined to any rules of Composition laid down by any that went before me, neither should I think (were I to pretend to lay down rules) that any who come after me were in any ways obligated to adhere to them, any further than they should think proper. So in fact I think it best for every Composer to be his own Carver."

Apparently there were plenty of people who thought Billings was not a bad Carver, for his choral compositions were performed more often than those of any other native composer for more than a generation. And when they fell out of style in the cities, they lived on in the country districts, being reprinted in many a rural songster for at least a hundred and fifty years. The fuguing tune style which he invented had its limitations. It was often crude and primitive. But it had courage and zeal, often moments of striking beauty, and sometimes, within its scope, produced genuine little masterpieces, such as "Montague" and "Evening Shade."

The religious and patriotic songs of William Billings and his followers, Andrew Law, Timothy Swan, Jacob Kimball, Oliver Holden, Jezaniah Sumner—and many others—were the characteristic music of America in its moment of birth, and as such are of great interest.

E. S.

THE LIBERTY SONG

Words by John Dickinson (1768); Music by William Boyce
Arrangement by Elie Siegmeister

Come join hand in hand, brave A - mer - i - cans all, And rouse your bold hearts at fair Li - ber-ty's call; No ty - ran - nous acts shall sup-press your just claim, Or stain with dis-hon - our A - mer - i - ca's name.

Chorus
In Free-dom we're born and in Free - dom we'll live, Our purs - es are _ read-y.

Stead-y, Friends, Stead-y. Not as Slaves,—but as Free men our mon-ey we'll give.

<table>
</table>

2

Our worthy Forefathers—Let's give them a cheer—
To Climates unknown did courageously steer;
Thro' Oceans, to deserts, for freedom they came,
And dying bequeath'd us their freedom and Fame.
CHORUS: In Freedom we're born, etc.

3

The Tree their own hands had to liberty rear'd;
They liv'd to behold growing strong and rever'd;
With transport they cry'd, "Now our witness we gain
For our children shall gather the fruits of our pain."
CHORUS: In Freedom we're born, etc.

4

Swarms of placemen and pensioners soon will appear
Like locusts deforming the charms of the year;
Suns vainly will rise, Showers vainly descend,
If we are to drudge for what others shall spend.
CHORUS: In Freedom we're born, etc.

5

Then join hand in hand, brave Americans all,
By uniting we stand, by dividing we fall;
In so righteous a cause let us hope to succeed,
For Heaven approves of each generous deed.
CHORUS: In Freedom we're born, etc.

6

All ages shall speak with amaze and applause,
Of the courage we'll show in support of our laws;
To die we can bear—but to serve we disdain,
For shame is to Freedom more dreadful than pain
CHORUS: In Freedom we're born, etc.

7

This bumper I crown for our Sovereign's health,
And this for Britannia's glory and wealth;
That wealth and that glory immortal may be,
If she is but just—and if we are but Free.
CHORUS: In Freedom we're born, etc.

THE LIBERTY SONG

JOHN ADAMS attended a banquet on August 14, 1769 and wrote in his
diary: "Dined with 350 Sons of Liberty in Robinson's Tavern in Dor-
chester. There was a large collection of good company. We had the
Liberty Song (Dickinson's) and the whole company joined in the
chorus." The tune of the song was the famous "Hearts of Oak."

This Liberty Song, besides being our first patriotic song, was the opening shot in the battle of ballads between patriots and Tories which preceded the outbreak of revolution. It was published in the *Boston Gazette*
of July 18, 1768. It also appeared in the various newspapers of New
England, where it became very popular.

WHAT A COURT HATH OLD ENGLAND

[*Tune of "Derry-down"*]
Arrangement by Elie Siegmeister

VIGOROUS

What a court hath old Eng - land of

fol - ly and sin, Spite of Chat-ham and Cam-den, Barre, Burke, Wilkes, and Glynn! Not con-

tent with the game act, they tax fish and sea, And A - mer - i - ca drench with hot

wa - ter and tea. Der - ry down, down, down der - ry down.

There's no knowing where this oppression will stop;
Some say "There's no cure but a capitol chop,"
And that I believe's each American's wish,
Since you've drenched them with tea, and depriv'd 'em of fish.
    Derry down, down, down derry down.

Three Generals these mandates have borne 'cross the sea,
To deprive 'em of fish and to make 'em drink tea;
In turn, sure, these freemen will boldly agree
To give 'em a dance upon Liberty Tree.
    Derry down, down, down derry down.

Then freedom's the word, both at home and abroad,
So out, every scabbard that hides a good sword!
Our forefathers gave us this freedom in hand,
And we'll die in defense of the rights of the land.
    Derry down, down, down derry down.

WHAT A COURT HATH OLD ENGLAND

A Tory satire which marked the ineffective efforts of the patriots in 1770, occasioned this reply from the Colonists. It was flung far and wide on broadsides and it added fuel to the rapidly rising flame of resentment when the British Parliament rejected the petition of 1775 and declared that a state of rebellion existed in America. Again an English tune, its hearty and muscular spirit emphasized by the characteristic refrain, "Down, Derry, Down," is the vehicle of the popular feeling. The song, fierce and satirical, was a recapitulation of grievances and a further incitement to war.

YOU SIMPLE BOSTONIANS*

1

You simple Bostonians, I'd have you beware
Of your Liberty Tree, I would have you take care,
For if that we chance to return to this town
Your houses and stores will come tumbling down.
    Derry down, down, down derry down.

2

Our fleet and our army, they soon will arrive—
Then to a bleak island, you shall not us drive,
In every house you shall have three or four,
And if that will not please you, you shall have half a score.
    Derry down, down, down derry down.

*This song was the Tory original to which "What a Court Hath Old England" was a reply.

YANKEE DOODLE

Composer: Unknown
Arrangement by Elie Siegmeister

2	4	6

2

And there we saw a thousand men,
As rich as Squire David;
And what they wasted ev'ry day,
I wish it could be savèd.

3

And there was Captain Washington
Upon a slapping stallion,
Agiving orders to his men;
I guess there was a million.

4

And then the feathers on his hat,
They looked so 'tarnal fine, ah!
I wanted peskily to get
To give to my Jemima.

5

And there they'd fife away like fun,
And play on cornstalk fiddles,
And some had ribbons red as blood,
All bound about their middles.

6

Uncle Sam came there to change
Some pancakes and some onions,
For 'lasses cake to carry home
To give his wife and young ones.

7

But I can't tell half I see,
They kept up such a smother;
So I took my hat off, made a bow,
And scampered home to mother.

The popular verse goes:

Yankee Doodle went to town,
Riding on a pony
Stuck a feather in his hat
And called it macaroni.

Yankee Doodle, doodle doo,
Yankee Doodle Dandy,
All the lads and lassies are
Sweet as sugar candy.

YANKEE DOODLE

THIS INSOLENT and satirical tune played a conspicuous part in the American Revolution. It was sung derisively by the English at the Yankees. They, in turn, struck up the tune as they marched the defeated British soldiers to prison. "They even enticed away the British band," says Marjorie Barstow Greenbie, "hired it themselves, and had it playing the obnoxious song." The Minute Men of Concord adopted it as their own, and when Cornwallis surrendered at Yorktown, it was to the accompaniment of "Yankee Doodle."

It is hard to think of a tune that is more typical of the lively, fresh, happy-go-lucky spirit of America.

CORNWALLIS'S COUNTRY DANCE

1

Cornwallis led a country dance,
The like was never seen, sir;
Much retrograde and much advance,
And all with General Greene, sir.
CHORUS: Yankee Doodle, *etc.*

2

Greene, in the South, then danced a set,
And got a mighty name, sir,
Cornwallis jigged with young Fayette
But suffered in his fame, sir.
CHORUS: Yankee Doodle, *etc.*

3

Quoth he, "My guards are weary grown
With footing country dances;
They never at St. James's shone
At capers, kicks or dances."
CHORUS: Yankee Doodle, *etc.*

4

His music soon forgets to play,
His feet can no more move, sir;
And all his bands now curse the day
They jigged to our shore, sir.
CHORUS: Yankee Doodle, *etc.*

5

Now, Tories all, what can ye say?
Come—this is not a griper:
That while your hopes are danced away,
'Tis you must pay the piper.
CHORUS: Yankee Doodle, *etc.*

CHESTER

Words and Music by William Billings (1770)
Arrangement by Elie Siegmeister

Let ty - rants shake their i - ron___ rods, And slav - 'ry clank___ her___ gall - ing___ chains. We fear them not___ we trust___ in___ God. New___ Eng - land's God _____ for - e - ver___ reigns.

Howe and Burgoyne and Clinton too,
With Prescott and Cornwallis joined,
Together plot our overthrow
In one infernal league combined.

3

The foe comes on with haughty stride,
Our troops advance with martial noise;
Their vet'rans flee before our youth,
And gen'rals yield to beardless boys.

4

When God inspired us for the fight,
Their ranks were broke, their lines were forced.
Their ships were shatter'd in our sight
Or swiftly driven from our coast.

CHESTER

"Chester," composed as a church hymn in 1770, was taken up by the Minute Men at the outbreak of the Revolution and used as a marching song. Chanted by thousands of foot-weary Continentals from Maine to Georgia, it became one of the most popular of our early patriotic anthems. It still breathes a fierce hatred of tyranny and the eternal spirit of American freedom.

The composer, William Billings, was vastly popular in the heroic days of the Revolution, but was later forgotten, died in poverty, and lies buried in an unknown grave somewhere in the vicinity of Boston Common. But his music, crude in some ways, remains full of the fresh and challenging spirit of early America.

BUNKER HILL
[THE AMERICAN HERO]

Words by Nathaniel Niles
Music by Andrew Law (1775)
Arrangement by Elie Siegmeister

Now, Mars, I dare thee, clad in smoky Pillars,
Bursting from Bomb-Shells, roaring from the Cannon,
Rattling in Grape Shot, like a Storm of Hailstones,
        Torturing Aether!

Still shall the Banner of the King of Heaven
Never advance where I'm afraid to follow:
While that precedes me with an open Bosom,
        War, I defy thee.

While all their Hearts quick palpitate for Havock,
Let slip your Blood Hounds, nam'd the British Lyons;
Dauntless as Death stares; nimble as the Whirlwind;
        Dreadful as Demons!

Fame and dear Freedom lure me on to Battle.
While a fell Despot, grimmer than a Death's Head,
Stings me with Serpents, fiercer than Medusa's:
        To the Encounter.

6

Life, for my Country and the Cause of Freedom,
Is but a Trifle for a Worm to part with;
And if preserved in so great a Contest,
        Life is redoubled.

BUNKER HILL

YOUNG ANDREW LAW had just received his B. A. from Rhode Island College in September 1775, when the battle of Bunker Hill made the good citizens of Boston realize that the war was definitely on. Law sat down and set to music the stately and sonorous "Sapphick" ode, "The American Hero," by Nathaniel Niles of Norwich, Connecticut. The timeliness of the song connected it immediately with the battle that had just been fought, and the public, ignoring Niles's title, called it, simply "Bunker Hill." As such it was widely sung and long remembered.

PAUL JONES' VICTORY

Arrangement by Elie Siegmeister

We had not cruised long before he espies
A large forty-four, and a twenty likewise,
Well manned with bold seamen,
Well laid in with stores,
In consort to drive us from England's old shores.
Hurrah! Hurrah! Our country forever, hurrah!

Paul Jones then said to his men, ev'ry one,
"Let ev'ry true seaman stand firm to his gun!
We'll receive a broadside from this bold Englishman
And like true Yankee sailors, return it again."
Hurrah! Hurrah! Our country forever, hurrah!

To us they did strike and their colors hauled down,
The fame of Paul Jones to the world shall be known;
His name shall rank with the gallant and brave,
Who fought like a hero our freedom to save.
Hurrah! Hurrah! Our country forever, hurrah!

PAUL JONES' VICTORY

"ON SEPTEMBER 23, with three men-of-war, he sighted a British warship off the English coast. One of Jones' vessels under a French commander turned and fled. But with two others, the Bonhomme Richard and Pallas, he fought and won a desperate engagement of three and one-half hours . . . it gave the American navy a baptism of glory"—Henry Steele Commager. The good rugged Celtic tune, with its Doric harmonies, is well suited to the story.

ODE TO THE FOURTH OF JULY

Words by Daniel George
Music by Horatio Garnett (1789)
Arrangement by Elie Siegmeister

'Tis done, the e - dict past, by Heav - en de - creed,— And
See haugh - ty Bri - tain send-ing hosts of foes,— With

Han - cock's name con - firms the glor - ious deed. On
ven - geance armed our free - dom to op - pose. But

this au - spi - cious morn was In - de - pen - dence born: Pro - pi - tious
Wash - ing - ton the great dis-pelled im-pend - ing fate, and spurned each

day! Hail the U - ni - ted States of blest A - mer - i - ca!
plan. A - mer - i - cans com - bine to hail the god - like man.

ODE TO THE FOURTH OF JULY

AMERICA'S FIRST Fourth of July as a nation was greeted by this song, composed by Howard Garnet for the celebration of 1789. That was the day also, of the adoption of the new Constitution. Garnet's obscurity as a composer is such that he is not mentioned again in the history of American music. He will nevertheless be well remembered for this piece of inspiration, which rises imposingly to its climax with the final apostrophe, "Let cannon roar and joyful voices shout Columbia's name." There are trumpets and drums in the music, and the jubilant Handelian figures of the accompaniment here provided, carry out this latent feeling.

ODE ON SCIENCE

ALTHOUGH Jezaniah Sumner, a small-town deacon, wrote the words and music of the long popular "Ode on Science" in 1798, fifteen years after the conclusion of the War of Independence, his song still twisted the lion's tail, still breathed stalwart defiance of the mother country. This song had a great vogue and was one of the most frequently reprinted. The title is a curious one, less readily understood today than in Sumner's time. The men of that period closely associated science with liberty, democracy, freedom from the thrall of church and state. The musical ideas furnish an interesting example of a composer who utilizes whatever current musical idioms may be in his head in order to drive home a dramatic message. It is about equally compounded of pretty English lyricism in the first and gentle part, and the ebullient vigor of a hornpipe in the ending. Mr. Siegmeister has made a free adaptation of the choral harmonies in his piano accompaniment.

ODE ON SCIENCE

Words and Music by Jezaniah Sumner (1798)
Arrangement by Elie Siegmeister

The morn-ing___ sun shines from___ the east, And spreads___his___ glor-ies___ to___ the west. All___ nat-ions with his beams___are___ blest, Where' -er___ his rad-iant___ light ap - pears. So Sci - ence

DAVID'S LAMENTATION

Words and Music by William Billings (1778)
Arrangement by Elie Siegmeister

* Implied chords

74

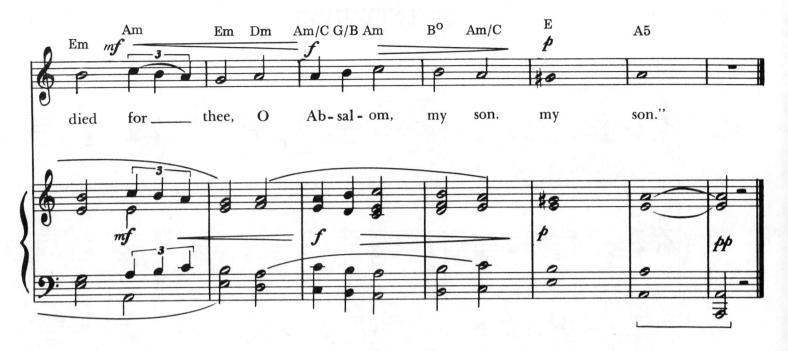

died for ___ thee, O Ab-sal-om, my son, my son."

DAVID'S LAMENTATION

WHEN BILLINGS ATTEMPTED, as he did, musical settings of the Song of Songs, he encountered difficulties. But when it came to the expression of sincere and often noble emotion he wrote with a genuineness and simplicity that were moving. This setting of the verse of David's Lamentation is not only practicable to sing for those who are not accomplished musicians, but it also expresses feeling with a dignity and earnestness that more celebrated composers might envy. The present harmonization follows carefully that of the choral setting.

PUTNEY HYMN

Arrangement by Elie Siegmeister

OWING to the lack of instruments in the churches, the scarcity of printed music, and attendant circumstances, congregational singing in New England by the beginning of the eighteenth century had sunk to a low level. To remedy this, itinerant deacons who specialized in teaching the elements of singing were sent from town to town. They would spend a few weeks in each community trying to set matters right and then would go on. These singing teachers were in many cases composers, and church music was the one channel which New England morality permitted them for self-expression. The number of the hymns they composed went into the thousands. In order to distinguish them one from another they would be called by the name of the village at which the teacher was staying when the hymn was written. In this way the names of hundreds of tiny Vermont, Massachusetts, and Connecticut hamlets are recorded, by anonymous composers, in the hymnals. That is the origin of the grave "Putney," the noblest of the New England hymns.

THE BEE

Arrangement by Elie Siegmeister

As Cu - pid in a gar - den strayed, Trans - port - ed with the dam - ask shade, A lit - tle bee un - seen a - mong The silk - en weeds his fin - ger stung.

* Passing chord = C G D B♭

78

As tears his beauteous cheeks ran down,
He stormed, he blowed the burning wound;
Then flying to a neighboring grove
Thus plaintive told the queen of love:

"Ah, ah, mama, ah me, I die!
A little insect, winged to fly—
It's called a bee, on yonder plain
It stung me. Oh! I die with pain."

Then Venus mildly thus rejoined,
"If you, my dear, such anguish find
From the resentment of a bee,
Think what those feel who'r' stung by thee."

THE BEE

A SONG of the more fragile, delicate type, charmingly written for voice and harpsichord, voicing the sentiments which must have gone well with powdered wigs, knee breeches, tallow candles and federalist sentiments, and a period and culture that are vanished. It first appeared in the American Musical Miscellany in 1798, which was "a collection of the most approved songs and airs, both old and new," printed by Daniel Wright & Co., Northampton, Massachusetts.

JEFFERSON AND LIBERTY

Arrangement by Elie Siegmeister

soul, and voice, For Jef - fer - son__ and Lib - er - ty.

2

No lordling here, with gorging jaws,
Shall wring from industry the food;
Nor fiery bigot's holy laws
Lay waste our fields and streets in blood!
CHORUS: Rejoice, *etc.*

3

Here strangers from a thousand shores,
Compelled by tyranny to roam,
Shall find, amidst abundant stores,
A nobler and a happier home.
CHORUS: Rejoice, *etc.*

4

Here Art shall lift her laurel'd head,
Wealth, Industry, and Peace divine;
And where dark, pathless forests spread,
Rich fields and lofty cities shine.
CHORUS: Rejoice, *etc.*

5

From Europe's wants and woes remote,
A friendly waste of waves between,
Here plenty cheers the humblest cot,
And smiles on every village-green.
CHORUS: Rejoice, *etc.*

6

Here, free as air, expanded space,
To every soul and sect shall be—
That sacred privilege of our race—
The worship of the Deity.
CHORUS: Rejoice, *etc.*

7

Let foes to freedom dread the name;
But should they touch the sacred tree,
Twice fifty thousand swords would flame
For Jefferson and Liberty.
CHORUS: Rejoice, *etc.*

8

From Georgia to Lake Champlain,
From seas to Mississippi's shore,
Ye sons of Freedom, loud proclaim—
"The reign of terror is no more."
CHORUS: Rejoice, *etc.*

JEFFERSON AND LIBERTY

JEFFERSON AND LIBERTY: homage to the plain man and champion of democracy whom the people loved so well, and by whom he was not held in less regard for riding to his inaugural in Washington on horseback and receiving ambassadors in his bedroom slippers. The song has much of historical significance, narrating, as it does, the public detestation of the Alien and Sedition Laws, which Jefferson had passionately swept away when he came into power. The music suggests a wild Irish jig.

Thar She Blows

[SEA CHANTIES]

"Start her, start her, my men! Don't hurry yourselves; take plenty of time—but start her! Start her like thunder-claps, that's all. . . . Start her now; give 'em the long and strong stroke, Tashtego. Start her, Tash, my boy—start her, all; but keep cool, keep cool—cucumbers is the word—easy, easy—only start her like grim death and grinning devils, and raise the buried dead perpendicular out of their graves, boys—that's all. Start her!"

From Herman Melville's "Moby Dick"

FROM THE BEGINNING, Americans have been a sea-going tribe. When the Pilgrims came to Plymouth, they planned to live by catching fish and shipping it back to Europe. The first food they found in the New World was clams taken from Plymouth Bay. It was ship-building and sea-borne commerce that built up early New England. Timber was plentiful in Maine and out of it shrewd Yankee traders began at an early date to build the great square-sterned whalers that sailed out of New Bedford and Nantucket in search of the valuable oil that was so important to early industry. Meanwhile Bangor, Portsmouth, New London, Boston were sending out the square-riggers that soon began to compete with British-owned boats in the European and West Indies trade.

Life on the early sailing vessels was hard. The Yankee skipper was a man who believed in rigid discipline, generally enforced by no milk-and-water methods. The cruelty on some of the boats earned for them the description of "hell afloat." The food was "chiefly salt beef, salt fish, slumgullion, a ration of lime juice, a ration of grog . . . and always hard-tack." *

The sailor's work was brutally hard, and never-ending: "swabbing down decks, mending tackle, manning the pumps, heaving the

lead, and always adjusting canvas to catch a favoring wind." *

Chanty-singing was, of course, not an American invention. Sailors had sung to help themselves at work ever since the days of the old Roman triremes. But the exciting period of the growth of the American navy from 1812 to 1860, the North Atlantic packet trade, the cotton traffic between Liverpool and the South, the height of the whaling industry, the golden days of the Yankee Clipper, and the shipping boom brought on by the gold rush around the Horn in '49—all of these brought ever more American men and ships to the sea and carried the practice of chanty-singing to its highest level.

Chanty-singing was not, as members of some choral societies may romantically imagine, a matter of giving vent to one's love of the sea in song. It was rather, as Joanna Colcord has pointed out, "a practical necessity in the work that daily and hourly went forward." † Everything on the old sailing boats was done by man-power and pulling together was essential if the ships were to be sailed. The singing of chanties with their vigorous and clearly-measured rhythms established the regular timing so necessary for the efficient execution of such tasks as weighing anchor, hoisting sail, manning the pumps and other work requiring split-second team-work.

The chantyman was that member of the crew whose voice, memory and skill in extemporizing apt or humorous lines singled him out above all the others. Most of the chanties were divided into solo phrases taken by the chantyman while the sailors were preparing their grip on the line, and a chorus, on which "all hands

* Linscott: "Folk Songs of Old New England."

* Linscott: "Folk Songs of Old New England."
† Colcord: "Songs of the American Sailorman."

gave a mighty pull and 'brought her home.' " *
Without the rhythm of the music, the heave or
drag would not have the absolute precision of
timing needed to throw the entire weight of
every man on the line at the same instant.

The chanties were of several varieties. The
"short-drag" chanties like "Haul on the Bow-
line" were used when only a few rapid, heavy
pulls were required. "Halyard chanties" (such
as "Blow, Boys, Blow") were used for the
longer and heavier tasks such as "catting" the
anchor and hoisting sail. The "Capstan" or
"Windlass" chanties were those used for a long,
steady process like hoisting anchor or "warping
ship" when the men wound the rope on the
capstan by walking around it, pushing the bars
before them. These were generally longer
songs, adapted to the tediousness and monotony of the work.

In addition to the chanties which were
actually sung at work, there were the "fo'c'sle
songs" sung for entertainment in the hours
when the crew was off duty. While the rhythm
and character of the chanties were determined
by the nature of the work to which they were
adapted, the fo'c'sle songs were of varied
nature. They might be ballads, patriotic or
vaudeville songs, or what not brought from
shore and in the course of time fitted out with
new words pertaining to sea life. They ranged
all the way from songs about ladies of easy vir-
tue, through epics of fishing and whaling, to
ballads of sea tragedies and victories of American naval heroes such as Paul Jones, Farragut,
and Decatur.*

There is still much difference of opinion
about the origin and even the spelling of the
word "chanty"—or "shanty," about the sources
of the tunes themselves, the English or American character of the songs. The beginnings of
many of the songs are lost in the mists of time,
and early records are practically nonexistent.
Chanties were sung on English vessels long before there was an American navy, and this has
led British collectors to assume that *all* chanties
must have originated in their country. But

how explain the singing of a song such as "Paul
Jones' Victory"—openly boasting of Yankee su-
periority—by British seamen? What is there
British about the lines,

*We'll receive a broadside from this proud
Englishman,
And like true Yankee sailors, return it again.
Hurrah! hurrah! Our country [America] for-
ever, hurrah!**

British authorities have suggested they may
have been new words fitted to an old English
tune. But then what of songs whose whole spirit
is Negro, like "A Dollar a Day" or "Run with
the Bullgine"; or minstrel-like chanties, and
those that resemble Stephen Foster, like "Sacramento"? "Shenandoah," one of the most beautiful and widely-sung of all chanties on ships
flying both the Union Jack and the Stars and
Stripes, speaks of crossing "the wide Missouri"
—which hardly flows through Kent or Cornwall.

The answer may be simple. American and
British boys worked interchangeably on ships
of both nations. In the early days the English
language and English songs were the heritage
of both. With the coming of independence and
the growth of our own navy, songs of distinctly
American origin, reflecting American experiences and view-points, were added to the store,
and British sailors working under a Yankee
chantyboy learned and sang such lines as:

*To us they [i.e., the British] did strike and
their colors haul down,
The fame of Paul Jones to the world shall be
known.
His name shall rank with the gallant and
brave
Who fought like a hero our country [i.e.,
America] to save.
Hurrah! Hurrah! Our country forever, hur-
rah!*

and thought nothing of it. The sailorman was
more concerned with the tune, the swing and
go of a song, than with its nativity.

Whether American or English in national-

* We are indebted to Joanna Colcord's book, "Songs of
the American Sailorman," for much of this material.

* A notation of this song as sung by a British sailor to
Percy Grainger is found among a manuscript group of folk-
songs collected in England by the eminent pianist, and now
in the New York Public Library.

ity, many of the songs have definitely Irish and Negro qualities. This is not surprising, for the sons of Erin and of the South had the full-throated or silvery voices that marked them out as obvious selections for the choice position of chantyman. It was natural that they should mingle familiar strains of their own people with the store of chanties which their memories held.

At any rate, whatever their origin or character, chanties have played a unique role in American life. They serve as enduring monuments to the great days of sailing the Yankee Clipper, and Moby Dick.

E. S.

BLOW, BOYS, BLOW

Arrangement by Elie Siegmeister

2

How do you know she's a Yankee liner?
Blow, boys, blow!
The Stars and Stripes float out behind her.
Blow, my bully boys, blow!

3

And who d'you think is the captain of her?
Blow, boys, blow!
Why, Bully Hayes is the captain of her.
Blow, my bully boys, blow!

4

Oh, Bully Hayes, he loves us sailors.
Blow, boys, blow!
Yes, he does, like hell and blazes.
Blow, my bully boys, blow!

5

And what do you think they've got for dinner?
Blow, boys, blow!
Pickled eels' feet and bullock's liver.
Blow, my bully boys, blow!

6

Blow, boys, blow, the sun's drawing water.
Blow, boys, blow!
Three cheers for the cook and one for his daughter.
Blow, my bully boys, blow!

BLOW, BOYS, BLOW

A HALLIARD SHANTY that originated in the old Congo slave trade. It
told of the brutal life aboard the early Yankee sailing boats. During the
Civil War the verse,

> *What do you think she's got for cargo?*
> *Old shot and shell, she breaks the embargo.*

was sung about ships carrying contraband.

The compactness of this shanty and its phrasing made it an ideal
song for jobs demanding quick tugs on the rope repeated at short
intervals.

CAPE COD GIRLS

Arrangement by Elie Siegmeister

LIVELY AND CHEERFUL

Oh, Cape Cod girls are ver-y fine girls, Heave a-way! Heave a-way! With Cod-fish balls they comb their curls, Heave a-way! Heave a-way! Heave a-way! my bul-ly, bul-ly boys, Heave a-way! Heave a-way! Heave a-way! and don't you make a noise, For we're bound for Aust-ral-ia.

Oh, Cape Cod girls they have no combs,
Heave away! Heave away!
They comb their hair with codfish bones,
Heave away! Heave away!
    CHORUS: Heave away, etc.

Oh, Cape Cod boys they have no sleds,
Heave away! Heave away!
They slide down hill on codfish heads,
Heave away! Heave away!
    CHORUS: Heave away, etc.

CAPE COD GIRLS

A SONG that manned many a capstan bar, with its tang of wave and spray. As for the girls of Cape Cod, and all the New England girls whom the men left behind them when they sailed the seven seas—let the author of *Moby Dick* speak:

"And the women of New Bedford, they bloom like their own red roses. But roses bloom only in the summer; whereas the fine carnation of their cheeks is perennial as the sunlight in the seventh heavens. Elsewhere, match that bloom of theirs, ye cannot, save in Salem, where they tell me the young girls breathe such musk, their sailor sweethearts can smell them miles off shore, as though they were drawing nigh the odorous Moluccas instead of the Puritanic sands."

BLOW THE MAN DOWN

Arrangement by Elie Siegmeister

HEARTILY, WITH MARKED RHYTHM

Oh, blow the man down, bul-lies. blow the man down! To me way, aye, blow the man down. Oh, blow the man down, bul-lies, blow him right down! Give me some time to blow the man down!

2

As I was a-walking down Paradise Street,
To me way, aye, blow the man down.
A pretty young damsel I chanced for to meet.
Give me some time to blow the man down!

* Symbols in italics for guitar with capo across 1st fret

3

She was round in the counter and bluff in bow,
To me way, aye, blow the man down.
So I took in all sail and cried, "Way enough now!"
Give me some time to blow the man down!

4

I hailed her in English, she answered me clear,
To me way, aye, blow the man down.
"I'm from the *Black Arrow* bound to the *Shakespeare*."
Give me some time to blow the man down!

5

So I tailed her my flipper and took her in tow,
To me way, aye, blow the man down.
And yardarm to yardarm away we did go,
Give me some time to blow the man down!

6

But as we were going she said unto me,
To me way aye, blow the man down.
"There's a spanking full-rigger just ready for sea."
Give me some time to blow the man down!

7

That spanking full rigger to New York was bound,
To me way aye, blow the man down.
She was very well manned and very well found,
Give me some time to blow the man down!

8

But soon as that packet was clear of the bar,
To me way aye, blow the man down.
The mate knocked me down with the end of a spar,
Give me some time to blow the man down!

9

And as soon as that packet was out on the sea,
To me way aye, blow the man down.
'Twas devilish hard treatment of every degree,
Give me some time to blow the man down!

10

So I give you fair warning before we belay;
To me way aye, blow the man down.
Don't ever take heed of what pretty girls say,
Give me some time to blow the man down!

BLOW THE MAN DOWN

THE TRADITIONAL TALE of the unfortunate adventures of many a sailor boy who found himself shanghaied aboard a ship with a tough-boned skipper as the result of the charms of a fair damsel. Speaking of its origin, Eloise Linscott* says: "... from the port of Liverpool, England, we have this most famous halyard chantey of the Atlantic packet ships. The earliest version of this song concerns the Black Ball line, which began its maritime service in 1818. The scorn with which the chanteymen looked upon these Western Ocean packets and the crews that manned them is vividly expressed here:

> *And when those packets were ready for sea,*
> *You'd split your sides laughing such sights you'd see,*
> *There were tinkers and tailors and soldiers as well,*
> *All shipped as sailors on board the Blue Bell.*

"The melody has remained the same through years of transition. 'Blow' as used here by the sailor means 'knock'. The street named in the song varies. The Winchester Street of some versions was the section where persons of rank lived; Paradise Street is said to have been a disreputable section along the waterfront."

* Eloise Linscott: "Folk Songs of Old New England."

THE BOSTON COME-ALL-YE

Arrangement by Elie Siegmeister

Come all ye young sail-or men, list-en to me,— I'll sing you a song of the fish of the sea. Then blow ye winds west-er-ly, west-er---ly blow,— We're bound to the south-'ard, so stead-y she goes.

2

Oh, first come the shale, the biggest of all,
He clumb up aloft and let ev'ry sail fall.
CHORUS: Then blow, *etc.*

3

And next come the mack'rel with his striped back,
He hauled aft the sheets and boarded each tack.
CHORUS: Then blow, *etc.*

From Joanna Colcord's Songs of American Sailormen, *published by W. W. Norton & Co., Inc.*

92

4

Then come the porpoise with his short snout,
He went to the wheel crying, "Ready! About!"
CHORUS: Then blow, *etc.*

5

Then come the smelt, the smallest of all,
He jumped to the poop, and sung out, "Topsail haul!"
CHORUS: Then blow, *etc.*

6

The herring come saying, "I'm king of the seas,
If you want any wind, why I'll blow you a breeze."
CHORUS: Then-blow, *etc.*

7

Next came the cod with his chuckle-head;
He went to the main-chains to heave at the lead.
CHORUS: Then blow, *etc.*

8

Last came the flounder as flat as the ground,
Says, "Damn your eyes, chuckle-head, mind how you sound!"
CHORUS: Then blow, *etc.*

THE BOSTON COME-ALL-YE

A WIDELY popular fo'c'sle song which began its life with the fishing fleet. We know from Kipling's *Captains Courageous* that under the title of "The Fishes" it was a favorite with the Banks fishermen. The chorus may have its origin in the Scotch fishing tune "Blaw the Wind Southerly." Here the sailor boy imagines what the fish would say if they could talk. The herring, the mackerel, the codfish express their views on life.

LOWLANDS

Arrangement by Elie Siegmeister

2

Lowlands, lowlands, away, my John.
A dollar and a half is a black man's pay,
My dollar and a half a day;
Five dollars a day is a white man's pay.

3

Lowlands, lowlands, away, my John.
The white man's pay is rather high,
My dollar and a half a day;
The black man's pay is rather low.
Lowlands, lowlands, away, my John.

* Symbols in italics for guitar with capo across 1st fret

"LOWLANDS," one of the most original of all songs of the sea, is nevertheless a strikingly collective expression of man in the presence of infinity. Cecil Sharp believes it to be compounded of the refrain of an old English ballad and variations bestowed upon it by Negro sailors out of Mobile. Americans and British shipped indiscriminately on vessels of both countries wherever the job was to be had that would take them off the beach. And this intermixture has made it impossible to say whether any given chanty is of American or English origin. This is a folk song, and it is by such interminglings and transmutations that a great folk song comes into being. How to harmonize it? The melodic line has a long sweep; the modal harmonies here employed are intended to suggest the expanse of mighty ocean.

SHENANDOAH
[THE WIDE MISSOURI]

Arrangement by Elie Siegmeister

Oh, Shen-an-doah, I long to hear you, A-way, my rol-ling riv-er! Oh, Shen-an-doah, I_ can't get near you. A-way, a-way, I'm bound a-way, 'Cross the wide Mis-sour-i!

2

Oh, Shenandoah, I love your daughter.
Away, my rolling river!
She lives across the stormy water.
Away, away, I'm bound away,
'Cross the wide Missouri!

3

For seven years I courted Sally,
Away, my rolling river,
For seven more I longed to have her,
Away, away, I'm bound away
'Cross the wide Missouri!

* Symbols in italics for guitar with capo across 1st fret

4

She said she would not be my lover.
Away, my rolling river!
Because I was a dirty sailor.
Away, away, I'm bound away,
'Cross the wide Missouri!

5

I'm drinkin' rum and chewin' terbaccer,
Away, my rolling river,
I'm drinkin' rum and chewin' terbaccer,
Away, away, I'm bound away,
'Cross the wide Missouri!

6

Oh, Shenandoah, I long to hear you,
Away, my rolling river,
A-coming back across the river,
Away, away, I'm bound away,
'Cross the wide Missouri!

SHENANDOAH

"SHENANDOAH" was an early land ballad about a trader who wooed the daughter of an Indian chief and then left her on the shores of the wide Missouri. The song was taken to sea, possibly by some of those roving lumberjacks who worked in the woods in winter and aboard ship during the summer. Without serious alterations, it became one of the most famous and widely sung of American shantys. It is that rare phenomenon, a slow, almost unrhythmical shanty.

RIO GRANDE

Arrangement by Elie Siegmeister

MODERATELY, WITH VIGOR

Oh, say, were you ev-er in Ri-o Grande? Way,___ you Ri-o!___ Oh, were___ you ev-er on___ that strand? For we're bound to the Ri-o Grande!___ And a-way,___ you Ri-o!___ Way,___ you Ri-o!___ Sing fare you well, my

pret-ty young girls, For we're bound to the Ri - o Grande!_____

2

Oh, say, were you ever in Rio Grande?
Way, you Rio!
It's there that the river runs down golden sand.
For we're bound to the Rio Grande!

CHORUS: And away, *etc.*

3

Oh, New York town is no place for me—
Way, you Rio!
I'll pack up my bag and go to sea.
For we're bound to the Rio·Grande!

CHORUS: And away, *etc.*

4

Now, you Bowery ladies, we'll let you know,
Way, you Rio!
We're bound to the South'ard, O Lord, let her go!
For we're bound to the Rio Grande!

CHORUS: And away, *etc.*

5

We'll sell our salt cod for molasses and rum—
Way, you Rio!
And get home again 'fore Thanksgiving has come.
For we're bound to the Rio Grande!

CHORUS: And away, *etc.*

RIO GRANDE

DURING THE MEXICAN WAR, Yankee ships sailed every ocean, some courting adventure by delivering contraband below the Rio Grande. This
capstan shanty grew up in those days and has been popular ever since.

A DOLLAR AND A HALF A DAY

Arrangement by Elie Siegmeister

But a dollar and a half is a black man's pay, way—
But a dollar and a half is a black man's pay,
My dollar and a half a day.

The black man works both day and night, way—
The black man works both day and night,
My dollar and a half a day.

4

But the white man he works but a day, way—
But the white man he works but a day,
My dollar and a half a day.

A DOLLAR AND A HALF A DAY

ANOTHER VERSION of "Lowlands," one of those sustained melodies hard
to imprison in any set bar-lines. The manner and tempo vary with every
singing. It was taken down from actual performance by Percy Grainger.

Ho, Boys, Ho

[PIONEER SONGS, WHITE SPIRITUALS, PLAY PARTIES]

AFTER THE REVOLUTION, and particularly after the War of 1812, the young country radiated enthusiasm and energy. A small upstart of a nation, it had just licked the greatest empire in the world and was ready for new adventures. It was expanding in all directions at once, sending its clippers out over the high seas and its population out into the uncharted land of the West. Footloose adventurers, farmers who had heard of fertile land to be had for the asking, immigrants from the troubled nations of the outside world, started out in whatever conveyance they could obtain. The stream of immigration, which had been steadily flowing since the War of Independence, now became a veritable torrent. Over mountains, on rivers, on foot, on horseback, in wagons, pushing carts before them, in river boats, whole families pulled up their stakes and set out for the Promised Land stretching before them in never-ending expanse.

Between 1770 and 1840 the westward movement grew from a handful of people to hundreds of thousands. Millions of acres were occupied by the moving hordes. McMaster tells us "reports from Lancaster (Pa.) state that 100 moving families had been counted going through the town *in a week,* and that the turnpike was fairly covered with bands of immigrants. At Zanesville (Ohio) 50 wagons crossed the Muskingum in one day." In spite of tremendous difficulties—roads that were quagmires, rivers that were often floods, attacks by the Indians—the settlers moved steadily on through the passes of Pennsylvania into the Ohio Valley, up through Ohio, Indiana, and Illinois, and down over the Cumberland Gap through Kentucky and Tennessee.

Davy Crockett is reported to have said to his wife one day, "There's some new settlers ten miles down the valley and I feel kind of crowded, so let's pull up and move on." Rarely did they stay put in the Promised Land; always there were new and better horizons farther on, new land for better herding, more fertile fields, less crowding. Abraham Lincoln's family went from Pennsylvania to Kentucky, where he was born in 1809. Seven years later they got on a raft and moved down the Ohio to Indiana. Fourteen years after that, his family moved again to Illinois. This was the rhythm of frontier life.

It was inevitable that this life in a wilderness, with its innumerable hardships and dangers, should develop a new type of man. He was energetic, hard-working, boastful and fearless. He was plain, disliked show or snobbishness, and since all he owned he had built with his own hands, he had a fundamental belief in himself and did not feel like taking orders from anyone.

It is plain to see that every aspect of this migration and this establishment of a new kind of life lent itself to the creation of song. Men on expeditions and men in danger, men on lonely frontiers and men in dark forests, sing. They sing for courage, for cheer and companionship, out of pride, out of sheer boisterousness. Women who care for children alone in the heart of the wilderness, with neighbors many miles off, croon their own lullabies and create their own work songs. Singing was one of the chief forms of recreation on the frontier. There were no theatres, no social gatherings, no time for such frippery. Men couldn't play cards, with the nearest neighbor twenty-five miles away, but people had their own voices and the treasury of song that they had brought along in their own memories. There must have been hosts of songs reflecting these early pioneer days, but few of them were recorded because people had no time or thought to give to such a thing as writing down music.

So the songs that have come down to us have arrived mainly by accident or because they persisted in other forms. The old song, for example:

> Come all ye fine young fellows
> Who have got a mind to range
> Into some far-off countree
> Your fortune for to change.
> We'll lay us down upon the banks
> Of the blessed O-hi-o,
> Through the wild woods we'll wander
> And chase the buffalo

would have been entirely forgotten had it not been taken up and made over into a play-party song, called "Shoot the Buffalo," in which form it is still sung today. Many songs were translated into spirituals and thus were recorded.

However, we still have a few of the original songs as they were sung in those days. They were the songs of the bullwhackers who drove the wagons, or the legends of the early *voyageurs* or fur traders, and the later professional boatmen who ferried the immigrants down the Ohio, Muskingum, and a dozen other streams, songs of early land boom experts and of lads and girls who were going off over the mountains in search of some faithless lover.

The pioneer songs that did get recorded were the religious songs and ballads. Musically, these were very little if at all, different from the folk songs. There was no established church on the frontier, no regular services, no fixed hymns. What religion there was came from the family Bible, which was always at hand, together with the rifle and axe, and from the circuit riding preachers, who, though in many cases not ordained by theological schools, yet felt the call of God strongly enough to brave hunger, thirst, Indians, wild animals, and the sometimes still wilder frontiersmen, to bring the Gospel into the very heart of the wilderness. Along with other ballads, frontiersmen would remember a few lines from some old hymn. With no set books to make them toe the mark,

these, with the addition of other phrases that would come to mind were soon fused and a new religious ballad or spiritual was born. Tunes flowed back and forth between the profane and religious ballads with the greatest of ease. The pioneers saw nothing incongruous in this, and indeed such a process has been going on ever since religion first started.

Or a spiritual might spring up this way: A circuit riding preacher during his long journey on horseback from one settlement to another, had plenty of time to think of what sermon he would preach and what hymn he would sing at the next meeting, which might be hundreds of miles off. Looking at the wilderness around him, what would be more natural than to take the forest, the trees, the skies, the presence of God in nature, as his theme? If he were apt at making verses, and many of them were, he might take some well-known tune as a starting point and fit religious words to it on this theme. At the next point of call, instead of singing the Doxology, he might sing his new hymn, and if it took, the frontiersman or his wife might go away humming it.

"Through All the World," "Poor Wayfaring Stranger" and "When Adam Was Created" are among the hundreds of spirituals which probably originated in some such manner. In many cases, of course, the pioneer himself, if he was a God-fearing man—and most of them were— might create such a religious song all on his own, without the help of any preacher, as a means of serving the Lord.

But perhaps the largest number of these songs grew up in that characteristic American institution, the camp meeting, which was a regular feature of frontier life. The announcement that a revival meeting was to be held generally would provoke tense excitement, for it was not only a religious gathering, but a social one as well, a chance to see his friends, trade, and later even go on drinking parties and hold games and contests of all sorts. Crowds would flock to the revival from miles around, and as the preacher delivered his sermon, which was usually burning with hell-fire and brimstone, the reactions of the mixed congregation were by no means demure. The listeners would shout, jump around, roll on the ground, scream with laughter and tears, fall into uncontrollable spasms and jerks, and into spontaneous singing. Needless to say, many of these songs were gibberish, but under the pressure of the exciting experience others developed a highly stimulating drive and lift. They were generally made up out of familiar phrases from the Scriptures, interspersed with hallelujahs, refrains of familiar songs, and phrases of common speech. When someone would strike up a refrain such as "We are bound for the Promised Land," the whole crowd would pile in with a roar that would make the wilderness shake.

Camp meetings songs had to be so simple that everyone, young and old alike, without any previous learning, could join in and be carried along. It is not surprising that we find familiar lines cropping up in one song after another, such as "I am bound for glory," "Say, brothers, will you join me?" "Shout Salvation, brothers," etc.

The verse was often given out by the leader, the crowd joining in only on the well-known refrain. It was at such camp meetings—and there were tens of thousands of them—that songs like the "Promised Land," reflecting the optimism of a growing America and of a country just opening up, were born. Many of the texts reflect the actual surroundings of the western frontier. Thus love of the new land is mirrored in "Whitestown"

> *Where nothing dwelt but beasts of prey*
> *Or men as fierce and wild as they,*
> *He bids th' oppress'd and poor repair,*
> *And build them towns and cities there.*
> *They sow the fields, and trees they plant,*
> *Whose yearly fruit supplies their want;*
> *Their race grows up from fruitful stocks,*
> *Their wealth increases with their flocks.*

The spiritual, "War Department," no doubt followed the close of one of the perennial Indian wars:

> *No more shall the sound of the war-whoops*
> *be heard,*
> *The ambush and slaughter no longer be*
> *fear'd.*
> *The tomahawk buried, shall rest in the*
> *ground,*
> *And peace and good-will to the nations*
> *abound.*

And "Liberty" expressed pithily the frontiersmen's most characteristic feeling:

> *No more beneath th' oppressive hand*
> *Of tyranny we mourn,*
> *Behold the smiling, happy land,*
> *That freedom calls her own.*

Were it not for the existence of the early singing-school teachers on the frontier, none of this music would have come down to us. They were professional musicians who followed the circuit preachers, generally in the slightly more settled regions, and earned their way by organizing religious singing semesters in the tradition of the early New England singing schools.

Singing schools of this type existed in western Tennessee and Kentucky more than a hundred years ago. Since the local teachers had to deal with untutored pupils, they simplified the difficult task of reading from music by using the old New England system of notation in which the shape of the notes indicated the pitch, even though the reader might know nothing of the lines and spaces of the clef.

Many of the early singing masters made their own, sometimes crude, but often distinctly original arrangements of well-known songs and published their own books. They were thus able to serve the Lord and realize an excellent profit as well. Mr. Billy Walker, A. S. H. (Author of the "Southern Harmony"—he said he would rather have the letters "A.S.H." after his name than the word "Pres." before it) sold over 600,000 copies of this book in the Midwest, an area most people would consider "that great musical desert." Collections such as "The Sacred Harp" have gone into many editions and are still used in these districts. Many of the songs have a distinct and powerful effect when sung, even though they look curious on paper. They have unusual harmonies which are often strange to the modern ear, and they violate conventional rules quite as radically as modern compositions. The spirituals in these songsters were home-grown and bred in the open air, and they take on a decidedly regional and distinctive American country style. "Singing Billy" Walker, and many other native country composers continued the tradition of William Billings' fuguing tunes. Though it seems incredible, these rather intricate pieces were actually sung by the raw pioneers, and if we are to believe George P. Jackson, they are still performed at the "Big Singings" in the South today. He tells us * that even youngsters in their teens can hold a part in these by no means simple contrapuntal pieces.

Another characteristic development of frontier life was the play-party song. Play parties were simply games played to the accompaniment of singing, varying all the way from simple steps like "Going to Jerusalem" and "Here Come Three Dukes A-riding," still played by children today, to intricate dance steps complete with calls, formations and turns, to such tunes as "Weevily Wheat," "Old Joe Clark," and Old Dan Tucker," very much like the square dances of today.

But it would never do to call them "dances." That would be sinful and the pioneers were a God-fearing people. Many a young bucko and his girl were haled before meeting charged with "dancing to devil-tunes." Since Puritan days, devil tunes were simply those played on a fiddle, banjo, or some other instrument. And to this day there are thousands in Oklahoma, Missouri and elsewhere who would not think of stepping out on a floor when a fiddle is playing. But so long as the music is merely their own singing, they will "play games," doing the same dance steps to the very same tunes from early evening to early morning.

In early days, play parties were an ideal means of solving the entertainment problem in

* G. P. Jackson: "White Spirituals in the Southern Uplands."

the simplest way available. In sparsely settled regions they gave people an opportunity to meet and enjoy themselves, and the frontier people held one on every possible occasion. When a new settler arrived, the word would go around, and men would come together from miles around to help with the house-raising. The weight of the logs made this a task requiring the combined efforts of a large crew, and this help was always cheerfully forthcoming. Corn huskings, log rollings, apple and pumpkin cuttings were other jobs that brought folk together. The women would make use of the opportunity for quilting, sewing, spinning thread, and preparing the community feast or barbecue, which always followed such gatherings. A play party was always sure to round out the evening. Several hours of singing and "playing" would generally wind up in drinking bouts for the married men and "sparking" for the younger folk.

What kind of music was sung at these parties? The tunes might be taken from anywhere and everywhere: old ballads, children's songs, wagon tunes, square dances, and at a later date, minstrel songs from the cities, army songs, and whatnot. But when sung at a play party, they all took on a characteristic lively swing, irresistibly gay and infectious, and full of the movement of sturdy legs and bodies. As memories were often short, and the evenings long, old verses got new twists and new ones were improvised on the spur of the moment. It was fun to sing out an unexpected new rhyme, and as the hour grew later, the sallies would often become more pointed and reckless.

Take her by the lily-white hand
And lead her like a pigeon.
Make her dance to 'Weevily Wheat'
And scatter her religion.

Some of the tunes furnish an ideal framework for new verses. "Skip to My Lou" is sung in 160 different versions in Oklahoma alone. Sometimes queer changes take place. "Weevily Wheat," which began its career hundreds of years ago with verses about bonnie Prince Charlie, now is sung to words about trading boats which serve the Southern plantations. Along with much nonsense, triviality and sheer fun, the songs reflect the migrations and the new environments, even in their titles: "Pig in the Parlor," "Way Down in the Paw Paw," "Hog Drovers Are We," "Shoot the Buffalo." They reflect an exuberant simplicity and joy in life that have kept them a living part of America even today.

E. S.

THE HUNTERS OF KENTUCKY

Arrangement by Elie Siegmeister

BRISK, GOOD-HUMORED

Ye gen - tle-men and la - dies fair who grace this fam - ous ci - ty, Just

lis - ten if you've time to spare while I re - hearse a dit - ty; And

for an op - por - tun - i - ty, con — ceive your - selves quite luck - y for

'tis not oft - en here you see a hunt - er from Ken - tuck - y,

O, Ken - tuck - y, the hunt - ers of Ken - tuck - y,

O, Ken - tuck - y, the hunt - ers of Ken - tuck - y.

2

You've heard I s'pose how New Orleans is fam'd for wealth and beauty,
There's girls of ev'ry hue it seems, from snowy white to sooty;
So Packenham he made his brags, if he in fight was lucky,
He'd have their girls and cotton bags, in spite of old Kentucky.

3

But Jackson he was wide awake, and wasn't scar'd at trifles,
For well he knew what aim we take with our Kentucky rifles;
So he led us down to Cypress swamp, the ground was low and mucky,
There stood John Bull in martial pomp, and here was old Kentucky.

4

A bank was rais'd to hide our breast, not that we thought of dying,
But that we always like to rest, unless the game is flying;
Behind it stood our little force—none wished it to be greater,
For ev'ry man was half a horse, and half an alligator.

5

They found at last 'twas vain to fight, where lead was all their booty;
And so they wisely took a flight, and left us all our beauty.
And now if danger e'er annoys, remember what our trade is,
Just send for us Kentucky boys, and we'll protect you, ladies.

THIS SONG was long a popular favorite because of the exploits of the Kentucky riflemen who under Old Hickory Jackson charged the British at New Orleans on January 8, 1815, with an axe in one hand, a spade in the other, and a rifle between the teeth.

For the rambunctious text the melody is exceedingly polite. Samuel Woodworth, author of "The Old Oaken Bucket," wrote the words in 1822.

STAR OF COLUMBIA

Words by Dr. Dwight
Music attributed to Miss M. T. Durham
Arrangement by Elie Siegmeister

Co - lum - bia, Co - lum - bia, to glor - y a - rise, The queen of the

world and the child of the skies, Thy gen - ius com - mands thee, with

rap - tures be - hold, While ag - es on ag - es thy splen - dors un - fold.

Thy reign is the last and the nob - lest of time, Most fruit - ful thy

soil, __ most in - vit - ing thy clime, Let __ crimes of the east __ ne'er en-

crim - son thy name. Be __ free - dom and sci - ence and vir-tue thy fame.

To conquest and slaughter let Europe aspire,
'Whelm nations in blood, or wrap cities in fire;
Thy heroes the rights of mankind shall defend,
And triumph pursue them and glory attend.

A world is thy realm, for a world be thy laws,
Enlarged as thy empire, and just as thy cause;
On freedom's broad basis that empire shall rise,
Extend with the main and dissolve with the skies.

STAR OF COLUMBIA

"A RISING NATION, spread over a wide and fruitful land, traversing all seas, with the rich productions of their industry, engaged in commerce with nations who feel power and forget rights, advancing rapidly to destinies beyond the reach of mortal eye. When I contemplate these objects, I shrink from the contemplation and shrink from the magnitude of the undertaking."

Jefferson's Inaugural Address.

THIS SONG, which may have already been current during Jefferson's presidency, radiates the energy of a young nation in its teens. The melody might well be a descendant of those old Scotch war songs brought into the Appalachians by the Highlanders. The present harmonization, in open fourths and fifths, is based on that made in 1835 by Billy Walker, a style suitable to the rugged quality of the text.

EL-A-NOY

Arrangement by Elie Siegmeister

Way down__ u-pon the Wa-bash, Sich land was nev-er

known,. If A-dam had passed ov-er it, The soil he'd sure-ly

own. He'd think it was the gar-den, He'd played in when a boy, And

straight pro-nounce it E-den, In the State of El-a-noy.

Chorus Bb / F

Then move your fam-ily west-ward, Good health you will en-joy, And

Dm/A Dm/G Dm/F C7/G F/A Am Dm

rise to wealth and hon-or, In the State of El - a - noy.

2

'Twas here the Queen of Sheba came,
With Solomon of old,
With an ass-load of spices,
Pomegranates and fine gold.

And when she saw this lovely land,
Her heart was filled with joy,
Straightway she said,
"I'd like to be a Queen in Elanoy!"
CHORUS: Then move, *etc.*

3

She's bounded by the Wabash,
The Ohio and the Lakes,
She's crawfish in the swampy lands,
The milk-sick and the shakes;

But these are slight diversions,
And take not from the joy
Of living in this garden land,
The State of Elanoy.
CHORUS: Then move, *etc.*

EL-A-NOY

WRITING OF ILLINOIS in 1818, Samuel Crabtree said in a letter to his brother: "This is a country for a man to enjoy himself, where you may see prairie sixty miles long and ten broad at two dollars an acre, that will produce from seventy to a hundred bushels of Indian corn per acre. I measured Indian corn more than fifteen feet high and some of the ears had from four to seven hundred grains. I believe I saw more peaches and apples rotting on the ground than would sink the British fleet, and they have such flocks of turkeys, geese, ducks and hens as would surprise you. The poorest family has a cow or two and some sheep. Good rye whiskey, apple and peach brandy, at forty cents per gallon, which I think equals the rum, excellent cider at three dollars per barrel of thirty-three gallons, barrel included."

THE UNCONSTANT LOVER

Arrangement by Elie Siegmeister

O— come, all my young lov-ers, Whom-so-ev — er wants to gao,— An' we'll all set-tle daown— On the O — hi — o.

An' we'll chaw aour terbacker,
An' smeoke aour pipes,
An' eat aour pertaties,
Whensoever they gits ripe.

Naow a meetin' are a pleasure,
An' a partin' are a grief;
But an unconstant lover
Is wusser nor a thief.

'Cos a thief he will rob ye
Of all thet you have;
But an unconstant lover
Will tote ye to yer grave!

THE UNCONSTANT LOVER

MANY WHO WENT down the Ohio Valley sought a plot of ground on which to settle. Others came for adventure, and still others to forget a broken heart. This song of a pioneer lass has overtones of both nostalgia and sarcasm in it.

WAY DOWN THE OHIO

A CAREFREE SONG of the early Ohio River traders, whom tradition represents as "happy-go-lucky fellows, swinging along in their canoes, and charming the birds off the trees."—Greenbie: *American Saga.*

WAY DOWN THE OHIO

LIVELY, WITH HUMOR

Way down the O - hi - o my lit - tle boat I steered,

In hopes that some pret - ty girl on the banks will ap - pear.

I'll hug her and kiss her, till my mind is at ease, And I'll

turn my back on her and court who I please

THE JOLLY WAGONER

Arrangement by Elie Siegmeister

ROLLICKING

When I first went a-wag-on-ing, a-wag-on-ing did go, I filled my par-ents' hearts full of sor-row, grief and woe, And man-y are the hard-ships that I have since gone through.— Sing wo, my lads, sing wo; drive on, my lads, I oh! Who would-n't lead the life of a jol-ly wag-on-er?

* Symbols in italics for guitar with capo across 1st fret

It is a cold and stormy night, and I'm wet to the skin;
I will bear it with contentment till I get into the inn,
And then I'll get to drinking with the landlord and his kin.
CHORUS: Sing wo, etc.

Now summer it is coming,—what pleasure we shall see;
The small birds are a-singing on every bush and tree,
The blackbirds and the thrushes all are whistling merrliee.
CHORUS: Sing wo, etc.

Now Michaelmas is coming,—what pleasure we shall find!
It will make the gold to fly, my boys, like chaff before the wind;
And every lad shall take his lass, so loving and so kind.
CHORUS: Sing wo, etc.

THE JOLLY WAGONER

THE PROFESSIONAL wagoners of early days played an important role in the building of America, for it was they who carried thousands of pioneer families over the Appalachian passes to the new lands in the mid-west. They were a hardy, strong-boned race, and many were the trials and dangers they had to face. The "bullwhackers" met up with Indians, wild animals, washouts, landslides and, worst of all—mud. Although they spent more time in lifting their wagons out of marsh holes and cursing the oxen than in singing, their tunes were plentiful and robust. "The Jolly Wagoner" was still heard not many years ago in the highlands of eastern Pennsylvania.

POOR WAYFARING STRANGER

Arrangement by Elie Siegmeister

116

go - ing o - ver Jor - dan, I'm on - ly go - ing o - ver home.

2

I know dark clouds will gather 'round me,
I know my way is rough and steep.
Yet beauteous fields lie just before me,
Where God's redeemed their vigils keep.

I'm going there to see my mother,
She said she'd meet me when I come,
I'm only going over Jordan,
I'm only going over home.

3

I'll soon be freed from every trial,
My body asleep in the old churchyard.
I'll drop the cross of self-denial,
And enter on my great reward.

I'm going there to see my brothers,
Who have gone before me one by one,
I'm only going over Jordan,
I'm only going over home.

POOR WAYFARING STRANGER

"IN 1785 I visited the rough and hilly country of Otsego where there existed not an inhabitant, nor any trace of road. I was alone, three hundred miles from home, without bread, meats or food of any kind; fire and fishing tackle were my only means of subsistence. I caught trout from the brook and roasted them in the ashes. My horse fed on the grass that grew by the edge of the water. I laid me down to sleep in my watch-coat, nothing but melancholy wilderness around me." So writes William Cooper, father of James Fenimore Cooper.

The desolation of the lonely traveller in the virgin forests of early America produced such a song as this one. This modal song with its poignant, sustained melody, is recorded as having been sung first about 1830, although it was probably known long before then. "Poor Wayfaring Stranger" is still heard in the Southern mountains today.

WHEN ADAM WAS CREATED

Arrangement by Elie Siegmeister

When A - dam was cre - a - ted, he dwelt in E - den's shade, As

Mo - ses has re - la - ted, be - fore a bride was made; Ten

thou-sand times ten thou - sand of crea - tures swarmed a - round, Be -

fore a bride was form - ed or a - ny mate was found.

* Symbols in italics for guitar with capo across 3rd fret

He had no consolation, but seemed as one alone,
Till, to his admiration, he found he'd lost a bone.
This woman was not taken from Adam's head, we know;
And she must not rule o'er him, 'tis evidently so.

This woman she was taken from under Adam's arm;
And she must be protected from injury and harm.
This woman was not taken from Adam's feet, we see;
And she must not be abused, the meaning seems to be.

This woman she was taken from near to Adam's heart,
By which we are directed that they should never part.
The book that's called the Bible, be sure you don't neglect,
For in every sense of duty, it will you both direct.

To you, most loving bridegroom; to you, most loving bride,
Be sure you live a Christian and for your house provide.
Avoiding all discontent, don't sow the seed of strife,
As is the solemn duty of every man and wife.

WHEN ADAM WAS CREATED

A MARRIAGE SERMON in song, this early white spiritual cites the Biblical story of the first couple to be joined in wedlock as the model of marital conduct. For generations its beautiful and homely counsel has been sung, usually to the simple modal melody cited here. Bearing out the connection between the sacred and the secular in the white spirituals, it is of interest to observe that the capstan shanty "The Banks of Newfoundland" has essentially the same tune.

THE PROMISED LAND

Words: Traditional; Music attributed to Miss M. Durham
Arrangement by Elie Siegmeister

LIVELY, JOYFULLY

On Jor-dan's storm-y banks I stand, And cast a wish-ful
eye, To__ Can-aan's_ fair and hap-py land, Where__ my pos-ses-sions
lie. I am bound for the prom-ised land,_____ I'm bound for the prom-ised
land Oh,__ who will_ come and go with me? I am bound for the prom-ised land. land..

2

There generous fruits that never fail
On trees immortal grow;
There rocks and hills and brooks and vales
With milk and honey flow.

CHORUS: I am bound, etc.

4

No chilling winds nor poisonous breath
Can reach that healthful shore;
Sickness and sorrow, pain and death
Are felt and feared no more.

CHORUS: I am bound, etc.

3

O, the transporting rapt'rous scene
That rises to my sight,
Sweet fields arrayed in living green
And rivers of delight.

CHORUS: I am bound, etc.

5

All o'er those wide extended plains
Shines one eternal day;
There God the Son forever reigns,
And scatters night away.

CHORUS: I am bound, etc.

6

When shall I reach that happy place,
And be forever blest?
When shall I see my Father's face,
And in his bosom rest?

CHORUS: I am bound, etc.

THE PROMISED LAND

TO THE early pioneer, the phrase, "the promised land" referred not only to the Heavenly pastures that lay beyond death, but also to the fertile earth that stretched beyond the Alleghenies. It was a phrase that recurred in conversation, in diaries, in letters written home. It was natural that it should spring up time and again in a score of camp meeting songs and spirituals. When the faithful sang of Heaven with its "sweet fields arrayed in living green" and its "wide extended plains" it was from the landscapes of Ohio, Indiana and Illinois that they borrowed their imagery.

The lively rhythm of this refrain sounded in many a wilderness camp-meeting during the "Great Southern and Western Revival" of the late eighteenth and early nineteenth century.

THE SAINT'S DELIGHT

Arrangement by Elie Siegmeister

When I can read my tit - le clear _ to man - sions in the
skies, I'll bid fare - well to ev - 'ry fear _ and dry my weep - ing eyes. I
Chorus feel like, I feel _ like I'm on my jour - ney home, _ I
feel like, I feel _ like I'm on my jour - ney home. I home.

Should earth against my soul engage,
And fiery darts be hurled,
Then I can smile at Satan's rage,
And face a frowning world.
CHORUS: I feel like, I feel like, *etc.*

Let cares like a wild deluge come,
Let storms of sorrow fall,
So I but safely reach my home,
My God, my heaven, my all.
CHORUS: I feel like, I feel like, *etc.*

There I shall bathe my weary soul
In seas of heavenly rest;
And not a wave of trouble roll
Across my peaceful breast.
CHORUS: I feel like, I feel like, *etc.*

THE SAINT'S DELIGHT

ONE OF THE loveliest of old camp-meeting songs, "The Saint's Delight"
no doubt delighted many among the early pioneers who were not quite
saintly. It was first published in 1835.

WONDROUS LOVE

Arrangement by Elie Siegmeister

SUSTAINED, MODERATELY SLOW

What won - drous love is this, Oh! my soul, oh, my soul! What won - drous love is this, Oh my soul! What won - drous love is this! That caused the Lord— of bliss, To bear the dread-ful curse for my soul, for my soul, To bear the dread - ful curse for my soul.

When I was sinking down, sinking down, sinking down;
When I was sinking down, sinking down;
When I was sinking down,
Beneath God's righteous frown,
Christ laid aside his crown for my soul, for my soul;
Christ laid aside his crown for my soul.

And when from death I'm free, I'll sing on, I'll sing on;
And when from death I'm free, I'll sing on.
And when from death I'm free,
I'll sing and joyful be,
And through eternity I'll sing on, I'll sing on,
And through eternity I'll sing on.

WONDROUS LOVE

THERE IS AWE in the mood of this white spiritual, harmonized in almost medieval manner by Billy Walker in his *Southern Harmony* of 1835. The constant empty parallel fourths and fifths, retained in the present arrangement, lend themselves admirably to this archaic-sounding music. It is strange that this type of harmonization, so similar to that of European composers of the twelfth and thirteenth centuries, was independently developed by Walker and other American mountain composers of a hundred and fifty years ago.

THROUGH ALL THE WORLD

Tune of "Captain Kidd"
Arrangement by Elie Siegmeister

Through all the world be - low, God is seen all a - round; Search
hills and val - leys through, There he's found. The grow-ing of the corn, The
li - ly and the thorn, The__ pleas - ant and for - lorn, All de-
-clare God is there, In the mead - ows dressed in green, There he's seen.

2

See springs of water rise,
Fountains flow, rivers run;
The mist below the skies
Hides the sun;
Then down the rain doth pour,
The ocean it doth roar,
And dash against the shore,
All to praise, in their lays,
That God that ne'er declines
His designs.

The sun, to my surprise,
Speaks of God as he flies;
The comets in their blaze
Give him praise;
The shining of the stars
The moon as it appears
His sacred name declares;
See them shine, all divine!
The shades in silence prove
God's above.

4

Then let my station be
Here on earth, as I see
The sacred One in Three
All agree;
Through all the world is made,
The forest and the glade;
Nor let me be afraid,
Though I dwell on the hill,
Since nature's works declare
God is there.

THROUGH ALL THE WORLD

PRESENT-DAY WRITERS of sacred music do not generally go to popular songs for their inspiration. But a hundred years ago, those who created hymns for use in frontier camp meetings did not hesitate to turn a profane tune to religious uses—if it was catchy enough.

The unknown poet who wrote the lovely pastoral verses of "Through All the World" had the most pious motives when he set them to the familiar tune of that bloodthirsty pirate Captain Kidd.* For the popularity of the tune certainly lightened the burden of the southern mountain hymn-singers whose spiritual zeal was greater than their note-reading ability. To ensure recognition of the melody, the song was even printed in hymn-books under the title "Captain Kidd," and is known as such in the South to this day. This white spiritual gives a charming image of the Appalachian wilderness as seen through the eyes of an early frontiersman, for whom the "meadows dressed in green," the "forest and the glade," the "growing of the corn," and the "mist below the skies" all declare "God is there."

The piano accompaniment retains the characteristic bare harmonies of "Singin' Billy" Walker's original vocal arrangement, published in his *Southern Harmony* in 1835 and sung ever since by hundreds of thousands in Georgia, Kentucky, Tennessee and the Carolinas.

* See p. 40 for the original words and another version of the melody of the "Captain Kidd" ballad.

WEEVILY WHEAT

Arrangement by Elie Siegmeister

I don't want none of your weev-i-ly wheat, I don't want none of your bar-ley, I want some flour and half an hour To bake a cake for Char-lie.

2

Charlie he's a fine young man,
Charlie he's a dandy;
He loves to hug and kiss the girls
And feed 'em on good candy.

3

The higher up the cherry tree,
The riper grows the cherry;
The more you hug and kiss the girls,
The sooner they will marry.

Take her by the lily white hand,
And lead her like a pigeon,
Make her dance to "Weevily Wheat,"
And scatter her religion.

5

Trading boats have gone ashore,
Trading boats are landing;
Trading boats have gone ashore
Loaded down with candy.

6

'Way down yonder in the maple swamp,
Where the water's deep and muddy,
We'll dance and sing till broad daylight,
And won't get home till Sunday.

7

If you love me like I love you,
We'll have no time to tarry,
We'll have the old folks flying around,
Fixing for us to marry.

8

I have got a sweet little wife,
A wife of my own choosing;
Hug her neat and kiss her sweet
And go no more a-courting.

WEEVILY WHEAT

THE FEET OF early New England settlers trod a lively measure to the sung verses of this play-party song, which originated from the period when Prince Charles tried to wear the crown of Britain, in 1745. Many were the songs written about him. This one has been variously treated by generations of Americans in different parts of the country. In the early 1800's pioneers danced to it in the maple swamps of Indiana, "where the water's deep and muddy." It reached the Southern plantations, where a verse about the "trading boats" that carried away the cotton was added. Whereas the New Englanders substituted their corn meal for British beef, the migrants to the west changed it to weevily wheat and barley.

SHOOT THE BUFFALO

Arrangement by Elie Siegmeister

Rise you up, my dear-est dear, And pre - sent to me your hand, And we'll
all run a - way To some far and dis - tant land, Where the
la - dies knit and sew, And the gents they plow and hoe, And we'll
ram - ble in the cane brake And shoot the buf - fa - lo.

2

Rise you up, my dearest dear,
And present to me your paw,
I'm sure you've got terbacker,
I'd like to have a chaw.

Oh, the rabbit shot the monkey
And the monkey shot the crow,
Let us ramble in the cane-break
And shoot the buffalo.

3

Where the women sit and patch
And the men stand and scratch,
We'll all meet together
In the old potato patch.

All the way from Georgia
To Texas I must go
To rally 'round the cane-brake
And shoot the buffalo.

Original verses to "Hunt the Buffalo"

1

Come all ye fine young fellows
Who have got a mind to range
Into some far off countree
Your fortune for to change.
We'll lay us down upon the banks
Of the blessed O-hi-o;
Through the wildwoods we'll wander,
And we'll chase the buffalo.

2

Come all ye fine young women
Who have got a mind to go,
That you may make us clothing
You can knit and you can sew.
We'll build you fine log cabins
By the blessed O-hi-o;
Through the wildwoods we'll wander,
And we'll chase the buffalo.

3

And should the dread wild Indians
By chance to us come near,
We'll all unite together,
And show we have no fear.
We'll bind ourselves together
And strike the fatal blow;
Through the wildwoods we'll wander,
And we'll chase the buffalo.

SHOOT THE BUFFALO

IN THE early nineteenth century there was a pioneer ballad, "Hunt the Buffalo," which invited footloose young men into the wildwoods to chase the hump-backed beast which apparently still ranged the banks of the "O-hi-o." Shortly afterward, some of the lines of this ballad were incorporated in a play-party song.

The buffalo has long since vanished not only from the shores of the Ohio, but even from the western plains, and with it "Hunt the Buffalo" disappeared. But youngsters in Oklahoma, Texas and Missouri still dance on Saturday nights as they sing to their young ladies to accompany them to "some fair and distant land" where they can "ramble through the canebrake and shoot the buffalo."

SKIP TO MY LOU

Arrangement by Elie Siegmeister

2

Gone again, skip to my Lou,
Gone again, skip to my Lou,
Gone again, skip to my Lou,
Skip to my Lou, my darling.

4

I'll get another one prettier than you,
I'll get another one prettier than you,
I'll get another one prettier than you,
Skip to my Lou, my darling.

3

Stole my partner, skip to my Lou,
Stole my partner, skip to my Lou,
Stole my partner, skip to my Lou,
Skip to my Lou, my darling.

5

Chicken on the haystack, shoo, shoo, shoo,
Chicken on the haystack, shoo, shoo, shoo,
Chicken on the haystack, shoo, shoo, shoo,
Skip to my Lou, my darling.

DIRECTIONS FOR DANCING

Balance all, skip to my Lou, etc.

Corners swing, skip to my Lou, etc.

Back to your partners, skip to my Lou, etc.

All promenade, skip to my Lou, etc.

SKIP TO MY LOU

"THE PLAY PARTY is a development of frontier life. . . . The square dance, to which the early settlers would have turned was often impossible because of lack of music. In the earliest settlements along the frontier, pianos and organs were unheard of, and violins were almost as rare. . . . Jigs and pigeon wings were frequently danced to the staccato rhythm of bones rattled by skilled hands or thimbled fingers on a tin washboard. But community dancing could not be had to such accompaniment, and as a result, the people turned to singing their simple directions for the dance movements." *

* Owens: Swing and Turn."

SWING ON THE CORNER

Arrangement by Elie Siegmeister

From **Folk Dances of Tennessee** by *McDowell & McDowell*, published by Edwards Brothers, Inc. Printed by permission.

134

waltz and swing, with a waltz and swing, Swing on the cor-ner with a

waltz and swing, And bal-ance to your pla-ces.

2

Take your partner and we'll all run away,
All run away, all run away,
Take your partner and we'll all run away,
And balance to your places.
CHORUS: Swing on, *etc.*

3

First young gent all around in town,
All around in town, all around in town,
First young gent all around in town,
And balance to your places.
CHORUS: Swing on, *etc.*

4

Take your partner all around in town,
All around in town, all around in town,
Take your partner all around in town,
And balance to your places.
CHORUS: Swing on, *etc.*

5

Next young lady all around in town,
All around, *etc.*

6

Take your partner and we'll all run away,
All run away, *etc.*

7

Next young gent all around in town,
All around, *etc.*

8

Take your partner and we'll all run away,
All run away, *etc.*

SWING ON THE CORNER

IN THIS play-party tune the directions for the dance movements, sung out
by the "caller," make the text. Each verse represents a different series of
steps. The melody has remained a favorite the country over from pioneer
times to this day.

Tooth-Ache in His Heel

WHILE PIONEER SONGS, spirituals and play-party tunes were developing in the newly settled country districts of the Midwest, an equally characteristic new form of music was growing up in the cities of the East, a form that was destined to produce America's greatest songster: Stephen Foster.

The minstrel show was an outgrowth of the native minstrel bands of the South. As James Weldon Johnson tells us, these could be found on almost every plantation. They consisted of a group of Negro entertainers, who were apt at cutting capers, playing the "bones" and the banjo, and performing comic songs, dances and impersonations with all the natural ease and vitality that is an organic part of their race.

Professional white comedians started, in the 1820's and '30's, to use the jokes, the "Ethiopian" ditties, the hoe-downs, the pigeon wings, and the other entertainments of these plantation companies. They appeared on the stage in black-face. According to tradition, it was "Daddy" Rice who really started the minstrel vogue which for over sixty years was the chief American form of entertainment, and the ancestor of vaudeville, the tap-dance, the musical comedy and Amos 'n Andy. Rice put on his "Jump Jim Crow" act in Louisville in 1830. The story goes that the comedian had watched a Negro stablehand humming a tune and doing some tricky steps. Borrowing his clothes, he reproduced the act on the stage and did so well that the original Jim Crow grew tired of waiting and came on the stage to demand his suit back. The audience apparently thought this was part of the show and roared with laughter.

Like many stories, this is probably too pat to be true. At any rate, the minstrel vogue grew rapidly. Companies of wise-cracking, fiddle-, bones-, and banjo-playing song and dance men in blackface were formed, such as the Virginia

Serenaders, the E. P. Christy Minstrels, Callender's Consolidated Minstrels, and the Ethiopian Serenaders. The new type of entertainment was immediately successful and profitable. Tours were made through all the principal cities and the managers vied with one another, as do the band leaders of today, for new numbers that would "pack them in." The slapstick turns of Sambo, Mr. Bones and the Interlocutor needed the backing of both "hot" and "sweet" tunes, and the characteristic lively, syncopated style and the sentimental "old plantation" style were born. Clever composers and arrangers who understood the popular taste and could turn out appropriate numbers plentifully, often to order, were much in demand.

The minstrel show, which was thus founded on basic, even though generally caricatured, folk origins, and on a sound democratic demand for light entertainment, was really the forerunner of the tradition of the rag-time, jazz and swing that have made American popular music the best in the world. The men and the songs it produced: Dan Emmett, Stephen Foster, James Bland, E. P. Christy, Cool White; and "Old Dan Tucker," "Old Zip Coon," "Oh Susanna," "My Old Kentucky Home," "Dixie," "Carry Me Back to Old Virginny," were America's first contributions that were popular abroad.

Of course, there were those who scorned the low-brow minstrel songs. A critic of 1858 assures us that:

"Such tunes, although whistled and sung by everybody, are erroneously supposed to have taken a deep hold on the popular mind; . . . the charm is only *skin-deep;* . . . they are hummed and whistled 'for lack of thought'; . . . (they) are not popular in the sense of musically inspiring, but . . . such a melody *breaks out* every now and then, like a morbid irritation of the skin." *

The melody referred to was "Old Folks at Home."

There were others who did not estimate Foster's songs at their true value, including Foster himself. He made a present of his "Oh Susanna" and two other songs to a music publisher, W. C. Peters, who published them as "Songs of the Sable Harmonists" and made $10,000 on them. Foster's name was not even mentioned on the copies.

Many a sigh has been heaved and many a homesick heart has beaten more quickly at the lines of "Swanee River." Yet when it was published, Foster had never been further south than the Ohio. He got the name "Swanee" from his brother, who had found it on the map.

When E. P. Christy, the famous minstrel entrepreneur, asked Foster to write songs for him, the agreement stipulated that Christy's, not Foster's, name was to appear on the first edition as composer. This is a practise which, alas, many another budding young song-writer has been obliged to submit to. Thus we find the following title-page:

MUSIC OF THE

ORIGINAL

CHRISTY

MINSTRELS

The oldest established Band in the United States

As arranged and sung by them with distinguished success

OH SUSANNA

OLD FOLKS AT HOME

With regard to one of his songs, Foster wrote to Christy:

"If you accept my proposition I will make it a point to notify you hereafter when I have a new song and send you the ms. on the same terms. . . . Thus it will become notorious that your band brings out all the new songs. You

* John S. Dwight in the *Journal of Music,* quoted by J. T. Howard in "Our American Music."

can state in the papers that the song was composed expressly for you. . . ."

And again:

"I regret that it is too late to have the name of your band on the title page, but I will endeavor to place it (alone) on future songs, and will cheerfully do anything else in my humble way to advance your interest."

Foster wrote many of his songs to order for Christy.

But, in 1852, six months after "Old Folks at Home" was written, Foster wrote to the bandleader, asking that his name be placed on the title page as composer:

"I find I cannot write at all unless I write for public approbation and get credit for what I write."

Twenty-one years later Oliver Ditson & Co. issued a reprint edition, still crediting words and music to Christy.

THE '49ERS

In a vigorous, thriving civilization, folk songs and professionally composed songs have a close relationship. Much of the energy of the minstrel music came from the strong folk element in it: from the fiddle jigs, banjo strains, plantation tunes of the South, to whose influence even Foster was not impervious. Now the time had come for the current to flow in the other direction, and it did—into the wagon ballads, Cape Horn chanties, and sagas of the Gold Rush. The rush for gold was a great human adventure, to inspire great and crazy songs; a comic and tragic epic of a nation on the loose: something fantastic for a Breughel or a Daumier to paint. Greenbie tells of it:

"When the word flashed over the mountains that this land . . . contained gold—gold in unlimited quantities, gold that could be washed out of the sands, picked out of the rocks with the fingernails—the wildest stampede in history began. Into the West they poured, in wagons, on horseback, on foot. Out of the harbors they dashed, in sailing boats, in steamers, in anything that could keep afloat. The news spread to Europe. The ports of the Atlantic were crammed with immigrants seeking transshipment. It ran down the coast of South America and up the other side, and almost all of Chile set sail at once. It flashed across Canada and the trappers dropped their pelts and beat it down the coast. It flashed from ship to ship in the Orient, and across the Pacific they came flying loaded with everybody from maharajahs to Chinese."

This fantastic migration could not help pouring out into song. Enthusiasts piled into overloaded leaky boats for the long journey around the Horn with song on their lips. Alkali Ike and Joe Bowers tramped over endless miles of desert singing "Ho for California!" to any one of a dozen tunes. Composed songs, popular stage or vaudeville hits, came back to the common folk and were twisted to fit the verses about the "Promised Land." Foster's "Oh Susanna" and "Camptown Races" were among the most parodied, and they echoed through Rocky Mountain passes to lines of every character.

Another chapter in the annals of American music had been recorded.

E. S.

WELCOME EVERY GUEST

[ROUND*]

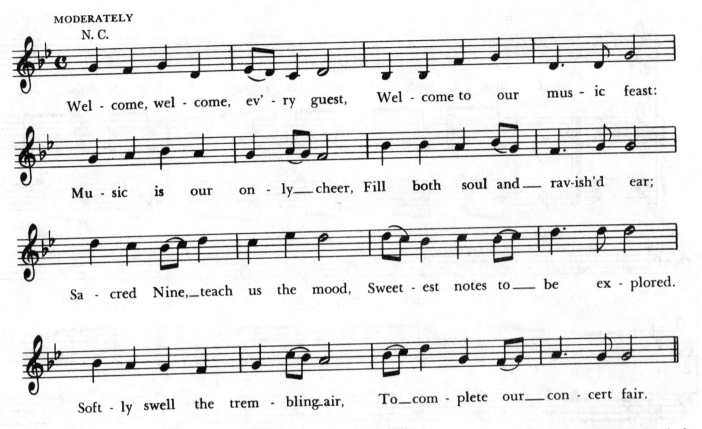

MODERATELY

N. C.

Wel - come, wel - come, ev' - ry guest, Wel - come to our mus - ic feast:

Mu - sic is our on - ly____cheer, Fill both soul and ___ rav-ish'd ear;

Sa - cred Nine,___teach us the mood, Sweet - est notes to ___ be ex - plored.

Soft - ly swell the trem - bling_air, To___com - plete our___con - cert fair.

* *This round is to be sung by four voices. The first singer starts alone; when he reaches the second line, the second singer starts at the beginning (the first singer continuing). When the second singer reaches the second line, the third singer starts, and so on. Each singer sings the complete round through twice.*

WELCOME EVERY GUEST

SOUTHERN SINGING SCHOOL TEACHERS, in order to vary the diet of spirituals and hymns on which they regaled their charges, occasionally sneaked into their hymnals a completely secular composition. Such is this lively ode to Dame Music, in the form of a round. This doubtless served not only to entertain the pupils, but was a painless introduction to the mysteries of contrapuntal singing.

OLD DAN TUCKER

IN 1830 DAN EMMETT composed this, one of the most popular of all minstrel songs, of which the chorus contains perhaps the first example of syncopation in black-face song. Though many verses assigned to him are in dialect, he is not a Negro, but a reckless, shiftless, debonair American, taking life as he finds it and in his frolics a hell-bender. In Steinbeck's *Grapes of Wrath* the tune played for the Oklahoma square dance described is "Old Dan Tucker."

OLD DAN TUCKER

Words and Music by Dan Emmett (1830)
Arrangement by Elie Siegmeister

You're too late to come to sup - per.

2

Old Daniel Tucker was a mighty man,
He washed his face in a frying pan,
Combed his head wid a wagon wheel,
An' died wid de toothache in his heel.
CHORUS: So, git out, *etc.*

3

Old Dan Tucker he got drunk,
He fell in de fire an' he kicked up a chunk;
De red hot coals got in his shoe
An' whee - ee! how de ashes flew!
CHORUS: So, git out, *etc.*

4

Old Dan Tucker's mother-in-law,
Was the ugliest thing I ever saw,
Her eyes stuck out an' her nose stuck in,
Her upper lip hung over her chin.
CHORUS: So, git out, *etc.*

5

Old Dan Tucker's back in town,
Swingin' the ladies all aroun';
First to the right and then to the left,
An' then to the gal that he loves best.
CHORUS: So, git out, *etc.*

6

I went to meetin' de udder day,
To hear old Tucker preach an' pray,
Dey all got drunk, but me alone,
I make ole Tucker walk-jaw-bone.
CHORUS: So, git out, *etc.*

7

Tucker is a nice old man,
He us'd to ride our darby ram,
He sent him whizzin' down de hill,
If he hadn't got up, he'd laid dar still.

OLD DAN TUCKER
(Down Rent Verses)

1

The moon was shining silver bright,
The sheriff came at dead of night
High on a hill an Indian true
And on his horn a blast he blew.
CHORUS:

2

Bill thought he heard the sound of a gun
He cried in fright, "O my race is run,
Better that I'd never been born
Than come within sound of that big horn."
CHORUS:

CHORUS:

Get out the way, Big Bill Snyder,
Get out the way, Big Bill Snyder,
Get out the way, Big Bill Snyder,
We'll tar your coat and feather your hide, sir.

LUBLY FAN

Words and Music by Cool White (1844)

As I was lumb - 'ring down de street, Down de street,

down de street, A pret - ty gal I chanc'd to meet, O she was fair to view.

Chorus

Den lub - ly Fan will you cum out to - night, Will you cum out to-night, will you

cum out to night, Den lub–ly Fan will you cum out to-night, An' dance by de lite ob de moon.

2

I stopt her an' I had some talk
Had some talk, had some talk,
But her foot covered up de whole side-walk
An' left no room for me.
CHORUS: Den lubly Fan, *etc.*

3

She's de prettiest gal Ibe seen in my life,
Seen in my life, seen in my life,
An' I wish to de Lord she was my wife,
Den we would part no more.
CHORUS: Den lubly Fan, *etc.*

4

Oh make haste, Fan, don't make me wait,
Make me wait, make me wait,
I fear you've kept me now too late,
Yes, dere's de ebening gun.
CHORUS: Den lubly Fan, *etc.*

LUBLY FAN

ANOTHER PERENNIAL minstrel favorite, this one took on a number of pseudonyms early in its career. It was composed in 1844 by Cool White, of the Virginia Serenaders, for his banjoist, Jim P. Carter, and was sung by him and the "Virginia Serenaders at their concerts throughout the United States with unbounded applause." In the same year a black-face comedian brought the song closer to home in New York by singing "Bowery gals" instead of "Lubly Fan, won't you come out to-night?" This practice was adopted by other minstrels on tour, and that is how the song became known as "Buffalo Gals," "Louisiana Gals," "Pittsburgh Gals."

The printed accompaniments to minstrel songs, like the sheet-music versions of present-day jazz, were far simpler than the music played in actual performance.

OLD ZIP COON
[TURKEY IN THE STRAW]

Words and Music attributed to Bob Farrell (1834)
Arrangement by Elie Siegmeister

O— ole Zip Coon he is a larn- ed sko- ler, O— ole Zip Coon he is a larn- ed sko- ler, O— ole Zip Coon he is a larn- ed sko- ler, Sings pos- sum up a gum tree an- coon- y in a hol- ler Pos- sum up a gum tree, coon- y on a stump

144

Pos - sum up a gum tree, coon - y on a stump,

Pos - sum up a gum tree, coon - y on a stump, Den___

o - ver dub - ble trub - ble, ___ Zip Coon will jump.

2

O it's old Suky blue skin, she is in lub wid me,
I went the udder arternoon to take a dish ob tea;
What do you tink now, Suky hab for supper,
Why chicken foot an possum heel, widout any butter.

3

Did you eber see the wild goose, sailing on de ocean,
O de wild goose motion is a bery pretty notion;
Ebry time de wild goose beckens to de swaller,
You hear him google google google google goller.

4

I tell you what will happin den, now bery soon,
De Nited States Bank will be blone to de moon;
Dere General Jackson, will him lampoon,
And de bery nex President, will be Zip Coon.

TURKEY IN THE STRAW

1

As I was a-gwine down the road,
Tired team and a heavy load,
Crack my whip and the leader sprung;
I says "Day-day," to the wagon-tongue.

CHORUS:

Turkey in the straw,
Turkey in the straw,
Turkey in the hay,
Turkey in the hay,
Roll 'em up and twist 'em up a high tuck-a-haw,
And hit 'em up a tune called Turkey in the Straw!

2

Went out to milk and I didn't know how,
Milked the goat instead of the cow.
A monkey sittin' in a pile of straw,
A-winkin' at his mother-in-law.
CHORUS: Turkey in the straw, *etc.*

3

Met Mr. Catfish comin' down stream,
Says Mr. Catfish, "What does you mean?"
Caught Mr. Catfish by the snout,
And turned Mr. Catfish wrong side out.
CHORUS: Turkey in the straw, *etc.*

4

As I came down the new-cut road,
Met Mr. Bullfrog, met Miss Toad,
And every time Miss Toad would sing,
Ole Bullfrog cut a pigeon wing.
CHORUS: Turkey in the straw, *etc.*

5

Oh, I jumped in the seat, and I gave a little yell,
The horses ran away, broke the wagon all to hell;
Sugar in the goard and honey in the horn,
I was never so happy since the hour I was born.
CHORUS: Turkey in the straw, *etc.*

ANOTHER LITTLE DRINK
(*Tune of "Old Zip Coon"*)

1

Oh, we had an old hen and she had a wooden leg,
And ev'ry morning she used to lay an egg.
She was the best old hen that we had down on the farm,
And another little drink wouldn't do us any harm.

2

Oh, we had an old cow and she had a swishy tail,
And when we milked her, we used a wooden pail.
She was the best old cow that we had down on the farm,
And another little drink wouldn't do us any harm.

THERE WAS AN OLD SOLDIER

(Tune of "Old Zip Coon")

1

OH!—There was an old soldier
    And he had a wooden leg,
    No terbaccy did he have,
    No terbaccy could he beg:
    T'other old soldier, a sly old fox,
    Always had terbaccy in his old terbaccy box.

2

SAID!—One old soldier,
    "Will ye give me a chew?"
    Said t'other old soldier,
    "I'll be danged if I do!
    Quit your loafin' round
    And git ter crackin'' rocks
    And ye'll allers have terbaccy
    In yer own terbaccy box!"

3

WELL—the one old soldier was a-feelin' very bad,
    He says, "I'll get even, I will, begad!"
    He goes to a corner,
    Takes a rifle from his peg,
    And stabs the other soldier
    With a splinter from his leg.

4

THERE—was an old hen
    And she had a wooden foot,
    And she made her nest
    By a mulberry root,
    And she laid more eggs than any hen on the farm;
And another wooden foot wouldn't do her any harm.

OLD ZIP COON

[*Turkey in the Straw*]

KNOWN TODAY as the classic American square dance tune, this song won its spurs in the days of Andrew Jackson as a burnt-cork melody. It was first sung by Bob Farrell in the Bowery Theatre, New York, on August 11, 1834, and was quickly spread throughout the country by travelling minstrel companies, who, like the dance bands of today, were quick to pick up the latest New York hits.

If any proof were needed of the deep hold its rakish line and perky rhythms have taken of the American mind, it would be the almost endless string of lyrics which have been fitted to this tune. Besides "Zip Coon" and "Turkey in the Straw" there are "My Grandmother Lived" (said to be of Irish origin) ; "There Was an Old Soldier," which dates from Civil War times; and "There Was a Little Hen," which dates from any drinking party after 2 A. M.

Besides its many offspring, this most American of all tunes also has relatives, perhaps ancestors, abroad. Among those with which it is still on speaking terms are the English "Haymaker's Dance" and the Irish "Rose Tree in Full Bearing."

WALK, JAW-BONE

Words and Music by S. S. Steele
Arrangement by Elie Siegmeister

* Symbols in italics for guitar with capo across 1st fret

148

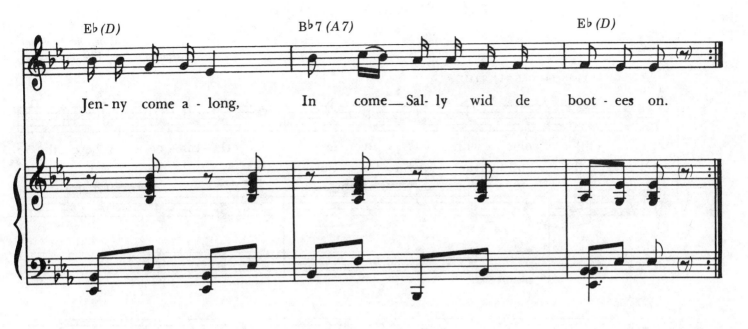

Jen-ny come a-long,   In come—Sal-ly wid de boot-ees on.

2	4
De corn de driver from me rob,	Dey made me a scar-crow in de field
An' he make me eat de cob.	And a buzzard come to get his meal.
I chaw de cob until my gums	But in his face I blowed my bref
Stick out like Carolina plums.	An' he was a case for ole Jim Death.
CHORUS: Walk, jaw-bone, etc.	CHORUS: Walk, jaw-bone, etc.

3	5
Dey fasten me up under de barn	Den down de bank I see'd a ship,
Dey feed me dar on leaves ob corn.	I slide down dar on de bone ob my hip,
It tickled my digestion so,	I crossed de brink an' yare I am
Dat I cotch de cholerophoby.	If I go back dar, I'll be damn!
CHORUS: Walk, jaw-bone, etc.	CHORUS: Walk, jaw-bone, etc.

WALK, JAW-BONE

As MANY of the minstrel songs were taken directly from Negro folk
originals, it is not surprising to find here, beneath the conventional
"Ethiopian" clowning and patter, an allegory of slavery and deliverance.
In an age when opponents of slavery were hounded, even in the North,
the minstrel comedian played the part of the court jester of old. Cavort-
ing about the stage in black-face he could mime the part of the runaway
slave and conceal many a stinging thrust in comedy.

One does not usually think of a Polish peasant as the composer of
American minstrel tunes. Yet that is exactly what happened in this case,
for the melody of "Walk-Jaw-Bone" is note for note that of the Polish
folk-dance, "The Krakoviak."

THE BURMAN LOVER

Music by John C. Baker
Arrangement by Elie Siegmeister

150

depths I'll rove, I'll gath-er the hon-ey-comb bright as gold, And
sky is blue,___ Should we ling-er a - noth-er day, Storms

chase the elk to his se-cret hold.
may a-rise and___ love de-cay. I'll chase the an-te-lope

o'er the plain, The___ ti-ger's cub I'll___ bind with a chain, And the

wild ga-zelle with her sil-ver feet, I'll give thee for a play-mate sweet.

151

ALABADO

Arrangement by Elie Siegmeister

2

And the pure Conception
Of the Queen of the Heavens
Who, Virgin Immaculate,
Is Mother of Eternal Word.

3

And the blessed Saint Joseph,
Chosen by God the Almighty,
For his reputed Father
Of His Son, the Divine Word.

4

This is for all ages,
And forever. Amen.
Amen. Jesus and Mary:
Jesus, Mary and Joseph.

2

*Y la limpia Concepción
De la Reyna los Cielos,
Que quedando Virgen pura,
Es Madre del Verbo Eterno.*

3

*Y el bendito San José,
Electo por Dios immenso,
Para padre estimativo,
De su Hijo el Divino Verbo.*

4

*Esto es por todos los siglos,
Y de los siglos, Amen.
Amen, Jesus y Maria:
Jesus, Maria, y José.*

ALABADO

ONE OF THE FEW remaining Spanish hymns which were brought to the Southwest and taught to the Indians by the missionary priests. When the '49ers came to California, songs like this were chanted in and around the missions. Even as it stands today, changed as it must be by time and memory, it retains the timeless flavor of century-old Gregorian chant.

SACRAMENTO

[DE CAMPTOWN RACES]

Arrangement by Elie Siegmeister

We've formed our band and we are well manned
Where the gold - en ore is rich in store,
Doo - da, doo - da! On the

jour - ney a - far to the Prom - ised Land.
banks of the Sac - ra - - men - to shore,
Doo - da, doo - da, day! Then

ho, boys, ___ ho, To Cal - if - or - nia go! There's

plent - y of gold, So I've been told, On the banks of Sac - ra - men - to!

s the gold is thar most anywhar, dooda, dooda,

nd they dig it out with an iron bar, dooda, dooda day.

nd whar 'tis thick with a spade or pick, dooda, dooda,

hey can shovel out lumps as heavy as brick, dooda, dooda day.

CHORUS: Then ho, boys, ho, to California go,
There's plenty of stones and dead men's bones
On the banks of Sacramento.

3

Oh, the land we'll save for the bold and brave, dooda, dooda,

Have determined there never shall breathe a slave, dooda, dooda day.

Let foes recoil for the sons of toil, dooda, dooda,

Shall make California God's Free Soil, dooda, dooda day.

CHORUS: Then ho, boys, ho, to California go,
No slave shall toil on God's Free Soil
On the banks of Sacramento.

DE CAMPTOWN RACES
(*by* STEPHEN FOSTER)

1

De Camptown ladies sing dis song,
Dooda, dooda!
De Camptown racetrack nine miles long,
Oh, dooda day.
See dem hosses round de bend,
Dooda, dooda!
Guess dat race'll never end,
Oh, dooda day.
CHORUS:
Gwine to run all night,
Gwine to run all day,
De hoss I fancy am de bobtail nag;
He'll walk away from de bay.

2

De long-tail'd filly an' de big black hoss,
Dooda, dooda!
Dey fly de track an' dey both cut 'cross,
Oh, dooda day.
De blind hoss stick in a big mud hole,
Dooda, dooda!
Can't touch bottom wid a ten-foot pole,
Oh, dooda day!
CHORUS:
Gwine to run all night,
Gwine to run all day,
De hoss I fancy am de bobtail nag;
He'll walk away from de bay.

SACRAMENTO

WHEN THE NEWS came from Sutter's Creek that there were gold nuggets as big as your fist to be picked up off the ground, the free-for-all rush started. Men packed into leaky sailing boats for the dangerous trip round Cape Horn to San Francisco; later, as Carl Sandburg has pointed out, these ships took thousands of the same passengers back.

Out of this mad Odyssey a song arose. At first it was sung with enthusiasm. Later, on the return voyages, bitter, sarcastic verses were sung to the same refrain. When the gold-rush fever died down, it remained as a shanty about windjammers and square-riggers.

All sorts and conditions of men started out in the mad rush. Among them were anti-slavery enthusiasts, who were drawn westward not only by the lure of gold, but by the desire to make the new territory Free Soil when it should join the Union as a state.

The similarity of the tune to that of Stephen Foster's "Camptown Races," written in 1850, is so striking that it is a question which was taken from the other. It is also possible that both were derived from the opening lines of the Negro spiritual, "Roll, Jordan, Roll."

Some of the verses of "Camptown Races," which may be sung to the same melody, are also given.

SWEET BETSY FROM PIKE

Arrangement by Elie Siegmeister

Oh, don't you re-mem-ber sweet Bet-sy from Pike, Who crossed the wide prair-ies with her lov-er Ike, With two yoke of cat-tle and one spot-ted hog, A tall shang-hai roost-er, an old yal-ler dog? Sing too-ral-i-oo-ral-i-oo-ral-i-ay.

Chorus

* Symbols in italics for guitar with capo across 3rd fret

They swam the wide rivers and crossed the tall peaks,
And camped on the prairie for weeks upon weeks.
Starvation and cholera and hard work and slaughter,
They reached California spite of hell and high water.
CHORUS: Sing-too-ral, *etc.*

The Injuns came down in a wild yelling horde,
And Betsy was skeered they would scalp her adored;
Behind the front wagon wheel Betsy did crawl,
And there she fought the Injuns with musket and ball.
CHORUS: Sing-too-ral, *etc.*

They soon reached the desert, where Betsy gave out,
And down in the sand she lay rolling about;
While Ike in great terror looked on in surprise,
Saying, "Betsy, get up, you'll get sand in your eyes."
CHORUS: Sing-too-ral, *etc.*

They went to Salt Lake to inquire the way,
And Brigham declared that sweet Betsy should stay;
But Betsy got frightened and ran like a deer,
While Brigham stood pawing the earth like a steer.
CHORUS: Sing-too-ral, *etc.*

The wagon tipped over with a terrible crash,
And out on the prairie rolled all sorts of trash;
A few little baby clothes done up with care
Looked rather suspicious, but it was all on the square.
CHORUS: Sing-too-ral, *etc.*

Long Ike and sweet Betsy attended a dance,
Where Ike wore a pair of his Pike County pants;
Sweet Betsy was covered with ribbons and rings,
Said Ike, "You're an angel, but where are your wings?"
CHORUS: Sing-too-ral, *etc.*

A miner said, "Betsy, will you dance with me?"
"I will that, old hoss, if you don't make too free;
But don't dance me hard. Do you want to know why?
Doggone ye, I'm chock-full of strong alkali."
CHORUS: Sing-too-ral, *etc.*

Long Ike and sweet Betsy got married of course,
But Ike, getting jealous, obtained a divorce;
And Betsy, well satisfied, said with a shout,
"Good-bye, you big lummox, I'm glad you backed out."
CHORUS: Sing-too-ral, *etc.*

SWEET BETSY FROM PIKE

LIFE ABOARD the covered wagons crossing the flats, the Rockies, the alkali desert, was no picnic. Songs serious, comic and grotesque enlivened many miles of endless monotony. This one relates the misfortunes of Ike and his Pike County Rose with sardonic undertones. Disappointed prospectors had at least one outlet: they could laugh at themselves and roar "Too-ral-i-oo-ral-i-oo-ral-i-ay" for all the prairies to hear.

Never was exquisite sentiment couched in more delicate language than:

"Good-bye, you big lummox, I'm glad you backed out."

JOE BOWERS

Arrangement by Elie Siegmeister

My name it is Joe Bow-ers, I've got a broth-er Ike, I came from old Mis-sou-ri, all the way from Pike; I'll tell you how it hap-pened I start-ed out to roam, And left my poor old mam-my so far a-way from home.

I used to love a gal thar, they called her Sally Black;
I axed her for to marry me, she said it was a whack;
"But," says she to me, "Joe Bowers, before we hitch for life,
You'd orter have a little home to keep your little wife."

3

Says I, "My dearest Sally, oh, Sally, for your sake,
I'll go to Californy and try to raise a stake."
Says she to me: "Joe Bowers, oh, you are the chap to win.
Give me a kiss to seal the bargin." And she threw a dozen in.

4

At length I went to minin', put in my biggest licks,
Come down upon the bowlders jist like a thousand bricks;
I worked both late and early, in rain, and sun and snow,
But I was workin' for my Sally, so 'twas all the same to Joe.

5

I made a very lucky strike, as the gold itself did tell,
And I saved it for my Sally, the gal I loved so well,
I saved it for my Sally, that I might pour it at her **feet**,
That she might kiss and hug me and call me something sweet.

6

But one day I got a letter from my dear kind brother Ike,
It came from old Missouri, sent all the way from Pike;
It brought me the gol-darndest news as ever you did hear;
My heart is almost busted, so pray excuse this tear.

7

It said my Sal was fickle, that her love for me had fled,
That she'd married with a butcher, whose hair was awful red;
It told me more than that—oh, it's enough to make one swear.
It said Sally had a baby, and the baby had red hair.

8

Now I've told you all that I could tell about the sad affair,
'Bout Sally marryin' the butcher, and the butcher had red hair.
Whether it was a boy or gal child, the letter never said,
It only said its cussed hair was inclinèd to be red.

JOE BOWERS

Sung in the 1850's by bull-whackers and mule drivers following the
Gold Rush to California, this was a favorite with Western regiments
during the Civil War. They would cheer loudly at the stanza relating
that "Sally had a baby and the baby had red hair." It was popular on
the vaudeville stage in the '50's and '60's.

THE DYING CALIFORNIAN

Arrangement by Elie Siegmeister

Lay up near-er, bro-ther, near-er, For my limbs are grow-ing cold And thy pres-ence seem-eth near-er, When thine arms a-round me fold.

2

I am dying, brother, dying;
Soon you'll miss me in your berth
For my form will soon be lying
'Neath the ocean's briny deep.

3

Listen, brother, catch each whisper,
'Tis my wife I'll speak of now;
Tell, Oh tell her how I missed her
When the fever burned my brow.

4

Oh, my children, Heaven bless them,
They were all my life to me;
Would I could once more caress them
Before I sink beneath the sea.

5

'Twas for them I crossed the ocean,
What my hopes were I'd not tell;
When I'm gone, Oh don't be weeping,
Brother, hear my last farewell.

"THERE'S PLENTY of stones and dead men's bones on the banks of Sacramento," one song of the '49ers relates, and history tells us that this was no exaggeration. For every man who reached the Promised Land, there was one or more claimed by the desert, the Indians, or by cholera, typhus, or the poisoned beef served aboard the overcrowded tubs that carried thousands on the sea route round Cape Horn.

"The Dying Californian," probably first sung as a stage song, struck a responsive note in the hearts of many a bereaved wife or daughter back east; so much so that it soon became a popular favorite. It has endured as a folk song, and is in the Southern shape note hymn books to this day.

OH SUSANNA!

Words and Music by Stephen Foster (1848)
Arrangement by Elie Siegmeister

2

I jumped aboard de telegraph,
And trabbelled down de riber,
De lectric fluid magnified,
And killed five hundred Nigger
De bullgine buste, de horse run off,
I really thought I'd die;
I shut my eyes to hold my breath,
Susanna, don't you cry.

CHORUS:

3

I soon will be in New Orleans,
And den I'll look all round,
And when I find Susanna,
I'll fall upon the ground.
But if I do not find her,
Dis darkie'll surely die,
And when I'm dead and buried,
Susanna, don't you cry.

CHORUS:

OH SUSANNA!

THIS SONG was a money-maker for almost everybody except Stephen Foster. At the time he became twenty-one, he gave a sample copy of "Oh Susanna" to E. P. Christy, the leader of a minstrel show. Christy turned it over to his New York publisher, modestly crediting himself as composer. Later a Louisville publisher, Peters, presented the song, together with "Old Uncle Ned," and made a neat profit of $10,000, while Foster never received a cent.

MY OLD KENTUCKY HOME

Words and Music by Stephen Foster (1853)

2

They hunt no more for the 'possum and the 'coon
On the meadow, the hill, and the shore;
They sing no more by the glimmer of the moon,
On the bench by the old cabin door:
The day goes by like a shadow o'er the heart,
With sorrow where all was delight,
The time has come when the darkies have to part,
Then, my old Kentucky home, good-night!

CHORUS: Weep no more, *etc.*

3

The head must bow and the back will have to bend,
Wherever the darky may go;
A few more days and the trouble all will end,
In the fields where the sugar-canes grow;
A few more days for to tote the weary load,
No matter, 'twill never be light,
A few more days till we totter on the road,
Then, my old Kentucky home, good-night!

CHORUS: Weep no more, *etc.*

JEANIE WITH THE LIGHT BROWN HAIR

Words and Music by Stephen Foster (1854)
Arrangement by Elie Siegmeister

* Symbols in italics for guitar with capo across 1st fret

war-bled them o'er; Oh!_____ I dream of Jean - ie with the

light brown hair,_____ Float - ing like a va - por, on the soft sum-mer air.

2

I long for Jeanie with the day-dawn smile,
Radiant in gladness, warm with winning guile;
I hear her melodies, like joys gone by,
Sighing round my heart o'er the fond hopes that die:—

Sighing like the night wind and sobbing like the rain,—
Wailing for the lost one that comes not again:
Oh! I long for Jeanie, and my heart bows low,
Never more to find her where the bright waters flow.

JEANIE WITH THE LIGHT BROWN HAIR

A RATHER UNSUCCESSFUL marriage to the daughter of a Pittsburgh phy-
sician, a Miss Jane McDowell, was the inspiration for this song. There
were periodic separations, and it is quite possible that the song was
written in a nostalgic moment when Foster found himself lonesome for
her. Whatever its origin, "Jeanie" retains its freshness and charm
throughout the years.

Year of Jubilo

[SONGS OF SLAVERY, THE CIVIL WAR, EMANCIPATION, NEGRO SPIRITUALS]

IN THE POPULAR MIND, and therefore in the song annals of this country, the Civil War, was a struggle to end slavery. Long before emancipation the Negro was singing of freedom.

At first it was freedom symbolized in religion: "The Great Jubilee" or "Dat Great Day in de Mornin' " or "Kingdom Come." Many of the finest spirituals come from the slave plantations and are expressed in terms of religious symbolism, but, as Frederick Douglass says in his autobiography: "A keen observer might have detected in our repeated singing of 'O Canaan, sweet Canaan, I am bound for the land of Canaan' something more than a hope of reaching heaven. We meant to reach the North, and the North was our Canaan.... On our lips it simply meant a speedy pilgrimage to a free state, and deliverance from all the evils of slavery."

Booker T. Washington expresses the same thought of the symbolism latent in the spirituals when he says in *Up from Slavery:* "Most of the verses of the plantation songs had some reference to freedom. True, they had sung those same verses before, but they had been careful to explain that the 'freedom' in these songs referred to the next world, and had no connection with life in this world. Now they gradually threw off the mask and were not afraid to let it be known that the 'freedom' in their songs meant freedom of the body in this world."

Another type of song which sprang from the servitude of the Negro was the work song, and many of these chants were of extraordinary beauty. A contemporary historian, William Francis Allen, said in *Slave Songs of the United States:* "I have stood for more than an hour often, listening to them, as they hoisted and lowered the hogsheads and boxes of their cargoes; one man taking the burden of the song (and the slack of the rope) and the others striking in with the chorus. They would sing in this way more than a dozen different songs."

Even such phenomena as the Underground Railway and the Abolitionist movement which preceded the Civil War were the subjects of many songs. The Underground Railway involved such anxiety and terror that it lent itself easily to dramatic musical interpretation. The song "Link O' Day" is an eloquent document of that institution, which was manned mostly by Quakers, religious enthusiasts, and other Abolitionist idealists. Anti-slavery singing circles were formed to spread the gospel, and special songs were written for them, generally to the tunes of old hymns. William Lloyd Garrison himself wrote many of these songs, and they were printed in the many pamphlets and "songsters" which appeared between 1840 and the Civil War.

But, just as any liberating movement inspires an avalanche of militant songs, the actual start of the Civil War roused the imagination of American song-writers. Every important event, every victory and defeat, produced its quota of songs: marching songs, rallying songs, songs of sentiment, weariness, and, finally, of immense jubilation when the conflict was over. They were sung by millions: in the camp, on the march, going into battle, at the fireside, and at patriotic meetings back home. Thousands of songs were written, and when the course of popular taste and historical evolution sifted them, a great number remained that may still be counted as moving and stirring music. Besides "The Battle Hymn of the Republic," "Tenting on the Old Camp Ground," "Dixie," and "When Johnny Comes Marching Home Again," there were many others that still live on after seventy-five years, notably: "The Battle Cry of Freedom," and "Tramp, Tramp, Tramp the Boys Are Marching." On the Northern side there was "Babylon Is Fallen," "Marching through Georgia" and "Kingdom Come." In the South, "Carolina," "The Southern Girl," and "The Bonnie Blue Flag."

Emancipation not only gave rise to a series of jubilant songs: "Slavery Chain," "Year of Jubilo," "No More Auction Block," and others; it also brought about a change in the status of the spirituals. Before the Civil War these songs were known and loved in the South. Now they obtained a new popularity in the North as well, and the spirituals began their long march toward general acceptance. There are definite landmarks in that march—the publication of *Slave Songs of the United States,* by Allen, Garrison and Ware, in 1867; the international tour of the Fisk Jubilee Singers in the 1870's; the use of Negro themes by Dvořák in the "New World Symphony" in the '90's; the concert arrangements and adaptations by Henry Burleigh, Nathaniel Dett, and Hall Johnson in the early decades of the present century; the concert careers of Paul Robeson and Roland Hayes; and finally the recognition of the artistry of such singers as Marian Anderson, Leontyne Price, William Warfield, and Shirley Verrett.

E. S.

HEAVE AWAY

Arrangement by Elie Siegmeister

MODERATELY, WITH GREAT VIGOR

Heave a - way,___ heave a - way!___ I'd rath - er court a yel - low gal Than

work for Hen - ry Clay. Heave a - way!___ Heave a - way! ____ Yel - low

gal, I want to go. I'd rath - er court a yel - low gal Than

work for Hen - ry Clay. Heave a - way!___ yel - low gal I want to go. ____

HEAVE AWAY

THIS NEGRO FIREMEN'S SONG is one of the very few work chants of slavery that have come down to us. Kane O'Donnell, who heard it in Savannah in 1840, said: "Each company has its own set of tunes, its own leader, and doubtless in the growth of time, necessity and invention, its own composer." The tune has a driving power and sweep that are extraordinary. It should be sung and the accompaniment played with exuberance.

GWINE TO ALABAMY

Arrangement by Elie Siegmeister

I'm gwine to Al-a-bam-y, _____ oh, _____

For to see my mam-my, ah. _____

2

She went from old Virginny, oh,
And I'm her pickaninny, ah.

3

She lives on the Tombigbee, oh,
I wish I had her wid me, ah.

4

But I'd like to see my mammy, oh,
Who lives in Alabamy, ah.

GWINE TO ALABAMY

"A GOOD SPECIMEN, so far as notes can give one, of the strange, barbaric songs one hears upon the Western steamboats," according to Allen, Ware and Garrison's *Slave Songs of the United States* (1867).

And to Henry F. Gilbert, who used it in his "Comedy Overture on Negro Themes," this was a melody "unusually wild and romantic in character, and withal of considerable nobility."

ABOLITIONIST HYMN

[*Tune: "Old Hundred"*]
Arrangement by Elie Siegmeister

WITH DIGNITY, NOT TOO SLOWLY

We ask not that the slave should lie As lies his mas - ter, at his ease, Be - neath a silk - en can - o - py Or in the shade of bloom - ing trees.

2

We ask not "eye for eye," that all,
Who forge the chain and ply the whip,
Should feel their torture; while the thrall
Should wield the scourge of mastership.

3

We mourn not that the man should toil
'Tis nature's need, 'tis God's decree;
But let the hand that tills the soil
Be, like the wind that fans it, free.

THE ABOLITIONIST MOVEMENT was decidedly unpopular in some parts of America, where respectable people had little patience with the Abolitionists. Frequently they were run out of town after their meetings were raided. In Philadelphia the meeting house of the Abolitionists was burned, and in Alton, Illinois, in 1837, Elijah Lovejoy, the editor of an Abolitionist paper, was murdered and his murderers acquitted. It was the heroism in the Abolitionist movement which led to such statements as William Lloyd Garrison's: "I am in earnest. I will not equivocate. I will not excuse. I will not retreat an inch—and I will be heard."

LINK O'DAY

From The Botsford Collection of Folk Songs. *Compiled and edited by Florence Hudson Botsford*

* Not suitable for chorded accompaniment

174

Get yeh far away, O!
An' leave yo' massa far behin',
'Fo de link o' day,
'Fo de link o' day.

CHORUS: Run yeh, etc.

Dere will come a time, O!
When we will all be free,
We will all be free.

CHORUS: Run yeh, etc.

LINK O' DAY

AN ELOQUENT runaway slave song which is part of the Abolitionist and Underground Railway record in American history.

"Many of the fugitives," Levi Coffin wrote in his reminiscences in 1877, "came long distances, from Alabama, Mississippi, Louisiana, and, in fact, from all parts of the South. Sometimes the poor hunted creatures had been out so long, living in woods and thickets, that they were almost wild when they came in . . . The pursuit was often very close, and we had to resort to various stratagems in order to elude the pursuers. Sometimes a company of fugitives were scattered and secreted in the neighborhood . . . at other times their route was changed and they were hurried forward with all speed. It was a continual excitement and anxiety . . ."

The song is presented in choral form, for which it seems best suited. "Link O Day" means daybreak. "Kentry" is country.

LINCOLN AND LIBERTY

Tune of "Old Rosin, the Bow"
Words: F. A. Simpson (1860)
Arrangement by Elie Siegmeister

VIGOROUSLY, MODERATELY FAST

Hur - rah for the choice of the na - tion!___ Our chief - tain so brave and so true;___ We'll go for the great re - for - ma - tion, For Lin - coln and Li - ber - ty, too.___ We'll go for the son of Ken -

tuck-y,— The he-ro of Hoo-sier-dom through;— The pride of the Suck-ers so luck-y, For Lin-coln and Li-ber-ty, too.—

They'll find what by felling and mauling,
Our rail-maker statesman can do;
For the people are ev'rywhere calling,
For Lincoln and Liberty too.
Then up with the banner so glorious,
The star-spangled, red white and blue,
We'll fight till our banner's victorious,
For Lincoln and Liberty, too.

Our David's good sling is unerring,
The Slavocrat's giant he slew,
Then shout for the freedom preferring,
For Lincoln and Liberty, too.
We'll go for the son of Kentucky,
The hero of Hoosierdom through;
The pride of the Suckers so lucky,
For Lincoln and Liberty, too.

LINCOLN AND LIBERTY

THE CAMPAIGN SONG of 1860.

"A man who had been on the roof and was engaged in communicating the results of the ballotings to the mighty mass of outsiders now demanded, by gesture at the skylight over the stage, to know what had happened. One of the secretaries, with a tally sheet in his hands, shouted: 'Fire the salute! Abe Lincoln is nominated!' "

"The City was wild with delight. 'Old Abe' men formed processions and bore rails through the streets. Torrents of liquor were poured down the throats of the multitude. A hundred guns were fired from the top of Tremont House." *Murat Halstead: "Caucuses of 1860"*

The same tune served for several other political campaigns, as those of Henry Clay and of Horace Greeley when he was running for the presidency against Ulysses S. Grant. The outcome of the latter campaign was accurately predicted in the variations of the following two lines:

"Then let Greeley go to the Dickens,

Too soon has he counted his chickens."

BATTLE HYMN OF THE REPUBLIC

[JOHN BROWN'S BODY]

Words by Julia Ward Howe (1861)
Arrangement by Elie Siegmeister

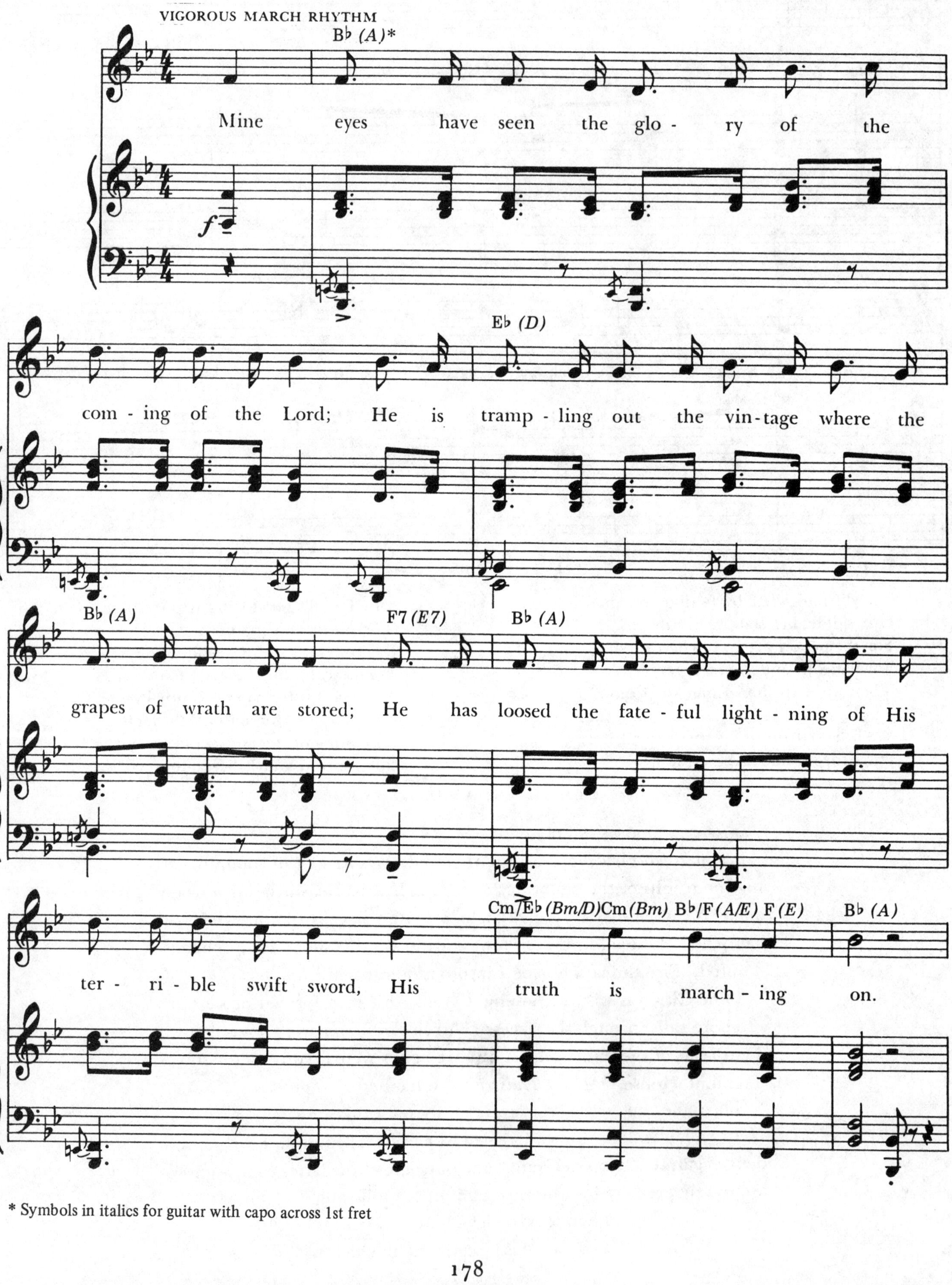

VIGOROUS MARCH RHYTHM
B♭ (A)*
Mine eyes have seen the glo - ry of the
f
E♭ (D)
com - ing of the Lord; He is tramp - ling out the vin - tage where the
B♭ (A) F7 (E7) B♭ (A)
grapes of wrath are stored; He has loosed the fate - ful light - ning of His
Cm/E♭ (Bm/D) Cm (Bm) B♭/F (A/E) F (E) B♭ (A)
ter - ri - ble swift sword, His truth is march - ing on.

* Symbols in italics for guitar with capo across 1st fret

I have seen Him in the watch-fires of a hundred circling camps;
They have builded Him an altar in the evening dews and damps:
I can read His righteous sentence by the dim and flaring lamps,
His day is marching on.

CHORUS: Glory, glory! Hallelujah, *etc.*

JOHN BROWN'S BODY

1

John Brown's body lies amould'ring in the grave,
John Brown's body lies amould'ring in the grave,
John Brown's body lies amould'ring in the grave,
His soul goes marching on!

CHORUS:

Glory, glory! Hallelujah! Glory, glory! Hallelujah!
Glory, glory! Hallelujah! His soul is marching on.

2

He captured Harper's Ferry with his nineteen men so true,
And he frightened old Virginia till she trembled through and through;
They hung him for a traitor, themselves the traitor crew,
But his soul is marching on!
CHORUS: Glory, glory, *etc.*

3

John Brown died that the slave might be free,
John Brown died that the slave might be free,
John Brown died that the slave might be free,
But his soul goes marching on!
CHORUS: Glory, glory, *etc.*

4

The stars of heaven are looking kindly down,
The stars of heaven are looking kindly down,
The stars of heaven are looking kindly down,
On the grave of old John Brown!
CHORUS: Glory, glory, *etc.*

THE JOHN BROWN saga inevitably found its way into American music. Hearken to his deathless words to the court at Harper's Ferry:

"This court acknowledges, as I suppose, the validity of the law of God. I see a book kissed here which I suppose to be the Bible. . . . It teaches me . . . to remember them that are in bonds, as bound with them.' I endeavored to act up to that instruction. . . . I believe that to have interfered as I have done—in behalf of His despised poor, was not wrong but right. Now if it is deemed necessary that I should . . . mingle my blood further with the blood of my children and with the blood of millions in this slave country whose rights are disregarded by wicked, cruel and unjust enactments—I submit; so let it be done!" And as it turned out, fatefully enough.

The spirit of these words was matchlessly embodied in the poem that Julia Ward Howe wrote on a night in December 1861, while she listened to the tramping of regiments on their way to the front, marching to the refrain of "John Brown's Body," and saw from the window of Willard's Hotel the campfires of the Union Army. Without waiting for dawn she wrote on the first piece of paper she could reach the poem which had formed itself in her half-conscious mind. (It is inscribed on a letterhead of the Sanitary Commission, to which her husband was attached at the time, and in that form is one of the greatest treasures of the Library of Congress.) A friend had expressed the wish that she might find new words for the marching song. "I have often prayed that I might," she had said. Now the words came. The stanzas were later sold to the editor of the *Atlantic Monthly* for five dollars and they were published in the issue of February 1862, under the title of "The Battle Hymn of the Republic."

Fatefully enough, it transpired that the melody carrying the verse that commemorates John Brown was taken from a hymn popular in Negro churches in the 1850's, sung to the words: "O brothers, will you meet us on Canaan's happy shore?" This melody, with its splendid swing, became the marching song which, according to John Tasker Howard,* was first sung by the Massachusetts Twelfth Regiment in the Civil War. The song spread like wildfire. It became the "Marseillaise" of the battlefields. And always, in the consciousness of the nation, it has kept marching on. On the night when a Negro smuggled into Libby Prison the news of Gettysburg the prisoners, in desperate plight, sang "The Battle Hymn of the Republic." Later, on a night in Washington, when Chaplain McCabe of the 122nd Ohio Regiment described this scene and again sang the song, Abraham Lincoln, in tears, asked that it be repeated. And on July 4, 1941 this same hymn to human liberty was intoned in St. Paul's Cathedral in London on the occasion of the unveiling of a memorial tablet to Billy Fiske, the flier, the first American to give his life in World War II.

* John Tasker Howard: "Our American Music: Three Hundred Years Of It." Thomas Y. Crowell Company, New York.

In his diary Charley White, the minstrel, has told us the story of the composition of "Dixie."

"One Saturday night in 1859, when Dan Emmett was a member of Bryant's Minstrels at Mechanics' Hall, New York, Dan [Bryant] said to Emmett: 'Can't you get us up a walk-around dance? I want something new and lively for next Monday night.' At that date, and for a long time after, minstrel shows used to finish up the evening performance with a walk-around dance, in which the whole company would participate. The demand for this special material was constant, and Dan Emmett was the principal composer of all, especially for the Bryant Minstrels. Emmett, of course, went to work, and as he had done so much in that line of composition, he was not long in finding something suitable. At last he hit upon the first two bars, and any composer can tell you how good a start that is in the manufacture of a melody. The next day, Sunday, he had the words commencing 'I wish I was in Dixie.' This colloquial expression is not, as most people suppose, a Southern phrase, but first appeared among the circus men in the North. In early fall, when nipping frost would overtake the tented wanderers, the boys would think of the genial warmth of the section they were heading for and the common expression would be, 'Well, I wish I was in Dixie.' This gave the title or catch line; the rest of the song was original. On Monday morning the song was rehearsed and highly recommended, and at night, as usual, the house was crowded and many of the auditors went home singing 'Dixie.' The song soon became the rage and several other minstrel organizations . . . applied to Emmett for copy and privilege of using it. . . . Not only was Emmett robbed of the copyright, but the authorship of it was disputed as well."

Emmett followed the stage until he was too old to perform and changes of fashion had made his entertainment out of date. In his eightieth year he was persuaded to tour with the minstrel show of Al Fields. When the orchestra struck up "Dixie" at the first performance, "he rose and, with old-time gestures and in a voice tremulous with age, sang the song." He was warmly welcomed in the South, but one such trip was enough for him; he retired to his shanty at Mount Vernon, Ohio, where he worked in his garden, chopped wood, and raised chickens. His receipts for his other songs besides "Dixie" amounted to one hundred dollars. But he was not a rebellious man.

Before his death he made the request that he be buried in the dress suit he had worn on tour with Al Fields's minstrels. As his body was lowered into the grave, the band played "Dixie."

The incomparable song became immediately popular, and, as it happened, was adopted in the Civil War as the war song of the Confederacy. Thereupon Emmett, a man of Union sympathies, was idolized in the South, and denounced in the North as a traitor. But after Appomattox a delegation waited on President Lincoln, who said: "I see you have a band with you. Play 'Dixie.' We have captured the Confederacy, and 'Dixie' now belongs to the Union."

DIXIE

Words and Music by D. D. Emmet (1859)
Arrangement by Elie Siegmeister

I__ wish I was__ in the land of cot - ton,

Old times there are not for - got-ten, Look a - way! Look a - way! Look a -

way! Dix - ie Land. In__ Dix - ie Land__ where I was born in, Ear - ly on one

frost - y morn - in', Look a - way! Look a - way! Look a - way! Dix - ie Land.

2

Sugar in de gourd and stony batter,
You'll grow fat and eber fatter,
    Look away, *etc.:*
Den hoe it down and scratch your grabble,
To Dixie's land I'm bound to trabble,
    Look away, *etc.:*

CHORUS: Den I wish, *etc.*

ABRAHAM'S DAUGHTER

Words and Music by Septimus Winner ("Alice Hawthorne")
Arrangement by Elie Siegmeister

LIVELY, RAMBUNCTIOUS

Oh, kind folks, list-en to my song, It is no i-dle stor-y; It's all a-bout a vol-un-teer Who's going to fight for glor-y. Now don't you think that I am right? For I am noth-ing short-er.

Chorus And I be-long to the Fire Zou-zous, And don't you think I

184

ought-er? We're go-ing down to Wash-ing-ton To fight for Ab-ra-ham's daugh-ter.

2

Oh, should you ask me who she am,
Columbia is her name, sir;
She is the child of Abraham,
Or Uncle Sam the same, sir;
Now if I fight, why ain't I right.
And don't you think I oughter?

CHORUS

The volunteers are pouring in
From ev'ry loyal quarter,
I'm going down to Washington,
To fight for Abraham's daughter.

3

But let us lay all jokes aside,
It is a sorry question;
The man who would these states divide,
Should hang for his suggestion.
One country and one flag, I say,
Whome'er the war may slaughter.

CHORUS

And I belong to the Fire Zou-zous,
And don't you think I oughter?
We're going down to Washington
To fight for Abraham's daughter.

ABRAHAM'S DAUGHTER

COMPOSERS as well as fighting men sprang up at Lincoln's call for volunteers, following the early reverses of the Union armies. It thus befell that Septimus Winner, one of the most successful song-composers of the day, produced one of the most widely circulated of the Civil War songs. It appeared under the signature of "Alice Hawthorne," which was one of many pseudonyms ("Percy Cruger," "Mark Mason," "Paul Stanton") that Winner attached to his published works. This versatile man, violinist, composer, arranger, and what not, born in Philadelphia, was also the creator of the ubiquitous "Listen to the Mocking Bird," "Whispering Hope," the duet sung in every parlor and at every church sociable, and literally hundreds of popular American ballads of the period. "Abraham's Daughter" was written specially for the "Fire Zou-zous," a dashing regiment of the place and time.

TENTING TO-NIGHT

Words and Music by Walter Kittredge (1862)
Arrangement by Elie Siegmeister

* Symbols in italics for guitar with capo across 1st fret

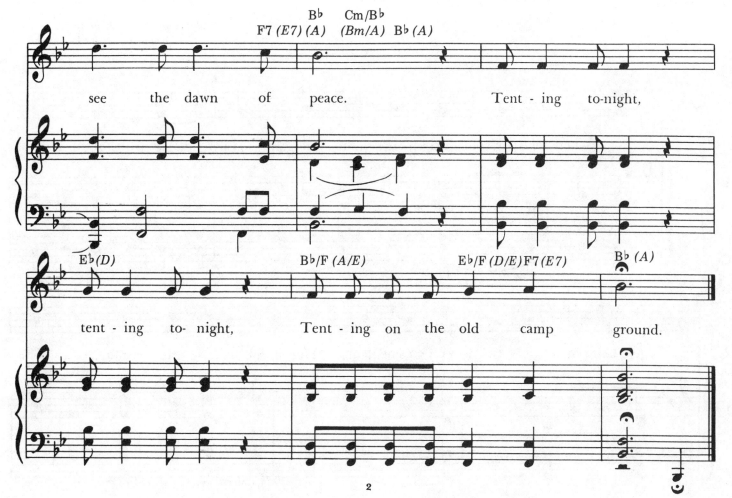

2

We've been tenting to-night on the old camp ground,
Thinking of days gone by,
Of the loved ones at home that gave us the hand,
And the tear that said, "Good-bye."
CHORUS: Many are the hearts, etc.

3

We are tired of war on the old camp ground,
Many are dead and gone,
Of the brave and true who've left their home,
Others been wounded long.
CHORUS: Many are the hearts, etc.

4

We've been fighting to-night on the old camp ground,
Many are lying near;
Some are dead, and some are dying,
Many are in tears.
CHORUS: Many are the hearts, etc.

TENTING TO-NIGHT

THIS SONG by Walter Kittredge, a ballad-singer from New Hampshire, was composed in 1862, just after he had been called to the front, and was sung by both sides in the Civil War. At first a publisher could not be found for it, but Kittredge's singing of it made it so popular that the Ditsons bought it, and the sheet-music sale ran into the thousands. Its simple melody has caused it to survive as a sentimental favorite.

WHEN JOHNNY COMES MARCHING HOME

Words and Music by Patrick S. Gilmore
Arrangement by Elie Siegmeister

* Implied chord

2

The old church bell will peal with joy,
Hurrah! Hurrah!
To welcome home our darling boy,
Hurrah! Hurrah!
The village lads and lassies say
With roses they will strew the way,
And we'll all feel gay
When Johnny comes marching home.

3

Get ready for the Jubilee,
Hurrah! Hurrah!
We'll give the hero three times three,
Hurrah! Hurrah!
The laurel wreath is ready now
To place upon his loyal brow
And we'll all feel gay
When Johnny comes marching home.

4

In eighteen hundred and sixty-one,
Hurrah! Hurrah!
That was when the war begun,
Hurrah! Hurrah!
In eighteen hundred and sixty-two,
Both sides were falling to
And we'll all drink stone wine,
When Johnny comes marching home.

5

In eighteen hundred and sixty-three,
Hurrah! Hurrah!
Abe Lincoln set the darkies free,
Hurrah! Hurrah!
In eighteen hundred and sixty-three
Old Abe set the darkies free,
And we'll all drink stone wine,
When Johnny comes marching home.

6

In eighteen hundred and sixty-four,
Hurrah! Hurrah!
Abe called for five hundred thousand more,
Hurrah! Hurrah!
In eighteen hundred and sixty-five,
They talked rebellion—strife;
And we'll all drink stone wine
When Johnny comes marching home.

WHEN JOHNNY COMES MARCHING HOME AGAIN

THERE WERE showmen of the stature of Joseph Papp and Harold Prince long before the latest Broadway extravaganzas. In 1869 and 1872, Patrick S. Gilmore, bandmaster of the Union Army, organized monster Peace Jubilees. They boasted an orchestra of more than 1,000 and a chorus of 10,000 voices, with cannon-fire to emphasize the rhythm of the music, and 100 real, in-the-flesh firemen to pound the anvils for the "Anvil Chorus" from *Trovatore*.

Gilmore claimed the authorship of the song "When Johnny Comes Marching Home Again." He is reported to have told a friend that he took down the melody when he heard a Negro singing the song. Even the most untutored audience, however, would suspect, upon hearing the song, that the Negro's name may have been Pat Reilly. That suspicion deepens when we learn that Gilmore himself came from Erin's Isle.

"Johnny" remains a rousing tune, one of the sturdiest in the whole American grab-bag.

ALL QUIET ON THE POTOMAC

Words by Lamarr Fontaine
Music by J. H. Hewitt
Arrangement by Elie Siegmeister

SLOW, FLOATING RHYTHM

"All qui-et a-long the Po-to-mac to-night," Ex-

cept here and there a stray Pick-et Is shot as he walks on his

beat to and fro By a rif-le-man hid in the thick-et. 'Tis

noth-ing, a pri-vate or two now and then Will not count in the news of the

* Symbols in italics for guitar with capo across 1st fret

bat - tle: Not an of - fi - cer lost, on - ly one of the men Moan - ing

out all a - lone the death rat - tle. "All qui - et a -

long _____ the Po - to - mac to - night." _____

2

"All quiet along the Potomac to-night,"
There the soldiers lie peacefully dreaming,
And their tents in the rays of the clear autumn moon
And the rays of the camp-fires are gleaming.

A tremulous sigh as the gentle night wind
Through the forest leaves slowly is creeping,
While the stars up above, with their glittering eyes
Keep guard o'er the army while sleeping.

"All quiet along the Potomac to-night."

3

Hark! Was it the night wind that rustles the leaves?
Was it the moonlight so wondrously flashing?
It looked like a rifle! "Ha! Mary, good-bye!"
And his life-blood is ebbing and plashing.

"All quiet along the Potomac to-night."
No sound save the sound of the river;
While soft falls the dew on the face of the dead,
The "picket's" off duty forever.

"All quiet along the Potomac to-night."

WEEPING, SAD AND LONELY
[WHEN THIS CRUEL WAR IS OVER]

Words by C. C. Sawyer
Music by Henry Tucker
Arrangement by Elie Siegmeister

* Symbols in italics for guitar with capo across 3rd fret

When the summer breeze is sighing,
Mournfully along,
Or when autumn leaves are falling,
Sadly breathes the song.
Oft in dreams I see thee lying,
On the battle plain,
Lonely, wounded, even dying,
Calling, but in vain.
CHORUS: Weeping, sad, *etc.*

WEEPING, SAD AND LONELY

"WEEPING, SAD AND LONELY" brought tears to so many eyes that the Army command finally had to forbid the soldiers of the Army of the Potomac to sing it. Septimus Winner, who had written "Abraham's Daughter," replied with his poem, "Yes, I Would This Cruel War Were Over"—on condition of a Union victory.

SLAV'RY CHAIN
[JOSHUA FIT DE BATTLE]

Arrangement by Elie Siegmeister

194

head bowed   down And my brok - en   flesh an'   pain (But breth - er - en),

2

I did know my Jesus heard me,
'Cause de spirit spoke to me—
And said, "Rise my chile, your chillun
And you too shall be free."

CHORUS: Slav'ry Chain, *etc.*

3

I done' p'nt one mighty captain
For to marshal all my hosts:—
An' to bring loving my bleeding ones to me
'An' not one shall be lost.

CHORUS: Slav'ry Chain, *etc.*

4

Now no more weary travelin'—
Cause my Jesus set me free—
An' dere's no more auction block for me
Since he give me liberty.

CHORUS: Slav'ry Chain, *etc.*

JOSHUA FIT DE BATTLE

Joshua fit de battle of Jericho, Jericho, Jericho,
Joshua fit de battle of Jericho,
And de walls, come tumblin' down.

You may talk about yo' King ob Gideon,
You may talk about yo' man ob Saul
Dere's none like good ol' Joshua
At de battle ob Jericho.

CHORUS: Joshua, *etc.*

2

Up to de walls ob Jericho
He marched with spear in han',
"Go blow dem ram horns," Joshua cried,
"Kase de battle am in my han'."

CHORUS: Joshua, *etc.*

3

Den de lam' ram sheep horns begin to blow,
Trumpets begin to shout,
Joshua commanded de chillun to shout,
And de walls come tumblin 'down.

CHORUS: Joshua, *etc.*

SLAV'RY CHAIN

OF THE MANY jubilant songs of liberty that followed the Emancipation
Proclamation and the end of the Civil War, few have remained in the
permanent repertoire of the Negro. Even "Slav'ry Chain," which was
sung in the 1870's, is known today only under the words of "Joshua Fit
de Battle of Jericho."

YEAR OF JUBILO

[KINGDOM COME]

By Henry C. Work
Arrangement by Elie Siegmeister

way. De mas - sa run, ha! ha! De dark - ey stay, ho! ho! It

mus' be now de King-dom com-in' An' de year ob Ju - bi - lo!

2

He' six foot one way, two foot t'udder
An' he weigh t'ree hundred pound,
His coat's so big he couldn't pay de tailor
An' it won' go half way round.
He drill so much dey calls him cap'n,
An' he gets so mighty tanned,
I 'spec he'll try to fool dem Yankees
For to tink he's contraband.
CHORUS:

3

De darkeys got so lonesome libin'
In de log hut on de lawn,
Dey move dere t'ings into massa's parlor,
For to keep it while he's gone.
Dar's wine an' cider in de kitchen
An' de darkeys dey'll hab some;
I 'spose dey'll all be confiscated,
When de Linkun soldiers come.
CHORUS:

4

De oberseer he make us trouble,
An' he dribe us round a spell;
We lock him up in de smoke-house cellar,
Wid de key t'rown in de well.
De whip is los', de han'-cuff broken,
But de massa'll hab his pay;
He's ole enough, big enough, ought to know better
Dan to went an' run away.
CHORUS:

IT IS HARD to think of the man who looked like both of the Smith Brothers as a writer of smash-hit tunes of his day. Yet Henry Clay Work, bearded and patriarchal, was seldom absent from the best-seller list in music.

"Marching Through Georgia," and "Babylon is Fallen" are rousing tunes, but "Kingdom Come" was Work's most successful song. After Lee's surrender the Northern army sang it as they marched into Richmond.

GO DOWN MOSES

Arrangement by Elie Siegmeister

Thus saith the Lord, bold Moses said;
    Let my people go;
If not I'll smite your first born dead,
    Let my people go.
CHORUS: Go down Moses, *etc.*

3

No more shall they in bondage toil,
    Let my people go;
Let them come out with Egypt's spoil,
    Let my people go.
CHORUS: Go down Moses, *etc.*

4

The Lord told Moses what to do,
    Let my people go;
To lead the children of Israel thro',
    Let my people go.
CHORUS: Go down Moses, *etc.*

5

When they had reached the other shore,
    Let my people go;
They sang a song of triumph o'er
    Let my people go.
CHORUS: Go down Moses, *etc.*

GO DOWN, MOSES

LAWRENCE GELLERT tells of coming upon two colored boys who were sitting on a third one in the middle of a road in Georgia and systematically removing his various articles of clothing. When Gellert bent down to help the victim jumped up:

"Tha's awright, boss. We's jes' playin' ' sp'ilin' de' Gypshuns.' "

"Despoiling the Egyptians," now a children's game, was, in slavery times, a very real wish on the part of those whose favorite Biblical heroes were Joshua, David, Moses, men who could stand up and say, "Let my people go."

"Go Down, Moses" is more than a song. It is the cry of a people.

DIDN' MY LORD DELIVER DANIEL?

Arrangement by Elie Siegmeister

Solo

He de-liv-ered Dan-iel from de lion's___ den,___

Jo-nah from de bel-ly ob de whale, An' de He-brew chil-lun from de

fi-ery fur-nace, An' why not ev-e-ry man?

D.C.

2

De moon run down in a purple stream,
De sun forbear to shine,
An' every star disappear,
King Jesus shall be mine.
CHORUS: Didn' my Lord deliver Daniel, *etc.*

3

De win' blows eas' and de winds blows wes',
It blows like de judgament day,
An ev'ry po' soul dat never did pray'll
Be glad to pray dat day.
CHORUS: Didn' my Lord deliver Daniel, *etc.*

4

Set my foot on de Gospel ship,
An' de ship begin to sail,
It landed me over on Canaan's shore,
An' I'll never come back no mo'!
CHORUS: Didn' my Lord deliver Daniel, *etc.*

DEEP RIVER

Arrangement by Elie Siegmeister

THE GOSPEL TRAIN

Arrangement by Elie Siegmeister

The fare is cheap and all can go,
The rich and poor is there;
No second class aboard this train,
No difference in the fare.
CHORUS: Get on board, *etc.*

3

I hear that train a-comin',
She sure is speedin' fast,
So get your tickets ready
And ride to heaven at last.
CHORUS: Get on board, *etc.*

THE GOSPEL TRAIN

THE GREEKS had their Pegasus, and Elijah his fiery chariot, but what can equal the Negro's image of this Gospel Train, "comin' round the curve" with all steam and brakes loosened, to carry rich and poor alike to heaven, with "no second class aboard this train, no difference in the fare"?

NEVER SAID A MUMBALIN' WORD

New Words and Music adaptation by John A. Lomax and Alan Lomax

Arrangement by Elie Siegmeister

VERY SLOW, WEARILY

Oh, dey whupped him up de hill,— up de hill,— up de hill,— Oh, dey whupped him up de hill — an' he ne-ver said a mum-ba-lin' word, Oh, dey whupped him up de hill — an' he ne-ver said a mum-ba-lin' word, He jes' hung—— down his head,—— an' he cried.

Oh, dey crowned him wid a thorny crown, thorny crown, thorny crown,
Oh, dey crowned him wid a thorny crown, an' he never said a mumbalin'
    word,
Oh, dey crowned him wid a thorny crown, an' he never said a mumbalin'
    word,
He jes' hung down his head, an' he cried.

3

Well, dey nailed him to de cross, to de cross, to de cross,
Well, dey nailed him to de cross, an' he never said a mumbalin' word,
Well, dey nailed him to de cross, an' he never said a mumbalin' word,
He jes' hung down his head an' he cried.

4

Well, dey pierced him in de side, in de side, in de side,
Well, dey pierced him in de side, an' he never said a mumbalin' word,
Well, dey pierced him in de side, an' he never said a mumbalin' word,
Den he hung down his head, an' he died.

NEVER SAID A MUMBALIN' WORD

IN AN ADDRESS delivered July 9, 1862, Mr. J. N. McKim said:

"I asked one of these blacks where they got these songs. 'Dey make
'em, sah!'

" 'How do they make them?'

" 'I'll tell you, it's dis way. My master call me up, and order me a short
peck of corn and a hundred lash. My friends see it, and is sorry for me.
When dey come to de praise-meeting dat night dey sing about it. Some's
very good singers and know how; and dey work it in—work it in, you
know, till they get it right; and dat's de way!' "

"Never Said a Mumbalin' Word" tells the story of many a "hundred
lash."

LITTLE DAVID

Arrangement by Elie Siegmeister

Lit - tle Da - vid, play on yo' harp, Hal - le - lu! Hal - le -
lu! Lit - tle Da - vid, play on yo' harp, Hal - le - lu! Lit - tle Dav - id
play on yo' harp, Hal - le - lu! Hal - le - lu! Lit - tle Da - vid,
play on yo' harp, Hal - le - lu! Da - vid was a shep - herd boy____

He killed Go-li-ath and shou-ted for joy.___ Lit-tle Da-vid,

Little David, play on yo' harp, Hallelu! Hallelu!
Little David, play on yo' harp, Hallelu!
Little David, play on yo' harp, Hallelu! Hallelu!
Little David, play on yo' harp, Hallelu!

2

Joshua was the son of Nun
He never would quit till the work was done.

CHORUS: Little David, *etc.*

3

Done told you once, done told you twice,
There's sinners in Hell for shootin' dice.

CHORUS: Little David, *etc.*

LITTLE DAVID

THIS IS ONE of the most familiar of spirituals, and an excellent example of the singing method that was common among large congregations.

James Weldon Johnson has pointed out in his autobiography that it was necessary to have someone with a strong voice who knew just the appropriate tune to sing and the appropriate time to sing it. The leader had to pitch it in the right key and he had to have all the leading lines memorized "because the congregation sings only the refrains and replies. Every ear in the church is fixed upon him, and if he becomes mixed in his lines or forgets them, the responsibility is directly on his shoulders."

THIS IS A SIN-TRYIN' WORLD

Arrangement by Elie Siegmeister

don't know whe-ther I'll ev - er get to Heav'n or no. ———

CHORUS:

O, this is a sin-tryin' world—(High Heavens!)
This is a sin-tryin' world—(Hard trials!)
This ís a sin-tryin' world—(Crown of Life!)
This is a sin-tryin' world.

2

Jordan's stream is chilly and wide;
None can cross but the sanctified.

CHORUS:

O, this is a sin-tryin' world—(Cold Jordan!)
This is a sin-tryin' world—(Deep and wide!)
This is a sin-trying' world—(Can't you cross it!)
This is a sin-tryin' world.

THIS IS A SIN-TRYIN' WORLD

IT IS VIRTUALLY IMPOSSIBLE to catch the spirit of true folk song on the printed page. "This Is a Sin-Tryin' World" represents one of those improvised revival-meeting spirituals that teem with excitement and tension. The cumulative emotion that goes into the half-sung, half-shouted interjections of "Oh, Jesus!," "Hard Trials!," the ecstatic voice of the leader and the crushing unison of the entire congregation in the chorus can only be interpreted and understood by those who have heard Negro revival meetings.

BLIND MAN

Arrangement by Elie Siegmeister

2

Cryin', "Help me, O Lawd, if you please!"
Cryin', "Help me, O Lawd, if you please!"
Cryin', "O Lawd, show me de way!"
Blin' man stood on de road an' cried.

3

When I was a sinner I stood on de road an' cried,
When I was a sinner I stood on de road an' cried,
Cryin', "O Lawd, show me de way!"
Blin' man stood on de road an' cried.

BLIND MAN

TRUE ART speaks to all men above barriers of place and language. This song seems to speak for all those who have cried out, "Show me the way!"

Courting, Love, and Children

[BALLADS OF EVERYDAY LIFE]

IT USED TO be pointed out by the fashionable critics of American culture that the Yankee was incapable of creating what every other race had produced—a body of native folk song. Various explanations for this were offered, usually by visiting lecturers at ladies' afternoon teas: that the American was by nature cold-blooded and unmusical; that he was too preoccupied with commercial and material success; that folk song was the product of a peasant class and could not be produced by an "individualistic" nation; that we lacked tradition, roots in the soil; and, finally, that we were too young, too hybrid, too immature as a people to have the "creative gift."

That was the first stage. After several dozens of volumes of native songs had been published, the visiting authorities finally were constrained to admit that yes, there was some local music in this country, but it could all be shown to be of foreign origin. Even that astute and catholic observer, Cecil Sharp, who did much to bring attention to and record the music of the Appalachian region, could not bring himself to see in it anything other than a residue of what the early settlers had brought over with them. Although he was the first to discover and publish songs such as "Ground Hog," "Kentucky Moonshiner," "John Hardy" and "Come all you Arkansas Girls" which are as American as corn pone, chewing tobacco or Boston baked beans, he assumed that they must naturally be the reflection of something that happened in England some centuries ago, and he published them all under the title, "English Folk Songs in the Southern Appalachians." Sharp, of course, found many descendants of the old English and Scotch ballads and folk songs still alive in the mountains; in fact he was the first to notice and point out that they were even more alive here than in his native England. But to him everything he heard here was English.

About 1930, as a result of Sharp's researches, and those of Lunsford, Lomax, Richardson, and many others, it began to be generally conceded that there was a certain amount of native production; but still, it was considered something peculiar to very restricted areas and to a very special type of American. In the general mind these were: (1) the hill-billy mountaineer, who was always supposed to be feudin', moonshinin' or sittin' around strummin' a banjo; (2) the cowboy who, of course, was always whoopee-ti-yoing it over the lone prairree; and, of course, (3) the southern Negro who was pictured as intoning spirituals all day long, while he picked cotton, interrupting occasionally only to shout, "Praise de Lawd!" or "Hallelujah!" While this picture may seem overdrawn, it is the one we still got from Hollywood some years back.

It is not long ago that this fiction of an uncreative, or of a musically limited America has collapsed. With the spread of interest and research it had been discovered that there is practically no part of this land without its treasure of folk and traditional song. Not only the mountains but the foot-hills, the flatlands, the tide-water regions, New England, the midwest, the far west; even the cities have yielded a rich harvest for those who know how to hear. Vermont, hitherto considered a dour and unmusical state, has yielded over 200 native tunes, many dealing with local events. Florida, of which nothing was known in the way of music, has recently turned in over a thousand songs! Ohio, Nebraska, Michigan, Oklahoma—spoken of only a few years ago by some of our snobbish high priests of intelligence as "the great intellectual desert," the "hinterland," the home of the "booboisie"—all these have yielded ballads old and new, songs, fiddle tunes, play party and square dances, prison wails, work songs, folk hymns, shanties and blues. The Library of Congress alone has, according to recent report, more than 15,000 phonograph discs of native song, which have scarcely begun to be studied, much less notated and made available. From Texas, John and Alan Lomax wrote of one family alone which had five hundred tunes in their repertory.

Far from being confined to any special place, or being the property of any particular set of Americans, our traditional music is hidden everywhere. Some of it gets around in the strangest ways. Mary Eddy told of recording one of the most attractive versions of the "Gypsy Laddie" ballad from the singing of a Russian Jew who had learned it in Utah while living among the Mormons. From Scotland to Salt Lake to the banks of the Wabash via the singing of someone who probably came from Minsk or Odessa!

One of the present authors, working in his study, was interrupted by the cry of a peddler outside his window. He notated the peddler's call, and when it was performed at a Town Hall concert a few months later, the reviewers singled it out as a characteristic bit of American folk-lore! Three songs were picked up during intermissions between rehearsals in the Columbia Broadcasting System studios in New York—where one might ordinarily expect the utmost sophistication—from professional singers who remembered them from father's or grandmother's singing back home in Indiana, Maine and Oklahoma.

Folk music, then, is a broad and general expression of our country. Folk songs tell of humble incidents of everyday life, treat universal themes in an American manner. They deal with courtship, love and marriage; the old maid and the scolding wife; the rocking cradle. There are animal songs and children's game songs, many of them evolved from the songs of adults.

Some of our folk songs are derived from ancient ballads. Others have the tang of the Green

Mountains, the Appalachians, the Ozarks. Their language and their musical line stem out of rural life. They tell us what happens in Podunk, Squash Hollow, Strawberry Point. In them we have portraits of brisk young lovers, hen-pecked husbands, lonely girls, children at play, saucy old maids, housewives who have to work from morning till night. They lead us through an Arkansas kitchen, an Ohio front room, a Vermont bedroom, and a Mississippi backyard.

In telling the story of America, these songs bring to life once more the traditional lore of world culture. Since Homer's day children have been singing of what the Blackbird told the Crow, of how the Frog and the Mouse got on together. Only here the blackbird has a Yankee twang and the frog courts the mouse with a Southern or Western drawl. Old Druidic rituals appear once more in the game song of the "Old Woman All Skin and Bones." Ancient mystic incantations may lie hidden in the nonsense refrains, "Scratch-a-fol-lee-fol-lol-i-dee-i-day," or "Ram yam gilliam, dandoo, ah," —although to the modern singer they are merely manifestations of a simple *joie de vivre*, like Shakespeare's "Hey Nonny Nonny," the cowboy's "Yippee-i-yay" or Tin Pan Alley's "Hi-de-ho."

But whether ancient or modern, the common song-lore of America cannot be crushed. Differing from the more sophisticated art, which can be sung only by trained interpreters and which it is easy to kill by bad performance, the traditional songs can't be killed by screechy, rattly or wheezy voices, or by "wrong interpretations."

Although temporarily submerged by the fabricated tunes of Tin Pan Alley, radio and Hollywood, these tunes can "take it." Unlike certain products of the Broadway musical assembly line whose life span has dwindled to a matter of weeks, genuine folk songs, like the old Model-T Ford, were built to last, to take all the bumps and knocks and come up sturdy and strong when the "top ten" of today's charts have turned to dust.

E. S.

THE CHICKENS ARE A-CROWING

Arrangement by Elie Siegmeister

My mother she will scold me, will scold me, will scold me,
My mother she will scold me for staying away all night.

3

My father he'll uphold me, uphold me, uphold me,
My father he'll uphold me and say I'd done just right.

4

I won't go home till morning, till morning, till morning,
I won't go home till morning, and I'll stay with the girls all night.

5

The chickens they are crowing, a-crowing a-crowing,
The chickens they are crowing, for it is almost daylight.

THE CHICKENS ARE A-CROWING

A PLAY PARTY tune from the Appalachians. The jaunty, irregular rhythm,
with its alternating of 2/4 and 3/4, is in authentic mountain style.

From Cecil Sharp's English Folksongs of the Southern Appalachians, *published by Oxford University Press.*
by Permission of Oxford University Press

WHEN BOYS GO A-COURTING

Arrangement by Elie Siegmeister

When boys go a-court - ing they dress up so fine, To
cheat the poor girls is all their de-sign. They'll sit there and tat - ter and
tat - ter and lie, They'll keep up the girls 'til they're read - y to die.
La - rey - wo, wo, _____ wo, la - rey - wo. _____

From Cecil Sharp's English Folksongs of the Southern Appalachians, published by Oxford University Press. by Permission of Oxford University Press

The girls they be wearied, they'll rise up and say:
"Boys, I'm sleepy, I wish you'd go away.
You're nothing but false-hearted and such I do scorn."
Before you go home you will lie in the barn.

CHORUS: Larey-wo, *etc.*

Next morning, next morning, the boys they'll rise,
Brush off the straws and wipe open their eyes,
They'll mount on their horses and home they will ride,
Like false-hearted fellows all puffed up with pride.

CHORUS: Larey-wo, *etc.*

When they get there they'll stagger and reel,
Sing: "Bless all the girls, how sleepy I feel,
No wife to control me, no children to brawl,"
How happy this young man keeps bachelor hall.

CHORUS: Larey-wo, *etc.*

WHEN BOYS GO A-COURTING

A LILTING TUNE proving that this is a man's world. One of the theories
of the origin of nonsense syllables refrains is that they were sung in
polite company to replace lines of Rabelaisian character. One wonders
what the original words of the phrase, "Larey-wo, wo, larey-wo," must
have been.

The song is sometimes used for dancing.

I MUST AND I WILL GET MARRIED

Arrangement by Elie Siegmeister

One morn - ing, one morn - ing, the weath-er be-ing fine, The moth-er and the daugh-ter walked out to take the air; And as they were a-walk-ing this maid be-gan to vow: "I must and I will get mar-ried, I'm in the no-tion now." now."

From Cecil Sharp's English Folksongs of the Southern Appalachians, *published by Oxford University Press.*
by Permission of Oxford University Press

"Oh daughter, oh daughter, 'tis hold your foolish tongue,
What makes you want to marry? You know you are too young."
"I'm sixteen now, dear mother, and that you must allow,
I must and I will get married, I'm in the notion now."

"Suppose you were to try, dear, and could not find a man?"
"Oh, never mind, dear mother, for there are Miller Sam.
He calls me milk and honey, goes milking of my cow,
I must and I will get married, I'm in the notion now."

"Suppose he were to fool with you as he has done before?"
"Oh, never mind, dear mother, for there are plenty more.
For there is Jack the farmer, goes whistling to his plough.
I must and I will get married, I'm in the notion now."

I MUST AND I WILL GET MARRIED

AND so, according to George Bernard Shaw, "a man chases a woman until she catches him."

IF YOU WANT TO GO A-COURTING

Arrangement by Elie Siegmeister

They haven't got sense to bake a pound of bread,
They'll throw on a log heap as high as my head,
They'll rake out the ashes and then they'll throw
A little of what's called dough, boys, dough,
A little of what's called dough, boys, dough.

3

When the supper comes on and they ask me to eat,
When they call on me to carve up the meat;
One old knife and one old fork,
I sawed about an hour and could not make a mark,
I sawed about an hour and could not make a mark.

4

One of the girls said, "Wait, Mister, wait."
Then just kept sawing till I got it on the plate,
Then just kept sawing till I got it on the floor,
Then up with my foot and kicked it out of door,
Then up with my foot and kicked it out of door.

5

The girls cried, "Mister, you'd better run,
Yonder comes my daddy with a double barreled gun!"
I'll stand my ground as brave as a bear,
I'll tangle my fingers with the old man's hair,
I'll tangle my fingers with the old man's hair.

IF YOU WANT TO GO A-COURTING

AN EPISODE of backwoods wooing, with a warning note on the obstacles,
both culinary and military, to be overcome. The perky tune is tough as
the meat that wouldn't carve, as determined as the pappy with his
double-barreled gun.

HE'S GONE AWAY

Arrangement by Elie Siegmeister

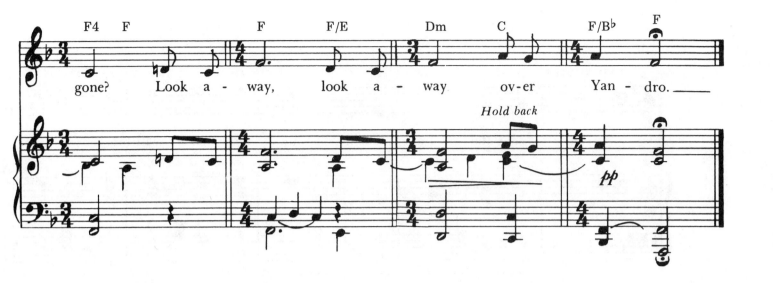

gone? Look a - way, look a - way ov - er Yan - dro. ____

2

He's gone away for to stay a little while,
But he's comin' back if he goes ten thousand miles.
Oh, it's pappy'll tie my shoes,
And mammy'll glove my hands,
And you will kiss my ruby lips when you come back!
Look away, look away over Yandro.

HE'S GONE AWAY

AN EXQUISITE mountain air with words descended from an old English ballad. As "The Lass of Rock Royal" it went:

> Oh, who will shoe my bonny feet,
> Or who will glove my hand,
> Or who will lace my middle waist,
> With a new-made London band?

The rhythm is so free, and the haunting melody so perfectly mated to the verse, that the bar lines which the editors have supplied seem stiff and superfluous.

I'M SAD AND I'M LONELY

Arrangement by Elie Siegmeister

Lyrics (under music, verse 1):

I'm sad and I'm lone-ly, my heart it will break, My sweet-heart loves an-oth-er, Lord I wish I wuz dead!____ My cheeks once were red as the bud on the rose. But now they are whit-er than the li-ly that grows.

Young ladies tak' wahnin', tak' wahnin' from me.
Don' waste your affections on a young man so free.
He'll hug you, he'll kiss you, he'll tell you more lies,
Than the cross-ties on the railroad, or the stars in the sky.

I'll build me a cabin in the mountains so high,
Where the blackbirds can't see me and hear my sad cry.
I'm troubled, I'm troubled, I'm troubled in mind;
Ef trouble don't kill me, I'll live a long time.

THE LONESOME GROVE

Arrangement by Elie Siegmeister

One day___ in a lone-some grove, Lit o'er my head a lit-tle
Do you___ see yon tur-tle- dove la-ment-ing on yon-der

dove, O lit-tle dove, you are not a- lone, Like you I am con-strained to
vine? She's mourn-ing for her own true love, Why should-n't I, too, mourn for

mourn. There is one thing that cheers my heart, That my dear Ma-ry's gone to
mine? My lit-tle dove, you're not a- lone, For with you I'm con-strained to

rest, And while___ tongue can move, She prayed, she prayed her Lord her par-don-ing love.
mourn, I once like you did have a mate, But like you now I'm des - o - late.

225

DANDOO

Arrangement by Elie Siegmeister

This old man came in from the plow,
Dandoo, dandoo,
This old man came in from the plow,
Dandoo, dandoo, ah,
This old man came in from the plow
And said, "Old woman, my breakfast, now!"
Ramyam gilliam dandoo, ah!

3

"There's a crust of bread upon the shelf,
Dandoo, dandoo,
There's a crust of bread upon the shelf,
Dandoo, dandoo, ah,
There's a crust of bread upon the shelf,
If you want any more, go cook it yourself!"
Ramyam gilliam dandoo, ah!

4

The old man walked to his sheep pen,
Dandoo, dandoo,
The old man walked to his sheep pen,
Dandoo, dandoo, ah,
The old man walked to his sheep pen,
And off he jerked a black sheep's skin,
Ramyam gilliam dandoo, ah!

5

He wrapped it round his wife, her back,
Dandoo, dandoo,
He wrapped it round his wife, her back,
Dandoo, dandoo, ah,
He wrapped it round his wife, her back,
And with a switch he made it crack!
Ramyam gilliam dandoo, ah!

6

"I'll tell my father and brothers three,
Dandoo, dandoo,
I'll tell my father and brothers three,
Dandoo, dandoo, ah,
I'll tell my father and brothers three
The way you've been a-whipping me."
Ramyam gilliam dandoo, ah!

7

"Go tell your father and all your kin,
Dandoo, dandoo,
Go tell your father and all your kin,
Dandoo, dandoo, ah,
Go tell your father and all your kin
How the old man tans his mutton skin."
Ramyam gilliam dandoo, ah!

DANDOO

THIS SONG is descended from the old Scotch ballad, "The Cooper o' Fife";
There was a wee cooper who lived in Fife,
Nickety, nackety noo noo noo,
And he has gotten a gentle wife,
Hey Willie Wallacky Now John Dougall Alane
Quo rushety roo roo roo.

The American text and melody express a more impudent spirit.

THE DEVIL AND THE FARMER'S WIFE

Arrangement by Elie Siegmeister

There was a man lived un-der the hill (whistle)_____

_____ If he ain't moved a-way___ he lives there still.

Chorus

Sing rite - ful - aw - ful - ay - ful - a - ni - go,

Rite - ful - aw - ful - a - ni - go lee.

2

This old man went out to his plow,
He hooked up his wife and his old white sow.
CHORUS: Sing rite-ful, *etc.*

3

One day the Devil came down to the field,
Said, "One of your family I'm going to steal."
CHORUS: Sing rite-ful, *etc.*

4

The old man cries out, "Oh I am undone,
For the Devil has come for my oldest son!"
CHORUS: Sing rite-ful, *etc.*

5

"No, t'aint your son I'm after now,
But that danged old rip that you call your wife!"
CHORUS: Sing rite-ful, *etc.*

6

He took the old woman right on to his back,
And down into hell he went, snappety crack!
CHORUS: Sing rite-ful, *etc.*

7

Nine little devils came, rattling their chains.
She up with a poker and knocked out their brains.
CHORUS: Sing rite-ful, *etc.*

8

"On now," said the Devil, "let's h'ist her up higher."
She up with her foot and kicked nine in the fire.
CHORUS: Sing rite-ful, *etc.*

9

The odd little devil peeped over the wall,
Saying, "Take her back, daddy, she'll kill us all!"
CHORUS: Sing rite-ful, *etc.*

10

The Devil he got her right on to his back,
And back to the farmer went, snappety crack!
CHORUS: Sing rite-ful, *etc.*

11

Says he, "Old lady, did you fare very well?"
Says she, "Old man, I flattened all hell!"
CHORUS: Sing rite-ful, *etc.*

12

The old man cries out, "I am to be cursed—
She's been down to hell and come back worse!"
CHORUS: Sing rite-ful, *etc.*

13

And now you see what women can do:
They can lick old men and devils too!
CHORUS: Sing rite-ful, *etc.*

THE DEVIL AND THE FARMER'S WIFE

AGE-OLD TALE of the "curst" henpecking wife, a ballad sung in innumerable versions in Old and New England and at least as far west as Missouri.   Aunt Molly Jackson said: "A lot of times it was sung by the farmers to skeer their wives up a little bit when they'd been quarrelin' and raisin' sand around, to make 'em afraid the same thing might happen to them."
The present version hails from New York's Catskill Mountains.

229

THE SINGLE GIRL

Arrangement by Elie Siegmeister

When I was sing-le, went dressed all so fine; Now I am mar-ried, go rag-ged all the time. I wish I was a sing-le girl a-gain. O Lord, don't I wish I was a sing-le girl a-gain.

2
When I was single, my shoes they did screak;
Now I am married, my shoes they do leak.

3
When I was single, I eat biscuit and pie;
Now I am married, it's eat corn-bread or die.

4
Three little babies, crying for bread,
With none to give them, I wish I was dead.

5
Wash their little feet and send them to school,
Along comes a drunkard and calls them a fool.

6
Dishes to wash, springs to go to,
When you are married, you've all to do.

THE SINGLE GIRL

A REALISTIC TALE of that forgotten woman, the old-fashioned housewife
who remembers wistfully the pleasures and freedoms of an earlier day.

GO TO SLEEPY

Arrangement by Elie Siegmeister

Go ter sleep, go ter sleep, Go ter sleep - y, mam - my's ba - by, When you wake you shall have cake, Go ter sleep - y, mam - my's ba - by.

2

Go ter sleep, go ter sleep,
Go ter sleepy, mammy's baby,
All de horses in de stable
B'longs ter mammy's little baby.

GO TO SLEEPY

A LOVELY DROWSY TUNE, hummed over many a cradle by both white and
Negro women of the South. The words are descended from much older
lullabies.

ITISKIT, ITASKIT

Arrangement by Elie Siegmeister

I - tis - kit, i -tas - kit, A green and yel - low bas - ket, I
wrote a let - ter to my love And on the way I dropped it,
Dropped it, dropped it, A lit - tle boy came a - long
Put it in his pock - et, Pock - et, pock - et.

A GAME SONG, known to children the country over. The tune is archaic and timeless. It is currently sung in slightly different versions as a nursery rhyme ("It's raining, it's pouring"); a lullaby ("Bye, Baby Bunting, daddy's gone a-hunting"); a taunting song ("Cry, baby, cry)"; as another game song ("Little Sally Sand"); and as a wishing song on rainy days ("Rain, rain, go away, Come again some other day, Little Willie wants to play").

LITTLE SALLY SAND

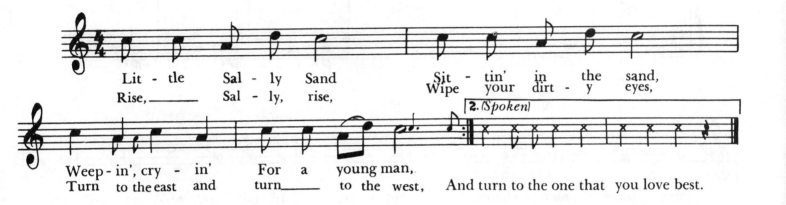

IT'S RAINING, IT'S POURING

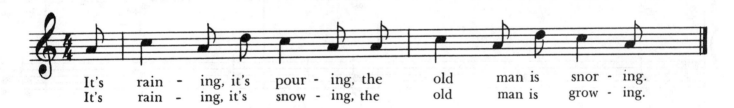

BYE, BABY BUNTING

HERE COME THREE MERCHANTS A-RIDING

Arrangement by Elie Siegmeister

Here come three mer-chants a - rid - ing, A - rid - ing, a - rid - ing, Here

come three mer - chants a - rid - ing, In - na - men, se - na - man, see.

2

What are you riding here for,
Here for, here for,
What are you riding here for,
Innamen, senaman, see.

3

We're riding here to get married,
Married, married,
We're riding here to get married,
Innamen, senaman, see.

4

You're awful dirty and ragged,
Ragged, ragged,
You're awful dirty and ragged,
Innamen, senaman, see.

5

We're just as good as you are,
You are, you are,
We're just as good as you are,
Innamen, senaman, see.

6

Which one of us will you have, sir,
Have, sir, have, sir,
Which one of us will you have, sir,
Innamen, senaman, see.

7

The fairest one that I can see, sir,
See, sir, see, sir,
The fairest one that I can see, sir,
Innamen, senaman, see.

HERE COME THREE MERCHANTS A-RIDING

WHEN THIS PLAY SONG is sung in company, it is the custom of the boys
and girls to take turns with the lines and answer each other. An old version of the ditty gave it the title of "Three Dukes A-riding."

OLD WOMAN ALL SKIN AND BONE

Arrangement by Elie Siegmeister

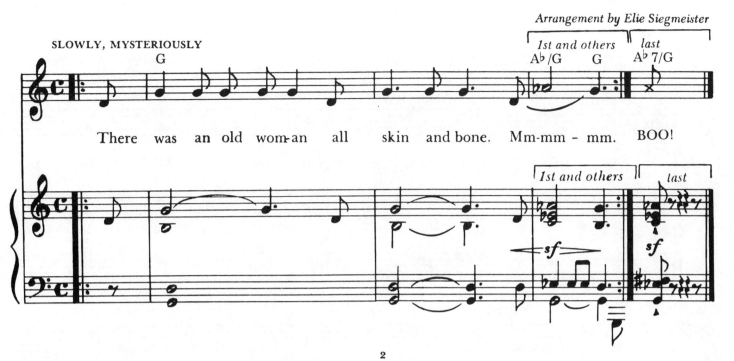

There was an old wom-an all skin and bone. Mm-mm – mm. BOO!

2
She went to the churchyard all alone. Oo-oo-oo

3
She looked up and looked down. Oo-oo-oo.

4
She saw a corpse lie on the ground. Oo-oo-oo.

5
"Father, father," so she said. Oo-oo-oo.

6
"Shall I look so when I am dead?" Oo-oo-oo.

7
The sexton to her made reply. Oo-oo-oo.

8
"Yes, my darling, by and by." BOO!

OLD WOMAN ALL SKIN AND BONE

THE VERSE has a gruesomeness in which children appear to delight. Especially do they delight in the screech supposed to come with the sight of the corpse.

To play the game, each object and person in the verses is represented by a player. The one who takes the part of the old woman approaches the corpse, which lies at the feet of the sexton. The players sing as the old woman walks toward the "churchyard," and the moaning chant is broken by the shrill scream of the corpse as it arises abruptly and gives chase to the other players. If the corpse can catch another player, that one becomes the old woman.

From Mrs. Charles H. Linscott's Folk Songs of Old New England. Permission granted.

THE BIRDS' COURTING SONG

Arrangement by Elie Siegmeister

* Symbols in italics for guitar with capo across 3rd fret

Tow -dy ow -dy, dil - do dum, Tol - lol - li - do dil - do day.

2

"Hi!" said the little leather-winged bat,
"I will tell you the reason that,
The reason that I fly in the night
Is because I've lost my heart's delight."

CHORUS: Towdy owdy, *etc.*

3

"Hi!" said the little mourning dove,
"I'll tell you how to regain her love,
Court her night and court her day,
Never give her time to say 'Oh Nay!' "
CHORUS: Towdy owdy, *etc.*

4

"Hi!" said the woodpecker, sitting on a fence,
"Once I courted a handsome wench,
She got scary and from me fled,
And ever since then my head's been red."
CHORUS: Towdy owdy, *etc.*

5

"Hi!" said the bluejay as she flew,
"If I was a young man I'd have two.
If one proved fickle and chanced for to go
I'd have a new string to tie to my bow."
CHORUS: Towdy owdy, *etc.*

THE BIRDS' COURTING SONG

THE ANIMAL SONG and the animal story are timeless. Seven centuries ago, our ancestors held their sides laughing at the antics of Reynard the Fox. More recently, children followed the adventures of Mickey Mouse with equal avidity. The song of the blackbird, the crow, the woodpecker who exhibit human frailties is a perennial favorite in country districts.

BARNYARD SONG

Arrangement by Elie Siegmeister

LIVELY

I had a cat and the cat pleased me, Fed my cat un-der

yon-der tree; Cat went "Fid-dle-i - fee."

Dog went "Bow wow," Cat went "Fid-dle-i - fee."

In successive verses repeat these two measures as often as needed to get in the cries of all the animals.

2

I had a dog and the dog pleased me—
Fed my dog under yonder tree;
Dog went "Bow-wow!"
Cat went "Fiddle-i-fee."

3

I had a hen and the hen pleased me—
Fed my hen under yonder tree;
Hen went "Ka, Ka."
Dog went "Bow-wow!"
Cat went "Fiddle-i-fee."

4

I had a hog and the hog pleased me—
Fed my hog under yonder tree;
Hog went "Krusi, Krusi."
Hen went "Ka, Ka."
Dog went "Bow-wow!"
Cat went "Fiddle-i-fee."

5

I had a cow and the cow pleased me—
Fed my cow under yonder tree;
Cow went "Moo, Moo."
Hog went "Krusi, Krusi."
Hen went "Ka, Ka."
Dog went "Bow-wow!"
Cat went "Fiddle-i-fee."

6

I had a sheep and the sheep pleased me—
Fed my sheep under yonder tree;
Sheep went "Baa, Baa."
Cow went "Moo, Moo."
Hog went "Krusi, Krusi."
Hen went "Ka, Ka."
Dog went "Bow-wow!"
Cat went "Fiddle-i-fee."

7

I had a goat and the goat pleased me—
Fed my goat under yonder tree;
Goat went "Maa, Maa."
Sheep went "Baa, Baa."
Cow went "Moo, Moo."
Hog went "Krusi, Krusi."
Hen went "Ka, Ka."
Dog went "Bow-wow!"
Cat went "Fiddle-i-fee."

BARNYARD SONG

THE OPPORTUNITY for zoological sound effects provided by this song has
made it a children's favorite throughout the land for many a year.

FROG WENT A-COURTIN'

Arrangement by Elie Siegmeister

2

He rode up to Miss Mousie's den,
uh-huh, uh-huh,
He rode up to Miss Mousie's den,
And said, "Miss Mousie, are you within?"
uh-huh, uh-huh.

3

"Yes," said Miss Mousie, "I'm within,"
uh-huh, uh-huh,
"Yes," said Miss Mousie, "I'm within."
"Raise the latch and please walk in."
uh-huh, uh-huh.

4

Frog took Miss Mousie on his knee,
uh-huh, uh-huh,
Frog took Miss Mousie on his knee,
And said, "Miss Mousie, will you marry me?"
uh-huh, uh-huh.

5

"Not without Uncle Rat's consent,"
uh-huh, uh-huh,
"Not without Uncle Rat's consent,"
"Would I marry the President."
uh-huh, uh-huh.

6

Uncle Rat he went to town,
uh-huh, uh-huh,
Uncle Rat he went to town,
To get his niece a wedding gown,
uh-huh, uh-huh.

7

What does he get for a wedding gown?
uh-huh, uh-huh,
What does he get for a wedding gown?
A piece of a hide of an old grey-hound,
uh-huh, uh-huh.

8

Where will the wedding supper be?
uh-huh, uh-huh,
Where will the wedding supper be?
Way down yonder in a hollow tree,
uh-huh, uh-huh.

9

What will the wedding supper be?
uh-huh, uh-huh,
What will the wedding supper be?
Two soup beans and a black-eyed pea,
uh-huh, uh-huh.

10

Frog took Miss Mousie down to dwell,
uh-huh, uh-huh,
Frog took Miss Mousie down to dwell,
Down in the bottom of an old deep well,
uh-huh, uh-huh.

11

Frog went swimming across the lake,
uh-huh, uh-huh,
Frog went swimming across the lake,
He got swallowed by a water-snake,
uh-huh, uh-huh.

12

A little piece of corn-bread a-laying on the shelf,
uh-huh, uh-huh.
A little piece of corn-bread a-laying on the shelf,
If you want any more you can sing it yourself!
uh-huh, uh-huh.

FROG WENT A-COURTIN'

ON NOVEMBER 21, 1550, a new song title was entered in the Register of
the London Company of Stationers: "A Moste Strange Weddinge of the
Frogge and Mouse." For four hundred and thirty years children of all
ages have not tired of singing about "Mr. Frogge," his sword and pistol,
and how he ended his adventures in the belly of a water-snake.

Cripple Creek to Old Smoky

[SOUTHERN MOUNTAIN SONGS, "BALLITTS," FIDDLE AND BANJO TUNES]

WHILE THE conventional picture that presented all genuine American folk music as "mountain songs" is one-sided and false, it would be equally wrong to go to the other extreme and neglect the special contribution to our native culture of the people of the Ozarks, and particularly of the Appalachian mountain country.

Almost all sections of the country have characteristic folk music. But the several thousand square miles included in the mountain districts of western Virginia, West Virginia, North and South Carolina, Kentucky and Tennessee have something no other part of our country can equal. It is music tangy as a crab-apple, ebullient as hard cider.

Some years ago it was quite the thing in certain circles to exclaim over these quaint mountaineers who still spoke Elizabethan English and sang ancient ballads of lords and ladies. But in 1917 Cecil Sharp, although he came over to collect just that sort of material, noted that the Appalachian country was not, as some have given the impression, a sort of animated musical waxworks, in which the dead memories of past centuries were miraculously preserved and resuscitated. He found it remarkable that it was not only old people who sang folk songs, as in England, but also children, boys in their teens, people of all ages. It struck him that here was a community in which, for one reason or another, the natural gift for ballad-making and improvisation had not been lost; where musical utterance through song, which in more "civilized" regions is the property of a select and trained elite, was still the common property of all.

Since Sharp visited the Appalachians, things have changed there. Electricity and concrete highways now pass through the remote valleys and folk singers show their wares not only in some lonesome grove but also at annual festivals which bring audiences from miles around and are broadcast on the radio. The lonely settlers have been bought out by lumber companies, or have gone to work in the mill towns.

But through all this, the characteristic mountain speech, dances and songs have not been lost. Girls and boys still kick a lively step and the fiddler and banjo player still get in their licks in square dance tunes such as "Cotton-eyed Joe," "Bucking Mule," "Cackling Hen," "Who Bit the Tater," "Cornstalk Fiddle," or "Old Joe Clarke," though the evening may begin with modern dances to the radio. "Ballits" of local doings: robberies, murders, love tragedies, like "McAfee's Confession," "Darling Cora," "Wild Bill Jones," or "John Hardy," continue finding their way around. Not long ago there were plenty of mountain troubadours like Bascom Lunsford, Jim Garland, Sarie Ogan and Aunt Molly Jackson, whose authentic sliding, gliding, high-pitched creaky voices told of new days in the mountains —of the coming of the good and bad years, of loving and working, of new heroes and bad men whose names got around over the grapevine telegraph of song to places where newspapers are still not common. Far from killing them off, "civilization" has widened the mountain balladeer's scope, given him new and more exciting subjects to put into song.

Although it has been much caricatured, the "mountain intonation" is still a live and original kind of musical speech. To the unaccustomed ear it is nothing but a shrill, flat, unappealing mannerism. But once you have broken down your concert hall prejudices, the particular vocal, nasal and guttural inflections—which are as difficult to describe in print as they are to set down in notes—have a charm and color that are unique. There is nothing fixed or static about this intonation. A song will be sung a little differently each time it is performed. Notes which seem like sharps at first hearing turn out to be naturals a second time; a third time they are in between; and on a fourth hearing they seem to glide back and forth between sharp and natural. This is as true of the mountain fiddler as of the singer.

The same is true of rhythmic values. A song which is in 3/4 time on Monday turns up in 4/4 on Tuesday. And on Wednesday it has a few measures of 3/4 and the rest in 5/4. To those accustomed to written music which is generally better behaved, all this is very confusing at first. But after a while the fascination of these ever-fluctuating, ever-growing and changing melodic and rhythmic patterns dawns on you, and you are won over. Here is the feeling of what music must once have been like, before it became a business. Here is a people, many of them musicians, who still possess that instinctive knack of putting simple experiences of life into an immediate and direct musical speech without thinking first of regulations, rules, "audience appeal" or market. Here is one of the musical well-springs of America.

E. S.

SOURWOOD MOUNTAIN

Arrangement by Elie Siegmeister

Chick - ens a- crow- in' on Sour - wood Mount - ain, Ho- dee - ing- dong- doo - dle - all - a - day. So man - y pret - ty girls I can't count 'em, Ho- dee - ing- dong - doo - dle - all - a - day.

2

I got a gal at the head o' the holler,
Ho-dee-ing-dong-doodle-all-a-day,
She won't come an' I won't foller,
Ho-dee-ing-dong-doodle-all-a-day.

3

My true love is a blue-eyed daisy,
Ho-dee-ing-dong-doodle-all-a-day.
If I don't get her I'll go crazy,
Ho-dee-ing-dong-doodle-all-a-day.

4

She sits up with old Si Hall,
Ho-dee-ing-dong-doodle-all-a-day.
Me an' Jeff can't go there at all,
Ho-deeing-dong-doodle-all-a-day.

5

Big dog bark an' the little one bite you,
Ho-dee-ing-dong-doodle-all-a-day.
Big gal court an' the little one marry you,
Ho-dee-ing-dong-doodle-all-a-day.

6

Geese in the pond and ducks in the ocean,
Ho-dee-ing-dong-doodle-all-a-day.
Devil's in the women when they take a notion,
Ho-dee-ing-dong-doodle-all-a-day.

7

Old gray goose goin' down the river,
Ho-dee-ing-dong-doodle-all-a-day.
If I'd been a gander I'd a-went with her,
Ho-dee-ing-dong-doodle-all-a-day.

SOURWOOD MOUNTAIN

THIS IS one of the gayest and most popular of all the mountain fiddle tunes. There are as many variants of this song as there are counties and communities in the Kentucky mountains.

OLD JOE CLARKE

Arrangement by Elie Siegmeister

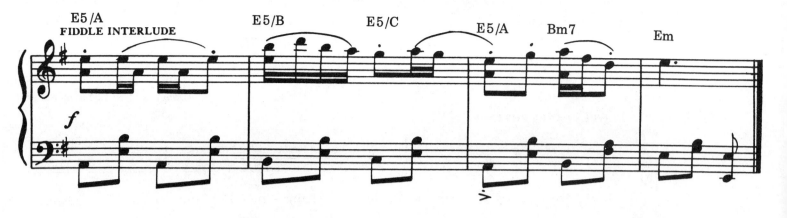

2

The funniest thing I ever saw
Was two old women fighting,
The one cried out: "It's no fair fight!"
The other one's a-biting."
CHORUS: Fare you well, etc.

3

When I was a little girl
I used to play with toys;
But now I am a bigger girl
I'd rather play with boys.
CHORUS: Fare you well, etc.

4

When I was a little boy
I used to want a knife;
But now I am a bigger boy
All I want is a wife.
CHORUS: Fare you well, etc.

5

Once I had a muley cow
Muley when's she's born;
Took a buzzard a thousand years
To fly from horn to horn.
CHORUS: Fare you well, etc.

6

Wish I was a sugar tree,
Standing in the middle of some town—
Ev'ry time a pretty girl passed,
I'd shake some sugar down.
CHORUS: Fare you well, etc.

7

Old Joe Clarke had a yellow cat
She would neither sing nor pray;
She stuck her head in a buttermilk jar
And washed her sins away.
CHORUS: Fare you well, etc.

OLD JOE CLARKE

ROBERT W. GORDON described in his article, "Some Mountain Songs from North Carolina," how he recorded tunes like "Old Joe Clarke."

"Long ago, even before you arrived, word of your coming has been spread. 'A furriner on his way up to Shelton's. Your recording phonograph and banjo have proclaimed you as ostensibly a 'musicioner' . . . Hardly have the first notes of the banjo sounded before they begin to appear. . . . At first it will be a bit hard to induce any one to play or sing for the phonograph, but once they have heard the living voice come back nothing can stop them. . . . One of the fiddlers and your host with the banjo have begun to play 'Old Joe Clarke.' Already two of the younger couples are dancing. The fiddler swings and sways as he plays. Your host begins singing the time-honored words his voice is rising sharp and clear above the music. As he comes to the chorus all join in."

CINDY

Arrangement by Elie Siegmeister

LIVELY DANCE RHYTHM

G6   D9

I wish I was an ap-ple, a hang-in' in the tree, And

G6   C   G/B   C   G

ev-'ry time my sweet-heart passed, she'd take a bite of me. She

Em   D9

told me that she loved me, she called me sug-ar plum, She

bring out left hand

G   C   C/D   G

throwed 'er arms a-round me,——— I thought my time had come.

Get a-long home Cin-dy, Cin-dy, Get a-long home Cin-dy, Cin-dy,

Get a-long home Cin-dy, Cin-dy, I'll mar-ry you some-time.

2

She took me to the parlor, she cooled me with her fan,
She swore that I's the purtiest thing in the shape of mortal man.
Oh where did you get your liquor, oh where did you get your dram?
I got it from a nigger, away down in Rockingham.
CHORUS: Get along home, etc.

3

Cindy got religion, she had it once before,
When she heard my old banjo, she 'uz the first one on the floor.
I wish I had a needle, as fine as I could sew,
I'd sew the girls to my coat tail, and down the road I'd go.
CHORUS: Get along home, etc.

4

Cindy in the springtime, Cindy in the fall,
If I can't have my Cindy girl, I'll have no girl at all.
Cindy went to the preachin', she swung around and around,
She got so full of glory, she knocked the preacher down.
CHORUS: Get along home, etc.

CINDY

"OLD TIMERS" believed that dancing to the fiddle or banjo was tanta-
mount to reserving a seat in Hell. But many of the mountain youngsters
like Cindy, just couldn't keep their feet virtuous when the twang of
the banjo was heard.

Cindy got religion, had it once before,
When she heard my old banjo, she 'uz the first one on the floor.

DARLING CORA

Arrangement by Elie Siegmeister

2

The first time I saw darling Corie,
She was standing on the banks by the sea,
With a .44 buckled around her,
And a banjo on her knee.

3

Go away, go away, darling Corie,
And do and best you can.
I will get me another woman,
And you can get you another man.

4

The last time I saw darling Corie,
She had a .44 in her hand,
Kill that revenue officer,
That took away her man.

5

Go away, go away, darling Corie,
Quit your hanging around my bed.
Whiskey has ruined my body,
Pretty woman has killed me stone dead.

* Symbols in italics for guitar with capo across 3rd fret

DARLING CORA

IN THE MOUNTAINS the moral law often took precedence over mere enactments recorded in statute books. A great deal of traditional and not so traditional balladry is concerned with the doings of bad men, "feudin', shootin', killin'." There are ballads dealing with "Bloody Breathitt," "Wild Bill Jones," "The Killin' in the Gap," "Poor Omie," and "The Fitch-Austin Feud." Whether "Darling Cora" records an actual or imaginary killing, its heroine was certainly someone not to be trifled with on a dark night.

Some years after adding this ballad to the others in this book, I felt there was more that could be done with it, and turned it into a one-act opera.

E. S.

GROUND HOG

Arrangement by Elie Siegmeister

AT A GOOD CLIP, TANGY

Shoul-der up your gun and call your dog,

Shoul-der up your gun and call your dog, A - way to the woods to

catch a ground hog, Ground hog.

1st and others *

last

FINE

* Play Interlude once after every two or three verses; or as often as desired.

FIDDLE INTERLUDE

2

Two in the cleft and one in the log,
Two in the cleft and one in the log,
See'd his nose, Lord, I thought I knew it was a hog.
Ground hog.

3

Sam cocked his gun and Dave pulled the trigger,
Sam cocked his gun and Dave pulled the trigger,
But the one killed the hog was old Joe Digger.
Ground hog.

4

They took 'im by the tail and wagged 'im to a log,
They took 'im by the tail and wagged 'im to a log,
And swore by gosh! he's a hell of a hog!
Ground hog.

5

Up stepped Sam with a snigger and a grin:
Up stepped Sam with a snigger and a grin:
"Whatcha goin' to do with the groun' hog skin?"
Ground hog.

6

Scrapes 'im down to his head and feet,
Scrapes 'im down to his head and feet,
By damn, Sam, here's a fine pile o' meat!
Ground hog.

7

Carried him to the house and skinned 'im out to bile,
Carried him to the house and skinned 'im out to bile,
I bet forty dollars you could smell 'im fifty mile.
Ground hog.

8

They put 'im in the pot and all begin to smile,
They put 'im in the pot and all begin to smile,
They eat that hog before he struck a bile.
Ground hog.

9

Run here, man, hit's bilin'-hot,
Run here, man, hit's bilin'-hot,
Sam and Dave's both eatin' outn the pot.
Ground hog.

10

The children screamed and the children cried,
The children screamed and the children cried,
They love groun' hog cooked and fried.
Ground hog.

11

Hello, mama, make Sam quit,
Hello, mama, make Sam quit,
He's eatin' all the hog, I can't git a bit.
Ground hog.

12

Hello, boys, ain't it a sin,
Hello, boys, ain't it a sin,
Watch that gravy run down Sam's chin!
Ground hog.

13

Hello, mama, look at Sam,
Hello, mama, look at Sam,
He's eat all the hog 'n' a-soppin' out the pan!
Ground hog.

14

Watch 'im, boys, he's about to fall,
Watch 'im, boys, he's about to fall,
He's eat till his pants won't button at all.
Ground hog.

WHAT WERE the boar-hunts of classical antiquity, the riding-to-hounds of the gentry of England, or the exploits of Teddy Roosevelt in darkest Africa, compared to this epic of the Kentucky mountains? There are those who would scarcely approve of the technique of "Soppin' out the pan," but it sounds as though a good time was had by all.

CARELESS LOVE

Arrangement by Elie Siegmeister

MODERATELY SLOW

Love, oh love, oh care - less love,

Love, oh love, oh care - less love, Oh it's love, oh love, oh care - less love You___ see what care - less love has done.

2
Once I wore my apron low,
Once I wore my apron low,
Oh it's once I wore my apron low
You'd follow me through rain and snow.

3
Now I wear my apron high,
Now I wear my apron high,
Oh it's now I wear my apron high,
You'll see my door and pass it by.

4

I cried last night and the night before,
I cried last night and the night before,
Oh I cried last night and the night before
Going to cry tonight and cry no more.

5

How I wish that train would come,
How I wish that train would come,
Oh it's how I wish that train would come
And take me back where I come from.

6

I love my mama and papa too,
I love my mama and papa too,
Oh I love my mama and papa too
But I'd leave them both to go with you.

7

It's on this railroad track I stand,
It's on this railroad track I stand,
Oh it's on this railroad track I stand
All for the love of a railroad man.

CARELESS LOVE

THE CLASSIC Southern version of an—alas!—eternal theme. The same motif appears in the Blues song, "Every night when the Sun Goes In," and W. C. Handy was the first of a series of composers who have turned "Careless Love" to account in more sophisticated versions.

WAY UP ON OLD SMOKY

Arrangement by Elie Siegmeister

Way up on old Smo-ky, _____ all cov - ered with snow, _____ I lost my true lov- er _____ by_ spark- ing too slow. _____ Now spark - ing is pleas-ure, _____ part - ing is grief, _____ but a false - heart- ed lov - er _____ is_ worse than a thief. _____

A thief he will rob you, will take what you have,
But a false-hearted lover will take you to your grave.
The grave will decay you, will turn you to dust,
There is not one girl out of a hundred a poor boy can trust.

3

They'll hug you and kiss you and tell you more lies
Than the cross-ties on the railroad or the stars in the skies.
They will tell you they love you, to give your heart ease,
And as soon as you back up on them, they'll court who they please.

Way up on old Smoky, all covered with snow,
I lost my true lover by sparking too slow.
Bury me on old Smoky, old Smoky so high,
Where the wild birds in heaven can hear my sad cry.

WAY UP ON OLD SMOKY

THERE IS a dry humor in the lines of this song, whose easy, lilting tune
is loved and sung all through the Appalachian country. It serves also as
the melody of "The Little Mohee."

KENTUCKY MOONSHINER

Arrangement by Elie Siegmeister

I've been a moon-shin-er for sev'n-teen long—years. I've spent all my mon-ey on whis-key and— beers. I'll go to some hol-ler, I'll put up my still, I'll— make you one gal-lon for a two dol-lar bill.

2

I'll go to some grocery and drink with my friends.
No women to follow to see what I spends.
God bless those pretty women, I wish they were mine.
Their breath smells as sweet as the dew on the vine.

3

I'll eat when I'm hungry and drink when I'm dry.
If moonshine don't kill me I'll live till I die.
God bless those moonshiners, I wish they were mine.
Their breath smells as sweet as the good old moonshine.

KENTUCKY MOONSHINER

A SONG of loneliness and the consolatory bottle. The scoops and slides, the free intonation, the indefinite floating rhythm of the tune, are in characteristic mountain style.

RYE WHISKEY
[CLINCH MOUNTAIN]

Arrangement by Elie Siegmeister

2

I'll eat when I'm hungry
And drink when I'm dry;
If whiskey don't kill me
I'll live till I die.

CHORUS:

Oh whiskey, rye whiskey,
I know you of old;
You rob my poor pockets
Of silver and gild.

3

If the ocean was whiskey
And I was a duck,
I'd swim to the bottom
And never come up.

CHORUS:

Oh whiskey, rye whiskey,
How sleepy I feel,
Oh whiskey, rye whiskey,
How sleepy I feel.

4

For work I'm too lazy
And beggin's too low,
Train robbin's too dangerous,
To gambling I'll go.

CHORUS:

Rye whiskey, rye whiskey,
Rye whiskey I cry,
If I don't get rye whiskey
I surely will die.

5

I've no wife to quarrel with,
No babies to bawl,
The best way of livin'
Is no wife at all.

CHORUS:

Oh whiskey, rye whiskey,
How I do love thee,
You killed my poor pappy,
Now, dang you, try me.

RYE WHISKEY

BACCHANAL atop Clinch Mountain after the first gallon of apple-jack or corn likker has gone down. What could old Bacchus have asked better than to be a duck at the bottom of a whiskey ocean?

EVERYBODY'S WELCOME

Arrangement by Elie Siegmeister

WITH ENTHUSIASM

Eve - ry - bo - dy's wel - come
Fath er you are wel - come
Moth - er you are wel - come
Sis - ter you are wel - come

Yes, yes, wel - come! Eve - ry - bo - dy's

wel - come,___ To the dy - ing Lamb! Oh Glo - ry!

Free Sal - va - tion! Oh Glo - ry! To the dy - ing Lamb.

From L. L. McDowell's *Songs of the Old Camp Ground*, published by Edwards Brothers, Inc.

O DEATH

Arrangement by Elie Siegmeister

SLOW AND HEAVY

What is this that I can see, Cold i-cy hands tak-ing
I'll lock your jaws till you can't talk, I'll bind your legs till

hold of me. For death has come you all can see Hell -
you can't walk. I'll close your eyes so you can't see, I'll

gate is op-en wide for me O death! O
bring you un-to me. O death!

death! Can't you spare me o-ver for a-no-ther year?

From *Ballad Makin' in the Mountains of Kentucky* by Jean Thomas, published by Henry Holt and Company, Inc. Printed by permission. Music arranged for publication by Walter Kob.

THERE ARE many in the mountains of Kentucky, who, while they are unable to read or write, know their Bible from cover to cover and can cite many a passage entire, both chapter and verse. This is the country where baptism is still by total immersion, where the pious gather in windowless log cabin churches for foot-washing rituals. It is in this region that the story is told of the preacher who ignored the Lord's call to preach, and was stricken and laid out for dead. But, stirring, he rose, stiff and cold, and begged the Lord, in these earnest and impressive lines, to spare him.*

* We are indebted to Mrs. Jean Thomas, author of *Ballad-Makin' in the Mountains of Kentucky*, for this story.

The Old Chizzum Trail

[WESTERN COWBOY, LUMBERJACK, RAILROAD SONGS]

THE ENDING of the Civil War released new energies for pushing further and completing the big job of the century: the opening of the Far West. The two decades following the conclusion of peace were the golden years of frontier adventure, when the last wild places were finally brought under control. While polite cosmopolitan novelists were mourning the passing of the age of romance, a generation of skilful, swaggering, hard-working fellows were living the experiences that were soon to be so romantically described in hundreds of dime novels and avidly followed by millions of small boys.

The 1870's and 1880's were the heyday of the cowboy. But while the Indian fights, train robberies, mail coach hold-ups and wild revels in clapboard saloons abound in the minds of Hollywood script writers, there were other realities in the cowboy's life: long days at the southern end of an endless herd of cows, choking hot prairie dust; long, cold sleepless hours of night-herding; unheroic losses of arm or leg in the crush of a thousand stampeding cattle; and, as the song tells us,

> . . . bacon and beans 'most every day;
> I'd as soon be eatin' prairie hay.

Opening up a huge country, in which any state was larger than two or three European countries, was a job which needed thousands of tough, raw-boned and careless men who could live hard and work harder. The West asked no passports and the men came from everywhere: from played-out farms and barren city streets; from jails and office desks. There were sailormen tired of the sea, and mountain boys who found it hard to grow corn on rocky hillsides. English, Irish, Negroes, Scandinavians, Germans, Czechs and Bulgarians, they came. They rode the round-ups and bedded cows down, and became American cowboys.

It was in the '60's and '70's that the railroads pushed through to Kansas and the grass began to be worn down on the old Chisholm Trail, the long drive from the Texas and Arkansas ranches up to the railroad shipping points and to the good grazing lands of Montana and Wyoming. John Lomax tells that between 1870 and 1890 one million mustang ponies were driven up the trail, along with twelve million head of cattle in herds of 1000 and 3000. The weeks and months on horseback on the long drive offered little to relieve the heat, the rain, the monotony, except thoughts of a grand bust-up to come at Dodge City—and song. Not all cowboys sang, nor did those who did sing pour out tunes one after another, as on a radio program. But often the jogging, loping, cantering rhythms of the horse would mold to a new pattern the flowing measures of a ballad or music hall tune remembered from the East, from Kentucky, from Ireland, or from the fo'c'sle of an ocean tramp. Cow calls, "ti yi's," "yeas," and "yippees," would fit into the musical scheme or form a new chorus to an old verse, and a cowboy song was in the making. Like the men who sang them, they came from everywhere, and made one grand jumble of styles. Yet the prairie life did something to them all, brought a distinctive color, a special accent, and a new subject matter: a unique style was born. Does it matter what the great-grandparents were of "Good-bye, Old Paint," or "The Night-Herding Song?" They are as pure-bred American as the comic strip, the buffalo nickel, or second generation Irish or Scandinavians.

Cowboy songs were often of a very practical nature. Those with sharp rhythmic cries were used to rally a sluggish herd; those with quiet rolling rhythms served as cattle lullabies, "to drown the wild sound" of coyotes or other animals which could startle nervous herds and might provoke a disastrous stampede. Other songs were sung around the campfire to pass the long night hours on the trail: of desperadoes, bucking bronchos, noble and not-so-noble love songs ("I Gave My Girl a Quarter," etc.). These songs were vociferous, sentimental, braggart and self-pitying.

Besides the cowboys, there were others who helped push the frontier back: lumberjacks and railroad men. Why songs should grow up around certain occupations and not others is sometimes hard to say, but in this case, isolated living in closely bound-up groups certainly played an important role. Life in the deep woods, cut off from the world for months at a time by winter snows, brought with it the same community feeling as existed on the old ranches.

Professional lumbering—that is, cutting timber for sale—migrated from Maine through Pennsylvania to Minnesota and Wisconsin. Its greatest heydey came in the '70's and '80's, and with it the flowering of the shantyboy songs. Like those of the cowboy, the shanty-boy songs are rambunctious and sentimental, tough and tearful in turn. The lumberjack had his hardships and dangers, too: broken legs and heads from falling trees, log jams on icy rivers, hard-headed bosses who forget to pay off when the snows were gone. On long winter nights, around the big-bellied stove, no one was more welcome than the shanty-boy minstrel—often Irish or Negro, as among shanty singers at sea. The shanty-boy singer would sing of it all in his own rough-hewn verses, using some old vaudeville or ballad tune, or, if they would not fit, a tune of his own making.

These old shanty-boy songs, many of them collected by Franz Rickaby on his long treks through the timber country just before lumbering became mechanized and changed into a large-scale industry, have the bleak, lonesome quality of the dark woods. Although still sung here and there by a few old-timers, their glory has gone with the work of the husky, raw-boned laughing boys who gave life to them a hundred years ago.

But for all the work of the cowboys and lumberjacks, it was the railroad men who really completed the picture of opening the West. Driving millions of spikes down into the sun-baked prairie, they brought with them the songs of the iron horse that soon were to drown the sound of the other songs. To those who have eyes and ears for the present as well as the past, the locomotive is as mythical and romantic a figure as any Minotaur of antiquity. The energy, the speed, the sense of creative power that those men who bridged the trackless wilds felt; the washouts, the wrecks, the train robberies—all are portrayed in the work-songs of the trackmen and the ballads of the boys who rode the caboose. To the railroad man, the locomotive is not an "it"; it is a "he" or a "she" who can be coaxed, cajoled and thundered at. She can be sung to in cooing tones, or bellowed at in a hoarse voice when passing the wrong switch. Railroad songs are the animal ballads of an age of coal and steel, and when the rails bridged the country the rhythm of the wheels and the song of the whistle replaced the plodding ballads of mule-drivers and the loping refrains of horsemen.

Railroad songs are Irish, German, Negro and Southern, as are the men who work in the roundhouse or sit up in the cab. They are an indispensable part of the ballad history of our country and their humor and fantasy, even in this age of miraculously streamlined flyers, are testimony to the fact that the machine does not always crush the humanity out of men, but can sometimes add to it very much indeed.

E. S.

266

COWBOY'S GETTIN'-UP HOLLER

New Words and new Music adaptation by John A. Lomax and Alan Lomax

Arrangement by Elie Siegmeister

RATHER SLOW BUT FREELY

Wake up, Ja-cob, day's a-break-in', Fry-in' pan's
Ba-con in the pan, Cof-fee in the pot, Git up now and

on an' hoe-cake bak-in'.
get it while it's hot.

COWBOY'S GETTIN'-UP HOLLER

JOHN A. LOMAX tells us this call is frequently heard in western camps. On Southern chain gangs, the caller sings out, "Wake up, boys, spit on a rock," or, "Wake, snakes, day is breakin'." All these calls may have come from or given birth to the line in that old spiritual.

"Wake up Jacob, day's a-breakin'."

THE CHISHOLM TRAIL

Arrangement by Elie Siegmeister

My feet are in the stirrups and my rope is at my side,
Show me a hoss that I can't ride.

CHORUS: Coma ti yi youpy, etc.

3

I'm up in the mornin' before daylight,
And before I sleep the moon shines bright.

CHORUS: Coma ti yi youpy, etc.

4

Oh! it's bacon and beans 'most every day,
I'd as soon be a-eatin' prairie hay.

CHORUS: Coma ti yi youpy, etc.

5

My slicker's in the wagon and I'm gettin' mighty cold,
And these long-horned sons-o-guns are gettin' hard to hold.

CHORUS: Coma ti yi youpy, etc.

6

I'll ride my horse to the top of the hill,
I'll kiss that gal, gol darn, I will.

CHORUS: Coma ti yi youpy, etc.

7

I went up the boss to draw my roll,
He had it figgered out I was nine dollars in the hole.

CHORUS: Coma ti yi youpy, etc.

8

I went up to the boss and we had a little chat,
I slapped him in the face with my big slouch hat.

CHORUS: Coma ti yi youpy, etc.

9

Oh, the boss says to me, "I'll fire you,
Not only you, but the whole damn crew."

CHORUS: Coma ti yi youpy, etc.

10

I'll sell my outfit just as soon as I can;
I won't punch cattle for no damn man.

CHORUS: Coma ti yi youpy, etc.

11

Goin' back to town to draw my money,
Goin' back home to see my honey.

CHORUS: Coma ti yi youpy, etc.

12

Well I'll sell my saddle and I'll buy me a plow,
And I'll swear begad, I'll never rope another cow.

CHORUS: Coma ti yi youpy, etc.

13

My seat is in the saddle and my saddle's in the sky.
An' I'll quit punchin' cows in the sweet bye and by

CHORUS: Coma ti yi youpy, etc.

THE CHISHOLM TRAIL

"THE SONG of the Chisholm trail is the cowboy classic; its simple beating
tune; its forthright couplets; its 'Comma-ti-yi-youpy'; its extemporane-
ous yelps, whoops and yips; its occasional departures from singing into
shouting, are as exciting as the clatter of horses' hooves on the hard
prairie," said Margaret Larkin in "Singing Cowboy."

269

NIGHT-HERDING SONG

Arrangement by Elie Siegmeister

2

I've circle-herded and night-herded too,
But to keep you together, that's what I can't do;
My horse is leg-weary and I'm awful tired,
But if you get away, I am sured to get fired,
Bunch up, little dogies, bunch up,
Hi-oo, hi-oo, hi-oo!

3

Oh, lay still dogies, since you have laid down,
Stretch away out on the big open ground;
Snore loud, little dogies, and drown the wild sound,
That will all go away when the day rolls around.
Lay still little dogies, lay still,
Hi-oo, hi-oo, hi-oo!

NIGHT-HERDING SONG

"THIS SONG is a good example of the jog trot rhythm found in many of
the cowboys' night-herding songs which were sung as a lullaby to the
herd. All night long the rider sleepily jogged around some two or three
acres of a deep-breathing, cud-chewing mass, singing or whistling to let
them know he was there. As long as the cattle heard the human voice,
they felt safe. Without it, the least noise in the extreme quiet might
cause a stampede." *

* Sires: "Songs of the Open Range."

I RIDE AN OLD PAINT

Arrangement by Elie Siegmeister

SLOWLY

I ride an old Paint,— I lead an old Dan,— I'm goin' to Mon-
tan' for to throw the hoo-li-an. They feed in the cou-lees, they
wa-ter in the draw, Their tails are all mat-ted, their backs are all
raw. Ride a-round, lit-tle do-gies, Ride a-round— them—

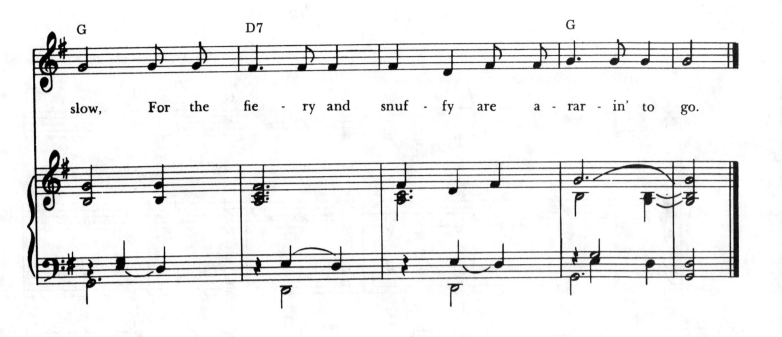

slow, For the fie - ry and snuf - fy are a - rar - in' to go.

2

Old Bill Jones had two daughters and a song.
One went to Denver and the other went wrong.
His wife she died in a poolroom fight,
Still he sings from mornin' till night.
CHORUS: Ride around, etc.

3

Oh, when I die, take my saddle from the wall,
Put it on my pony, lead him out of his stall.
Tie my bones to his back, turn our faces to the West,
And we'll ride the prairie that we love the best.
CHORUS: Ride around, etc.

I RIDE AN OLD PAINT

COWBOYS WERE a hard-bitten lot, but the toughest frequently revealed a
tender streak. There is touching sentiment in the picture of this bucko's
bones riding west "on the prairie that we love best." A coulee is a depression in the prairie; a draw, almost a ravine.

273

THE RAILROAD CORRAL

Arrangement by Elie Siegmeister

WITH A LIVELY SWING

We're up in the morn-ing ere break-ing of day, The chuck wag-on's bus-y, the flap-jack's in play, The— herd is a - stir ov - er hill - side and vale, With the night rid - er's— crowd-ing them in-to the trail.

2

Come take up your cinches, come shake out your reins.
Come wake your old broncho and break for the plains.
Come roust out your steers from the long chapparal,
For the outfit is off to the railroad corral.

3

The sun circles upward, the steers as they plod
Are pounding to powder the hot prairie sod
It seems, as the dust makes you dizzy and sick,
That we'll never reach noon, and the cool shady creek.

4

So tie up your kerchief and ply up your nag
Come, dry up your grumbles, and try not to lag;
Come on with your steers from the long chapparal,
We're far on the road to the railroad corral.

5

Come, shake out your rawhide and snake it up fair;
Come, break your old broncho to take in his share;
Come from your steers in the long chapparal,
For 'tis all in the drive to the railroad corral.

6

But the longest of days must reach evening at last,
The hills all climbed, the creeks all past.
The tired herd droops in the yellow light;
Let them loaf if they will, for the railroad's in sight.

THE RAILROAD CORRAL

A JOYFUL TUNE, sung when nearing the goal of the long, dusty trip up the trail. The railroad corral was the point at which the cattle were shipped, and after weeks, or sometimes months of following, guarding, pacifying them, the cowboys were glad to see their charges on the way to the stockyards. The rhythm of the song is that of galloping. Chapparal is a growth of low, thorny shrubs; cinch, a saddle girth.

GOOD-BYE, OLD PAINT

Arrangement by Elie Siegmeister

EASY, LOPING RHYTHM

Good - bye, old Paint, I'm a - leav - ing Chey - enne; Good
bye, old Paint, I'm a - leav - ing Chey - enne; I'm a -
leav - ing Chey - enne, I'm off to Mon - tan'. Good -
bye, old Paint, I'm a - leav - ing Chey - enne.

Good-bye, Old Paint, I'm a-leaving Cheyenne;
Good-bye, Old Paint, I'm a-leaving Cheyenne;
Old Paint's a good pony, he paces when he can;
Good-bye, old Paint, I'm a-leaving Cheyenne.

3

Good-bye, Old Paint, I'm a-leaving Cheyenne;
Good-bye, Old Paint, I'm a-leaving Cheyenne;
Go hitch up your hosses and give them some hay,
And seat yourself by me so long as you stay.

4

Good-bye, Old Paint, I'm a-leaving Cheyenne;
Good-bye, Old Paint, I'm a-leaving Cheyenne;
My hosses ain't hungry, they won't eat your hay,
My wagon is loaded and rolling away.

5

Good-bye, Old Paint, I'm a-leaving Cheyenne;
Good-bye, Old Paint, I'm a-leaving Cheyenne;
My foot's in the stirrup, my bridle's in my hand;
Good morning, young lady, my hosses won't stand.

GOOD-BYE, OLD PAINT

A GOING-AWAY SONG in the persistent rhythm of a loping horse, it leaves
us wondering why this cowboy was so intent on "a-leavin' Cheyenne."
"Old Paint" was often used as a "good-night" song at cowboy dances,
something like the familiar "Good-night, ladies." Tradition had it that
as long as anyone remembered another verse, the dance still went on.

BURY ME NOT ON THE LONE PRAIRIE

Arrangement by Elie Siegmeister

2

"O bury me not on the lone prairie,
Where the wild coyotes will howl o'er me,
In a narrow grave just six by three;
O bury me not on the lone prairie!

3

"O bury me not on the lone prairie,
Where the wild coyotes will howl o'er me,
Where the buzzard beats and the wind goes free;
O bury me not on the lone prairie!

4

"O bury me not on the lone prairie,
In a narrow grave six foot by three,
Where the buffalo paws o'er a prairie sea;
O bury me not on the lone prairie!

5

"O bury me not on the lone prairie,
Where the wild coyotes will howl o'er me,
Where the rattlesnakes hiss and the crow flies free;
O bury me not on the lone prairie!

6

"O bury me not," and his voice failed there,
But we took no heed of his dying prayer;
In a narrow grave just six by three
We buried him there on the lone prairie.

BURY ME NOT ON THE LONE PRAIRIE

THIS CLASSIC of the plains has been harmonized, parodied, yodeled by so many college, bar-room and radio quartets that the "lone prair-ee" has become the cliché of every synthetic cowboy song and singer. Yet the original "Bury Me Not" has genuine pathos, desolation and the cynicism of tough-skinned men. It is sung to several melodies. Choice among them is difficult.

A SHANTYMAN'S LIFE

Arrangement by Elie Siegmeister

Oh a shan - ty - man's life is a wear - i - some life Al - though
some think it void of care. _____ Swing - ing an ax from
morn - ing till night, In the midst of the for - ests so drear. _____
Ly - ing in the shan - ty__ bleak and__ cold While the cold,__ storm - y

wint-ery winds blow,_____ And as soon as the day-light doth ap - pear, To the wild woods we must go._____

Oh, the cook rises up in the middle of the night,
Saying, "Hurray, brave boys, it's day."
Broken slumbers ofttimes are passed
As the cold winter night passes away.
Had we rum, wine, or beer, our spirits for to cheer
As the days so lonely do dwine,
Or a glass of any shone while in the woods alone
For to cheer up our troubled minds.

3

But when spring it does set in, double hardships then begin,
When the waters are piercing cold,
And our clothes are dripping wet and fingers benumbed,
And our pike-poles we scarcely can hold.
Betwixt rocks, shoals, and sands give employment to all hands
Our well-banded raft for to steer,
And the rapids that we run, oh they seem to us but fun,
For we're void of all slavish fear.

A SHANTYMAN'S LIFE

THE FOLLOWERS of every craft or profession are generally convinced their trade is the most tedious, dreariest of all. There is an old cowboy song which goes: "A cowboy's life is a dreary life, He's driven through heat and cold." The railroad man sings: "There's many a man killed on the railroad and cast in a lonely grave," while Gilbert and Sullivan in "The Pirates of Penzance" tell us: "A policeman's lot is not a happy one." Here a shanty-boy tells his troubles.

THE JOLLY LUMBERMEN

Arrangement by Elie Siegmeister

Come all you jol - ly lum - ber - men and lis - ten to my song.__ But do not get un - eas - y,__ for I won't de - tain you long;__ Con - cern - ing some jol - ly lum - ber - men who once a - greed to go__ And spend a win - ter re - cent - ly on Col - ley's run, I oh.__

We landed in Lock Haven in the year of sev'nty three
A minister of the gospel, one evening said to me,
"Are you the party of lumbermen that once agreed to go
And spend a winter pleasantly on Colley's run, I oh?"

3

"Oh yes, we'll go to Colley's run, to that we will agree
Provided you pay good wages, our passage to and fro
Then we'll agree to accomp'ny you to Colley's run, I oh.
Then we'll agree to accomp'ny you to Colley's run, I oh."

4

"Oh yes, we'll pay good wages, your passage to and fro,
Provided you will sign papers to stay the winter through
But, mind you, if you get homesick and back you swear you'll go
You'll have to pay your own passage down from Colley's run, I oh."

5

'Twas by that 'tarnel agreement that we then agreed to go—
Full five and twenty in number, all able-bodied men.
The road it was a pleasant one; by train we had to go,
Till we landed at McFarling's tavern, full seventeen miles below.

6

But there our joys were ended, our troubles they began;
The captain and the foreman came following up the run.
They led us in every direction thru some places I did not know
Among the pines which grew so tall on Colley's run, I oh.

7

Our hearts were clad with iron, our soles were shod with steel
But the usages of that winter would scarcely make a shield
For our grub the dogs would laugh at, and our beds were wet with snow
God grant there is no worse hell on earth than Colley's run, I oh.

8

But now the spring has come again and the ice-bound streams are free
We'll float the logs to Williamsport, our friends we'll haste to see.
Our sweethearts they will welcome us, and bid others not to go
To that God-forsaken gehooley of a place of Colley's run, I oh!

THE JOLLY LUMBERMEN

THIS SONG, formerly sung in Pennsylvania about a place called "Colley's
Run," was derived from an older Maine lumbering song, "Canaday-I-O,"
which, according to Eloise Linscott, was based on a still older English sea
song, "in turn derived from an older love song, "Caledonia," first printed
in 1800. The song followed the timber west and was sung in the Lake
states camps of the nineties; and the refrain concerned "Michigan-I-O"
instead of "Canaday-I-O." Finally it was taken still farther west to the
prairies, where it became the cowboy song, "The Buffalo Skinners."

PAT WORKS ON THE RAILWAY
[PADDY WORKS ON THE ERIE]

New Words and new Music adaptation by John A. Lomax and Alan Lomax

Arrangement by Elie Siegmeister

In eighteen hundred and forty-two
I left the old world for the new,
Bad cess to the luck that brought me through
To work upon the railway.
CHORUS: Fi-li-me, etc.

3

When we left Ireland to come here
And spend our latter days in cheer,
Our bosses, they did drink strong beer,
And we worked on the railway.
CHORUS: Fi-li-me, etc.

4

Our contractor's name it was Tom King.
He kept a store to rob the men—
A Yankee clerk with ink and pen
To cheat Pat on the railway.
CHORUS: Fi-li-me, etc.

5

It's "Pat, do this," and "Pat, do that!"
Without a stocking or a hat,
And nothing but an old cravat,
While Pat works on the railway.
CHORUS: Fi-li-me, etc.

6

One Monday morning to our surprise,
Just half an hour before sun-rise,
The dirty divil went to the skies
And Pat worked on the railway.
CHORUS: Fi-li-me, etc.

PAT WORKS ON THE RAILWAY

THE SONG tells of the tough job that faced the Irish laborers who built the first transcontinental railroad in the 1860's. Sung on the Union Pacific it spread to the vaudeville stage, where it became a stock "Irish" number. It was even sung as a sea chanty for many years.

STATE OF ARKANSAS

New Words and new Music adaptation by John A. Lomax and Alan Lomax

Arrangement by Elie Siegmeister

came — to Ar - kan - sas.   sas.

2

I landed in St. Louis
With ten dollars and no more,
I read the daily papers
Till both my eyes were sore.
I read the evening papers
Till at last I saw
Ten thousand men were wanted
In the State of Arkansas.

3

I worked six weeks for the son-of-a-gun,
Jesse Howard was his name;
He was six feet seven in his stocking feet
And taller than any crane.
His hair hung down in strings over
His long and lantern jaw.
He was the photograph of all the gents
Who live in Arkansas.

4

He fed me on corn-dodgers,
As hard as any rock,
Until my teeth began to loosen
And my knees began to knock;
I got so thin on sass'fras tea
I could hide behind a straw,
And indeed I was a different man
When I left old Arkansas.

5

Farewell to swamp angels,
Canebrakes and chills,
Farewell to sage and sass'fras,
And corn-dodger pills;
If I ever see this land again,
I'll give to you my paw;
It will be through a telescope
From here to Arkansas.

STATE OF ARKANSAS

THIS SAGA of the migratory railroad worker in the Ozarks is one which
has been told—with changed names and occupations—of a half-dozen
states and employers. In none of the variants can the feeling be described
as subtle.

On the Job

[FARMER, BOATMAN, ROCK-PILE, PEDDLER SONGS]

COMMON FOLK know what it means to "sing for your supper." The Minnesota reaper, the Maine teamster, the hand laying rails in the desert, the youngster working a push-boat up a Tennessee River, the New Orleans dock-hand, have found the need to sing at or about their work. Sometimes happy, sometimes bitter, sometimes laughing and sometimes strictly practical, these songs tell the story of the adventures and hardships of the many people whose hands have shaped the destiny of this country.

In this country it is the Negro who has made the widest use of the group work-song. The tradition goes back to plantation days when, moving steadily down rows of cotton, breaking rocks on a mountain road, or toting bales on the levee, large groups of slaves would lift their voices and bodies in unison under the rhythmic guidance of a leader. After Emancipation the work-song tradition persisted and grew among southern railroad gang laborers.

Natalie Curtis Burlin vividly described a typical "Hammering Song":

"In the mines of Virginia this 'Hammerin' Song' chimed with the ringing of the hammer as the men chanted the . . . refrain which gave rhythm and pace to monotonous toil. The improvised verses were usually started by the 'header' or headman, who received extra pay for his good voice, his quick musical fancy and his ability to keep the men singing and thus working in unison. 'An' as soon as we'd git started a-*singin'*,' a Negro explained, 'We'd forgit we was ti-yerd, an' so long as the header would keep de song a-goin', we'd keep ohn a-hammerin' an' a-*hammerin'*!'

". . . Usually it is the leader who sings alone, for the worker must keep his lungs full while swinging the heavy hammer. Yet some-times the men break into harmony, joining in after the first words . . . and it is just this extraordinary fusion of the rhythm of men's toiling bodies with the beat of music that makes the work-chants of the Negro typical. . . ." *

The conditions of group work in the outdoors thus gave rise not only to the typical harmonized style of the Negro work-song, but also to elements of that special type of singing formerly referred to as "hot intonation." Isolated from contact with city-made and city-tuned instruments, the Negro singer developed a more flexible type of intonation based on the natural scale, intermingled with quarter tones, slides, grunts, shouts, sharp "hanhs"—violent exhalations of breath accompanying the descent of the hammer or pickaxe—and with an absolutely unique musical quality. All these colors of the Negro work-song were taken over and amplified into the Blues, Jazz and into the "hot" playing of Sidney Bechet and Louis Armstrong.

Because of its striking choral form, the work-music of the Negroes has received ample and deserved attention, which has, however, tended to obscure the songs of the white American worker. These have tended to be individual songs *about* work, not necessarily sung on the job, but at almost any time. Except in the case of the old sea shanties, there is little evidence that the white worker ever sang in gangs. At the beginning, Americans were a footloose people, not bound to the soil, rarely, in the early days, tied down for long to any one spot. In consequence, his songs of work had nothing of the fixity of an established style about them, but took on the characteristics of a shifting, migrating people.

* From Book IV of the Hampton Series of "Negro Folk Songs."

Carl Sandburg has compared the Erie Canal Song to the Song of the Volga Boatmen. In spirit, maybe—but in form what a world of difference. The Russian song, so steady, fixed in its measures, is the work chant of chained prisoners, serfs bound for life to one job and to one endless plodding pace. The tune of the "Canawllers," with its shifting syncopation, its ennobled ragtime pulse is the song of men free to come and go, to change from one job to another, picking up music hall strains on the way. So other work-songs have given and taken motifs from the minstrels, from vaudeville, from old ballads, from spirituals. The fascinating hybrids that resulted make for much of the charm of American work-music.

While in the hammering or cotton-picking song, whose main function is to set the pace for work movements, the rhythm is the main factor and the verses are often a sequence of half-remembered, patched together phrases, often making very little sense, in the ballad that tells about work, the text is of major importance. Every man knows most intimately the hardships and annoyances of his own particular job, and it is never the sailor who sings, "Oh, for a life on the ocean wave!" Song is an ideal outlet for unspoken grievances, and it is not surprising that the sharecropper sings of the voracious boll weevil, the boatman of a strong current, the mill worker of meager income, and the prisoner of the hardship of cracking rocks.

One peculiarly American job not usually thought of in musical terms is that of the promotion man. The technique of modern advertising, with its streamlined use of musical motifs as radio theme songs for gasoline, soap, and breakfast foods, had its forerunners in the Hamlin musical troupes who toured the length and breadth of the land, drawing crowds to their Wizard Oil spiels by singing humorous and sentimental songs. More direct musical salesmanship may be found in the song cries of street peddlers from Brooklyn to New Orleans, that were familiar to every housewife. And more often than not the peddler with the best cry had the best sales.

The songs and ballads of Americans on the job are powerful, trivial, gay, sarcastic, and matter-of-fact by turns. They reveal to us much about the plain day-to-day feelings of millions of average, day-to-day people. They stand as a lyric testimony to the imagination and creative power of the men who built the nation.

E. S.

LOOK OVER YONDER

Words and music by Lawrence Gellert
Arrangement by Elie Siegmeister

2

I was a-hamm'ring, huh,
Hamm'ring away last December.
I was a-hamm'ring, huh,
Hamm'ring away last December.
Wind was so cold,
Oh my Lord, wind so cold.

* Symbols in italics for guitar with capo across 3rd fret

3

Can't you all hear them, huh,
Cuckoo birds all a-holl'ring.
Can't you all hear them, huh,
Cuckoo birds are all a-holl'ring,
Sure sign of rain,
Oh my Lord, sure sign of rain.

4

My little woman, huh,
She keep sending me letter,
My little woman, huh,
She keep sending me letter.
Don't know I'm dead
Oh my Lord, don't know I'm dead.

5

Sometimes I wonder, huh,
Wonder if other people wonder.
Sometimes I wonder, huh,
Wonder if other people wonder.
Just like I do,
Oh my Lord, just like I do.

LOOK OVER YONDER

THIS TYPICAL ROCK-PILE SONG from a Georgia prison is harsh and eloquent with toil. Gangs of Negroes will chant rhythmical refrains like this for hours, as they work. The fall of the hammer is accompanied by the sharp exhalation "hunh!" which marks the pulse of the song.

THE FARMER COMES TO TOWN

Arrangement by Elie Siegmeister

When the farm-er comes to town with his wag-on brok-en down, Oh, the farm-er is the man who feeds them all. If you'll on-ly look and see, I think you will a-gree That the farm-er is the man who feeds them all.

Chorus The farm-er is the man,___ the farm-er is the man,

Lives on cred-it till the Fall. With the in-terest rate so high, it's a won-der he don't die, For the mort-gage man's the one who gets it all.

2

When the lawyer hangs around, while the butcher cuts a pound,
Oh the farmer is the man who feeds them all.
And the preacher and the cook go a-strolling by the brook,
Oh the farmer is the man who feeds them all.
CHORUS: The farmer, *etc.*

3

When the banker says he's broke, and the merchant's up in smoke,
They forget that it's the farmer feeds them all.
It would put them to the test if the farmer took a rest;
Then they'd know that it's the farmer feeds them all.

CHORUS

The farmer is the man, the farmer is the man,
Lives on credit till the Fall;
And his pants are wearing thin, his condition it's a sin,
He's forgot that he's the man who feeds them all.
CHORUS: The farmer, *etc.*

THE BALLAD OF THE BOLL WEEVIL

Arrangement by Elie Siegmeister

FAST GUITAR STYLE

Oh, de boll wee - vil am a lit - tle black bug, Come from Mex - i - co, dey say. Come all de way to Tex - as, Jus' a- look - in for a place to stay, Jus' a - look - in' for a home,____ ____ jus' a- look - in' for a home. ____ ____ home. ____

1st and others

last

De first time I seen de boll weevil,
He was settin' on de square.
De next time I seen de boll weevil,
He had all of his fam'ly dere,
Jus' a-lookin' for a home, jus' a-lookin' for a home.

De farmer take de boll weevil,
An' he put him in de hot san';
De weevil say, "Dis is mighty hot,
But I'll stand it like a man.
Dis'll be my home, dis'll be my home."

De farmer take de boll weevil
An' he put him in a lump of ice.
De weevil say to de farmer,
"Dis is mighty cool an' nice,
Dis'll be my home, dis'll be my home."

De boll weevil say to de farmer,
"You can ride in dat Fohd machine,
But when I get through wid yo' cotton
Can't buy no gasoline.
Won't have no home, won't have no home."

De merchant got half de cotton,
De boll weevil got de res'
Didn't leave de farmer's wife
But one ol' cotton dress,
An' it's full of holes, an' it's full of holes.

De farmer say to de merchant,
"We's in an awful fix,
De boll weevil et all de cotton up
An' left us only sticks.
We got no home, we got no home."

De farmer say to de merchant,
"I want some meat an' meal."
"Get away from here, you son of a gun,
You got boll weevils in yo' fiel',
Goin' to get yo' home, goin' to get yo' home."

De farmer say to de merchant,
"We ain't made but only one bale,
And befoh we'll give you dat one,
We'll fight and go to jail,
We'll have a home, we'll have a home."

THE BALLAD OF THE BOLL WEEVIL

"THE BOLL WEEVIL is a promising subject for balladry, since he furnishes many romantic motifs. He is an outlaw, hunted in every field. He has apparently superhuman powers of resistance to hardship, exposure, and attacks from man, the individual, and from organized society. He has an extraordinary cunning and trickery, can outwit and flout man, and go his way despite all human efforts to outwit him." *

This "ballet" was sung so widely throughout the cotton states that it might be considered the theme song of the Southern share-cropper. It was probably of Negro origin.

* Dorothy Scarborough: "On the Trail of Negro Folk Songs."

TEAMSTER'S SONG

Arrangement by Elie Siegmeister

Come all you bold ox team-sters, Wher-ev-er you may be, I
hope you'll pay at-ten-tion And lis-ten un-to me.

2

It's of a bold ox teamster,
His name I'll tell to you,
His name was Johnny Carpenter,
He pulled the oxen through.

3

He took with him six bags of meal
And his bunk chains also,
All for to bind his spruce and pine
While hauling through the snow.

4

Says Carpenter unto Flemmons,
"I'll show them to haul spruce,
For my oxen in the snow, you see,
Are equal to bull moose!"

5

Now the crew that tend those oxen,
Their names to you I'll tell;
The jobber's name was Crowley—
The boys all knew him well.

6

Old Duke and Swan all on the pole
So vigorous they do lug,
While Swan's the head with a collar and hames,
And a pair of leather tugs.

7

Old Brighty in the hovel lay,
They say his feet are sore.
But it was a strain that caused his pain,
And now he'll haul no more.

8

He tried to keep his oxen fat,
But found it was no use;
For all that's left is skin and bones,
And all the horns are loose.

9

Now to conclude and finish
I'm going to end my song.
I hope I haven't offended you
If I've said anything wrong.

TEAMSTER'S SONG

"Sung by Samuel Young of North Anson, Maine, who learned it when, as a lumberjack, he 'drove the river' for twenty-two years, on the Connecticut, Androscoggin, Penobscot, and Kennebec rivers.... He is known far and wide as the lumberjack who can sing all night and never repeat himself....

"Logging operations were begun in South Berwick Township, Maine, in 1631. Either oxen or horses were used for hauling. The bunk chains mentioned in the song are used to bind the logs onto the sled, or, as the lumberjack says, the 'bunk.' Ox teamsters were also known as bullwhackers and were said to have the prize vocabulary of strong language. The tally board was the record kept in camp to count the logs; to 'run another turn' was to make another trip. 'Hovel' is the lumberman's term for the lumber-camp barn.

"This is a fine example to show the mixture of Irish, French, Canadians, and Yankees who made up the logging crews."*

* Eloise Linscott: "Folk-Songs of Old New England."

GOIN' UP THE RIVER

Arrangement by Elie Siegmeister

Go - in' up the ri - ver from Cat - letts - burg to Pike,
work - in' on a push - boat for old man Jef - fry's Ike. Jane.

2

Working on a push boat
For fifty cents a day;
Buy my girl a brand new dress
And throw the rest away.

3

Working on a push boat
Water's mighty slack;
Taking sorghum 'lasses down
And bringing sugar back.

4

Pushing mighty hard, boys,
Sand-bar's in the way,
Working like a son-of-a-gun
For mighty scanty pay.

5

Going down big Sandy
With Pete and Lazy Sam,
When I get to Catlettsburg,
I'll buy myself a dram.

6

Working on a push boat,
Working in the rain;
When I get to Catlettsburg,
Goodbye, Cynthie Jane.

GOIN' UP THE RIVER

PUSHING BARGES was a slow, endless job on Kentucky's Big Sandy as
on any river. This song has the drowsy rhythm of poling, and the
random thoughts that will pass through men's heads as they work for
hour after hour on end.

From Ballad Makin' in the Mountains of Kentucky by Jean Thomas, published by Henry Holt and Company, Inc. Printed by permission. Music arranged for publication by Walter Kob.

I LIVED IN A TOWN

Arrangement by Elie Siegmeister

I lived in a town___ way down South___ By the name of Ow-ens-b'ro, And worked in a mill with the rest of the trash, As we're oft-en called,___ you know.

2

We rise up early in the morn,
And work all day real hard
To buy our little meat and bread
And sugar, tea and lard.

3

Our children they grow up unlearned,
No time to go to school,
Almost before they've learned to walk,
They learn to spin or spool.

4

The folks in town who dress so fine—
And spend their money free,
Will hardly look at a factory hand
Who dresses like you or me.

5

Just let them wear their watches fine—
And gems and pearly strings,
But when our day of judgment comes,
They'll have to share their pretty things.

I LIVED IN A TOWN

THE MOUNTAIN PEOPLE of Kentucky who came down to work in the mill towns brought with them their traditional music. Often they put new words to the old tunes, reflecting their changed lives. "I Lived in a Town," set to the melody of an old mountain hymn, was quoted by Grace Lumpkin in her novel "To Make My Bread."

THE ERIE CANAL

Words and music by William S. Allen
Arrangement by Elie Siegmeister

I've got a mule,___ her name is Sal,___ Fif-teen years on the
We bet-ter get a-long on our way, old gal,___ Fif-teen miles on the

Er - ie Can - al.___ She's a good old work-er and a good old pal,
Er - ie Can - al,___ Cause you bet your life___ I'd ne - ver part with Sal,

Fif - teen years on the Er - ie Can - al. __ We've hauled some barg - es
Fif - teen miles on the Er - ie Can - al. __ Git up there, mule, here

THE ERIE CANAL

For years the Erie Canal served as the main artery of communication and trade between the Atlantic Ocean and the Great Lakes. Between Albany and Buffalo, "Lumber, coal and hay" and a hundred other commodities flowed in a never-ending stream. The canal boat mule-drivers in their pull past the "inland towns with the sea-going names"—Brockport, Middleport, Gasport, Lockport—found relief in cadences molded by the tedium of the long haul.   Carl Carmer reported that "riders on the slow canal boats got many a bruised cranium from failing to heed the warning cry of the 'hoggie' or mule driver—'Low Bridge, Everybody Down.'"

BARBER'S CRY

Lath-er and shave, Lath-er and shave, Lath-er and shave, Sham-poo and shear.

CHARCOAL MAN

Arrangement by Elie Siegmeister

Mah mule is white, mah chah-coal is black, I sells mah chah-coal_ two bits_ a sack_ Chah-coal,_ chah-coal._

BARBER'S CRY AND CHARCOAL MAN

THE SHOUTS and calls of peddlers were part of the color of the big city. Housewives often told the time of day by the regular appearance of the "Cash clothes!", the "Banan'!" or the "Junk!" man. The Barber's cry and the call of the Charcoal man were both heard in the South, home of many colorful street cries.

THE SHOEMAKER

Arrangement by Elie Siegmeister

LIVELY, CHEERFUL

I am a shoe-mak-er by my trade, I'll work in rain-y weath-er, Be-sides two pair I've made to-day Of a side and a half of leath-er. Whack de loo-de-dum, Whack de loo-de-doo-de, Whack de loo-de-dum, Kate, you are my darl-ing. darl-ing.

From Cecil Sharp's English Folksongs of the Southern Appalachians, published by Oxford University Press. by Permission of Oxford University Press

2

Go hand me down my pegging awl,
I stuck it right up yonder,
Go hand me down my sewing awl
To peg and sew my leather.
CHORUS: Whack de loo-de dum, *etc.*

3

Oh, I have lost my shoemaker's wax,
And where do you think I'll find it?
Oh, ain't that enough to break my heart,
Oh right here, Kate, I've found it.
CHORUS: Whack de loo-de dum, *etc.*

THE SHOEMAKER

IN THE EARLY 1900's shoes were still hand-made in the remoter Tennessee valleys, as they had been for hundreds of years before the invention of the shoe machine. This is an interesting example of a handicraft song, a type grown rare in America since the growth of large-scale machine work. The ballad of an American Hans Sachs.

SHINE ON

Words and Music by Luke Schoolcraft
Arrangement by Elie Siegmeister

2

Monkey dressed in soldier's clothes,
Sing a little hoe-down Jordan,
Went out one day to shoot some crows,
Oh! Jerusalem.
The crows they all die fly away,
Sing a little hoe-down Jordan,
The monkey will shoot some other aay,
Oh! Jerusalem.
CHORUS: Shine on, shine on, etc.

3

Down in the hen-house on my knees,
Sing a little hoe-down Jordan,
I thought I heard a chicken sneeze,
Oh! Jerusalem!
'Twas only a rooster saying his prayers,
Sing a little hoe-down Jordan,
A-singin' a hymn to the hens upstairs,
Oh! Jerusalem!
CHORUS: Shine on, shine on, etc.

DURING THE 1880's, before the techniques of modern advertising, the Hamlin Wizard Oil Company was pioneering in new methods of parting man from his money. Its oil was guaranteed to cure every ailment from cholera morbus to flat feet. Wizard Oil concert troupes toured the country in wagons, stopping in town squares to regale the populace with the latest minstrel songs, humorous and sentimental ditties. "Shine On," one of the favorite of the Hamlin troupes, retailed the lament of the slave who despaired of winning freedom.

Big Men and Bad Men

[NATIVE HEROES AND DESPERADOES]

WRITERS HAVE told us the age of fantasy, of myths, legends and giants is dead. Possibly in many countries it is. But if we look at the story of our own land—not as written in history books, but as told in the speech, tales and songs of Americans who made the country —we find fantasies wilder than any ever before dreamed of; fairy tales and giants more colossal than any ever imagined; demons who tamed the lightning, harnessed the whirlwind and took the tornadoes in tow. Carl Carmer in his fascinating book, "The Hurricane's Children," pointed out that American fairy tales, unlike those of practically any other country, do not deal at all with the "little people," with elves, pixies, brownies or fairies. They are all about *big* people, whose footprints when filled with water make the Great Lakes; whose hammer-strokes make the mountains ring; whose lassos rope a thousand steers at one throw.

Wise men tell us that the myths and legends of a people symbolize their unconscious dreams and aspirations. In our case, there was nothing unconscious about it; the land was big and wild, the dream of clearing it, taming it, making it habitable was gigantic, heroic.

Davy Crockett, one of those frontiersmen who were "half horse, and half alligator, and the rest snapping turtle," told bigger whoppers, about grinning coons crazy, or grinning the knots off trees; of a muley cow so big "it took a buzzard a thousand years to fly from horn to horn." But the biggest whopper of all was Davy himself, getting elected to Congress as a prank, fighting the Indians, then sticking up for them in Washington, singing, "Won't You Come into My Bower?" as he picked off advancing Mexicans at the Alamo.

Said Carmer:

"At the end of a hard day's work the American cowboys or miners or lumberjacks or applepickers have had their fun out of making up stories about men who could do jobs that just could not be done, in an impossibly short time, with one hand tied behind them."

Such a story was the yarn that must have come after a long rainy spell in the North woods about Paul Bunyan who got caught in a rain so thick that water-spouts reached right up into the sky. He jumped in one, swam up it until he reached the top, and turned it off.

Kemp Morgan, Mike Fink, Febold Feboldson, Tony Beaver, Johnny Appleseed—these were the heroes of a race of movers and doers, of a people that finds no job too big, no odds too great to be taken and licked. From one of them Carl Sandburg culled that classic phrase: "We'll fight till hell freezes over, and then write on the ice, 'Come on, you b - - - - - ds!'"

With bigness comes simplicity. Thomas Jefferson, who believed in that fantastic thing, democracy, enough to make it work, received the British ambassador in his bedroom slippers. Abraham Lincoln, according to the story, would have entertained the politicians, bankers and clergymen, who were to swing the Presidential nomination for him, in similar fashion had it not been for the prompt and efficacious intervention of his wife.

These are the men who symbolize America, who live in the hearts of the people, in story and in song. Then there are legendary figures who grow out of the doings of real men: such as the crazy apple-planter who turned the Ohio Valley from an empty wilderness to a garden of apple-trees. Johnny Appleseed was the male Ceres or Demeter of a race of Yankee planters. There is the immortal saga of man against the machine, of his death-struggle and symbolic victory: the giant John Henry, about whom songs have grown abundantly. Then there is the music of villains and desperadoes, from the diamond-studded stock market juggler, Jim Fisk, to those western bandits like Sam Bass, Billy the Kid and Jesse James, who "robbed from the rich to give to the poor."

Each of these in his time lived out a real life on earth. But in song they became not one but many men, they became all men, all Americans. No more fantastic than the Kentucky pioneers, the Mississippi River captains, the '49ers rounding Cape Horn, of the past, or those Americans of today who sit through the whole Antarctic winter, follow a solar eclipse down to Central Africa, or spend thirty years in a laboratory tracking down a microbe no one has yet heard of, they tell us more of the spirit in which this country was conceived and brought into being than all the history books, political speeches and newspaper editorials put together.

E. S.

OLD ABE LINCOLN

Arrangement by Elie Siegmeister

2

Old Jeff Davis tore down the government,
Tore down the government, tore down the government,
Old Jeff Davis tore down the government,
Many long years ago.

3

But old Abe Lincoln built up a better one,
Built up a better one, built up a better one,
Old Abe Lincoln built up a better one,
Many long years ago.

OLD ABE LINCOLN

ALTHOUGH HE HAD RISEN to the highest office any American can attain,
to the people in the backwoods, the dwellers in the swamps and to those
who roamed the canebreak the man in the tall top-hat and frayed shawl
was still "Old Abe" who came out of the wilderness.

* Symbols in italics for guitar with capo across 1st fret

JOHN HENRY

Arrangement by Elie Siegmeister

Listen to my story___ 'tis a story___ true;

'Bout a might-y man, John Hen-ry was his name, And John

Hen-ry was a steel-driv-er too, Lawd, Lawd, John

Hen-ry was a steel-driv-er too.

2

John Henry's woman, Lucy, dress she wore was blue;
Eyes like stars an' teeth lak-a marble stone,
An' John Henry named his hammah "Lucy" too, Lawd, Lawd,
An' John Henry named his hammah "Lucy" too.

3

Lucy came to see him, bucket in huh han';
All the time John Henry ate his snack,
O Lucy, she'd drive steel lak-a man, Lawd, Lawd,
O Lucy, she'd drive steel lak-a man.

4

One day Cap' Tommy told him how he'd bet a man;
Bet John Henry'd beat a steam-drill down,
Jes' 'cause he was th' best in th' lan', Lawd, Lawd,
Jes' 'cause he was th' best in th' lan'.

5

John Henry, tol' Cap' Tommy, lightnin' in his eye;
"Cap'n bet you las' red cent on me,
Fo' I'll beat it to th' bottom or I'll die," Lawd, Lawd,
Fo' I'll beat it to th' bottom or I'll die."

6

Sun shined hot an' burnin', wer'n't no breeze at-tall;
Sweat ran down like watah down a hill
That day John Henry let his hammah fall, Lawd, Lawd,
That day John Henry let his hammah fall.

7

John Henry kissed his hammah, white man turned on steam;
Li'l Bill held John Henry's trusty steel,
'Twas th' biggest race th' worl' had ever seen, Lawd, Lawd,
'Twas th' biggest race th' worl' had ever seen.

8

White man tol' John Henry, "Niggah, damn yo' soul,
You might beat dis steam drill o' mine
When th' rocks in this mountain turn to gol'," Lawd, Lawd,
"When th' rocks in this mountain turn to gol'."

9

John Henry tol' th' white man, tol' him kind-a sad,
"Cap'n George, I want-a be yo' fr'en;
If I beat yo' to th' bottom, don' get mad," Lawd, Lawd,
"If I beat yo' to th' bottom, don' get mad."

10

Cap' Tommy sees John Henry's steel a-bitin' in;
Cap'n slaps John Henry on th' back,
Says, "I'll give yo' fifty dollars if you win," Lawd, Lawd,
Says, "I'll give yo' fifty dollars if you win."

11

John Henry, O John Henry, blood am runnin' red!
Falls right down with his hammah to th' groun'
Says, "I've beat him to th' bottom but I'm dead," Lawd, Lawd,
Says, "I've beat him to th' bottom but I'm dead."

12

John Henry kissed his hammah, kissed it with a groan,
Sighed a sigh an' closed his weary eyes,
Now po' Lucy has no man to call huh own, Lawd, Lawd,
Now po' Lucy has no man to call huh own.

13

Lucy ran to see him, dress she wore was blue;
Started down th' track an' she nevah did turn back,
Sayin', "John Henry I'll be true—true to you," Lawd, Lawd,
Sayin', "John Henry I'll be true—true to you."

14

John Henry, O John Henry, sing it if yo' can,
High an' low an' ev'rywhere yo' go,
He died with his hammah in his han'! Lawd, Lawd,
He died with his hammah in his han'!

JOHN HENRY

WHETHER JOHN HENRY ever really lived or is just a legend that came out of the hearts of his people, he is known, loved, and sung about by Negro workmen everywhere. Although there are some Negroes in the South who may not know the name of the President, there are few who cannot tell you the story of John Henry.

His ballad is sung in dozens of versions. They have him driving steel on the Air Line, the K. C., the Frisco, the C. and O. railroads; they call his woman Lucy, Delia Ann, Polly Ann; he is "sittin' on his pappy's knee" or holding his little son "in de palm of his han'." It is a seven-, and nine- or ten-pound hammer that is the death of him. But on this they all agree: John Henry battled with the steam drill which threatened to "beat him down"; toiled mightily from dawn to sunset; beat the machine as the sun went down, and "died wid a hammer in his han'."

The dignity of this song, its color, its dramatic power mark it as one of the masterpieces of folk creation, as one of the most important American contributions to balladry.

JOHNNY APPLESEED

Lyrics by Rosemary Benét
Music by Elie Siegmeister

* Not suitable for guitar accompaniment

gnarled as could be, But rud-dy and sound_____ as a good_ ap-ple
cum - ber his head, but wore a tin pan _____ on his white hair in -

tree.
stead.

For fif - ty years o-ver of har - vest and dew, _
A fine_ old man_ as ripe as a pippin, _

He plan - ted his ap - ples_____ where no ap-ples grew. __ The
His heart still_ light _____ and his step still skipping. _ He

winds of the prai - rie might blow thru his rags, But he car-ried his seed
nest - ed with owl, ____ with bear cub and possum, and knew all his orchards,

3

The stalking Indian, the beast in its lair,
Did no hurt while he was there,
For they could tell, as wild things can,
That Jonathan Chapman was God's own man.

Why did he do it? We do not know
He wished that apples might root and grow.
He has no statue, he has no tomb,
But he has his apple trees still in bloom.

Johnny Appleseed! Johnny Appleseed!

"IN 1806 Johnny Appleseed had expanded his operations. Down the Ohio he went, with two boats lashed together, bearing apple seed. Stopping here and there, wherever he found settlers, he started a little nursery. From the Ohio he branched off into the Muskingham, and thence up the White Woman Creek, and into the Mohican, and into the Black Fork. Later with his seeds in leather bags on his back, he tramped the trail from Fort Duquesne to Detroit by way of Fort Sandusky, starting nurseries all along the line. Thus for more than half a century Johnny Appleseed went just ahead of the oncoming farms with his little nurseries from which they could get trees, through Ohio, into Indiana, to Fort Wayne. A hundred thousand miles of the Northwest he thus provided with orchards."

From Marjorie Barstow Greenbie's "American Saga"

I have always thought there must be a song somewhere about this unique character of American history and folk lore. Not finding any, I wrote one.

E. S.

JOHN HARDY

Arrangement by Elie Siegmeister

John Har-dy was a brave and a des-per-a-ted boy, Said he car-ried two guns ev-er' day. He shot him a man in the Shaw-nee_ camp, An' I saw John Har-dy git-tin' a- way, po' boy, I saw John Har-dy git-tin a - way. John game.

2

ohn Hardy was a-standing by the dark sea bar;
He was unconcerned in the game,
A yeller gal threw down a fifty cents, sayin',
"Deal John Hardy in the game," po' boy, sayin',
"Deal John Hardy in the game."

3

ohn Hardy stepped up with the money in his hand,
Saying, "I have money to play.
An' the one who wins this yeller gal's money,
 have powder to blow him away!" Lord, Lord!
"I have powder to blow him away!"

4

The cards was dealt an' the money on the board,
Dave Campbell won that twenty dollar bill.
John Hardy drew his pistol, an' he took sure aim an' fired,
An' he caused Dave Campbell's brains to spill, Lord, Lord!
He caused Dave Campbell's brains to spill!

5

John Hardy had twelve miles to go,
An' six of them he ran,
He ran till he came to the river bank,
Then he fell on his bosom an' he swam, Lord, Lord!
He fell on his bosom an' he swam.

6

John Hardy went to this big, long town,
When he thought he was out of the way,
Up stepped a marshal and taken him by the hand,
Says, "Johnny, come and go with me," po' boy,
Says, "Johnny, come and go with me."

7

John Hardy had a father and mother,
He sent for them to go his bail.
No bail was allowed for murderin' a man,
So they shoved John Hardy back in jail, po' boy,
So they shoved John Hardy back in jail.

8

Johnny Hardy was standin' in his cell,
With the tears runnin' down his eyes,
"I've been the death of many a poor man,
And now I'm ready to die, O Lord,
And now I'm ready to die.

9

"I've been to the east and I've been to the west
I've been this wide world round,
I've been to the river and I've been baptised,
So take me to my hanging ground, O Lord,
So take me to my hanging ground.

JOHN HARDY

SOME FOLK BALLADS arise out of fantasy and imagination, but many, if not most, are narratives based on actual happening. For some time John Hardy, the hero of this ballad, was thought to be a symbolic or legendary character, sometimes confused with John Henry. But some years ago a diligent searcher showed that the Negro bad man had actually lived in West Virginia, that the incidents recounted in the ballad had a solid foundation in fact.

John Hardy worked for the Shawnee Coal Company. He murdered a man in an argument over a crap game, was caught after a chase, convicted and hanged in the town of Welch, McDowell County, West Virginia, on January 19, 1894. His story was made into a ballad, which spread into many states and is still sung to-day.

319

JESSE JAMES

Arrangement by Elie Siegmeister

MODERATELY

Jes - se James was a lad who__ killed man-y a man. He__ robbed the Glen - dale train. He__ stole from the rich and he gave to the poor; He'd a hand and a heart and a brain. Poor Jes-se had a wife to__ mourn for his life; Three child-ren, they were

brave; But that dir - ty lit - tle cow-ard___ that

shot Mis - ter How-ard___ Has laid poor___ Jes - se in his grave.

2

It was Robert Ford, that dirty little coward;
I wonder how he does feel,
For he ate of Jesse's bread and he slept in Jesse's bed,
Then laid poor Jesse in his grave.

CHORUS: Poor Jesse, etc.

3

Jesse was a man, a friend to the poor,
He never would see a man suffer pain;
And with his brother Frank he robbed the Chicago bank,
And stopped the Glendale train.

CHORUS: Poor Jesse, etc.

4

It was on Saturday night, Jesse was at home
Talking with his family brave;
Robert Ford came along like a thief in the night
And laid poor Jesse in his grave.

CHORUS: Poor Jesse, etc.

5

This song was made by Billy Gashade,
As soon as the news did arrive;
He said there was no man with the law in his hand
Who could take Jesse James when alive.

CHORUS: Poor Jesse, etc.

"IF AMERICA ever had a Robin Hood, it was the bandit and train robber,
Jesse James, whose life and death are celebrated in this ballad. . . .
Like all thieves of folk lore, he was kind to the poor. Old Timers will
tell you he always helped a fellow who was down on his luck." *Margaret
Larkin: "Singing Cowboy"*

Shortly before his death, Jesse was living in retirement under the assumed name of "Mr. Howard." He was hanging a picture on the wall,
when Robert Ford, a member of Jesse's gang, and a guest in his house-
hold, shot him from behind, for the sake of the reward. This is one of
the very few ballads in which the author, in this case, one Billy Gashade,
reveals his identity.

Heart-Throbs and Monkeyshines

[OLD-TIME FAVORITES AND CRAZY CAPERS]

*Warm from my Breast surcharg'd with grief
& Woe,
These Melancholy Strains spontaneous flow.*

The grand leap of a whale . . . up the falls of Niagara is esteemed, by all who have seen it, as one of the finest spectacles in nature.

THUS DID Benjamin Franklin, over one hundred and eighty years ago, apply two formulas that have come to be the mainstay of the American entertainment industry ever since: powerful sentiment and tall-story nonsense. From the early colonial broadside ballads and tavern singers through the minstrel shows, on through the works of Mark Twain, the early nickelodeon shows, Will Rogers and the comic strip to the latest Cream of Mush radio program, the combination of home, mother, love and parting, with outrageous punning, gagging, pie-throwing, darn-fool humor, has invariably tugged at the American heart and purse-strings. Politicians get elected to office by mastering its technique: Abe Lincoln won over the constituents of Sangamon County by using it in his front door speeches. Salesmen with their foot in the door always try it; lawyers work it on case-hardened juries; even doctors cure patients by first making them laugh and then saying, "Do it for the sake of the old folks!"

American hearts have always beaten indignantly at the story of the poor orphan child, the whipped horse, the faltering steps of the homeless wanderer, the deceived maiden. But at the proper moment they have always been able to execute a lightning switch to the most outrageous parodies of the same.

John Hill Hewitt told of one of the renditions in 1839 of that throbbing classic, "Wood-man, Spare That Tree" by its composer, Henry Russell:

"He had finished the last verse. . . . The audience was spell-bound for a moment, and then poured out a volume of applause that shook the building to its foundation. In the midst of this tremendous evidence of their boundless gratification, a snowy-headed gentleman, with great anxiety depicted in his venerable features, arose and demanded silence. He asked, with a tremulous voice: "Mr. Russell, in the name of Heaven, tell me, was the tree spared?' 'It was, sir,' replied the vocalist. 'Thank God! Thank God! I breathe again!' and then he sat down, perfectly overcome by his emotions." *

A few years later, students at New York University were singing, to the same tune, "Oh Barber, Spare Those Hairs!"

Audiences have wept to many another refrain, whose very titles today are enough to moisten an uninhibited eye: "The Old Arm Chair," "Oh, No, We Never Mention Her," "The Brave Old Oak," "Those Locks, Those Ebon Locks," "Rock Me to Sleep, Mother," "The Lost Letter," "She Sleeps in the Valley," and "The Inebriate's Lament." And then, shortly afterwards they devoured such elegant tomfoolery as "Root Hog or Die," "Kafoozalem," "Throw Him Down, McCloskey," "Abdul the Bulbul Ameer," and "You Never Miss the Water Till the Well Runs Dry."

Perhaps the haywire, monkeyshine spirit was the necessary antidote to too much weepy close harmony of the lavender-and-lace days. At any rate, it is only necessary to turn on the TV set to realize that both still reign in the American soul. And when the high-powered symphonic passion of the latest studio ar-

* Quoted by J. T. Howard in "Our American Music."

322

rangements and the fabricated smartness of the quick-paced gag songs have begun to pall, it might be time to switch off the dials and drift back to "Darling Nelly Gray," "Go Get the Axe," "The Elephant and the Flea," and many another immortal classic.

E. S.

RED RIVER VALLEY

Arrangement by Elie Siegmeister

WITH AN EASY FLOW

From this val - ley they say you are go - ing;_____ We will miss your bright eyes and sweet smile, For they say you are tak - ing the sun- shine_____ That__ bright - ens our path - way a while.

CHORUS:

Come and sit by my side if you love me,

Do not hasten to bid me adieu,

But remember the Red River Valley

And the girl that has loved you so true.

Won't you think of the valley you're leaving?
Oh how lonely, how sad it will be,
Oh think of the fond heart you're breaking,
And the grief you are causing me?

CHORUS: Come and sit, etc.

3

I have promised you, darling, that never
Will a word from my lips cause you pain;
And my life, it will be yours forever
If you only will love me again.

CHORUS: Come and sit, etc.

RED RIVER VALLEY

EVERY ONCE in a while a little known folk tune is "discovered" by some Broadway tunesmith and turned into a Tin Pan Alley or concert favorite. "Itiskit, Itaskit" and "Short'nin' Bread" are two older examples that come to mind. Sometimes the opposite happens: the people take for their own a current Broadway favorite, and turn it into a folk song. Fifty years ago the New York song, "In the Bright Mohawk Valley" spread throughout the South and the West, where the name of the stream was changed to Red River. Although long since forgotten on Broadway, it has become the permanent property of folks in rural districts throughout the country.

DARLING NELLY GRAY

Words and Music by B. R. Hanby
Arrangement by Elie Siegmeister

There's a low green val-ley on the old Ken-tuck-y shore, There I've
One_____ night I went to see her but "she's gone" the neigh-bors say, The_____

whiled man - y hap - py hours a - way,
A-
white man _____ bound her with his chain,
They have

sit - ting and a-sing - ing by the lit - tle cot-tage door, Where
tak - en her to Geor - gia for to wear her life a - way, As she

lived my _ darl - ing Nel - ly Gray.
toils in the cot - ton and the cane.

DARLING NELLY GRAY

THE RECENT restoration of the house in which Benjamin R. Hanby lived, in Westerville, Ohio, about thirteen miles northeast of Columbus, on Ohio Highway No. 3, is remindful of the environment which produced this popular song, in 1855 or 1856. Hanby, son of an Abolitionist minister, saw many sorrowful things when escaping slaves passed through a home which was a station of the "Underground Railroad." The story, however, which was responsible for "Darling Nelly Gray" was read in a newspaper. It told of how a Negro slave, Nellie Gray, was torn from the arms of her beloved and taken to a Kentucky auction block, where she was sold to a Georgia plantation-owner. Songs of this sort, sentimental as they were sincere, were built to last. This one stands up after more than a century of constant use.

LISTEN TO THE MOCKING BIRD

Words and Music by Alice Hawthorne
Arrangement by Elie Siegmeister

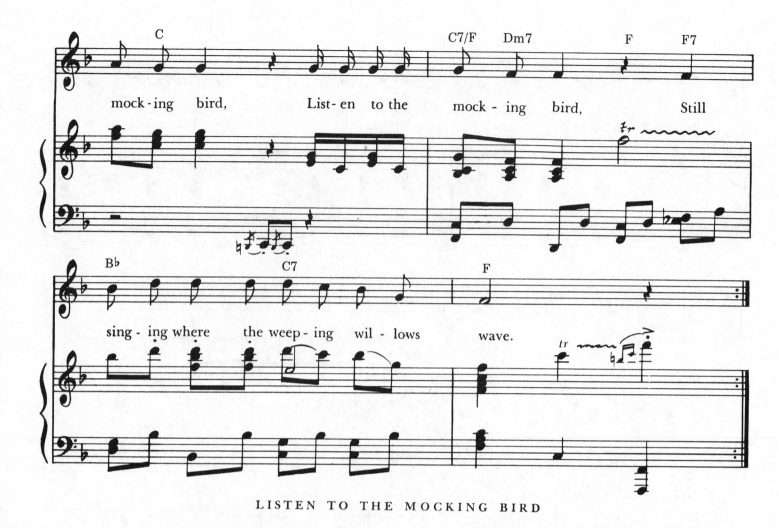

LISTEN TO THE MOCKING BIRD

IN THE DAYS of the Civil War and after, sentimental songs about the cruelty of the war, home and mother flourished. Septimus Winner, who used the pen name Alice Hawthorne, was the author of the text and music of this song. It was sung everywhere, in the home and the barber shop, by bird-call specialists in vaudeville houses, and diamond-studded prima donnas, trilling impossibly high notes.

GO GET THE AXE

(Extra Verses)

2

Peepin' through the knot-hole
Of grandpa's wooden leg,
Why do they build the shore so near the ocean?
Who cut the sleeves
Out of dear old daddy's vest,
And dug up Fido's bones to build the sewer?

3

A horsey stood around
With his feet upon the ground,
Oh, who will wind the clock when I am gone?
Go get the axe,
There's a fly on Lizzie's ear,
But a boy's best friend is his mother.

I fell from a window,
A second-story window,
I caught my eyebrow on the window-sill.
The cellar is behind the door,
Mary's room is behind the axe,
But a boy's best friend is his mother.

GO GET THE AXE

Arrangement by Elie Siegmeister

FAST AND CHOPPY (!)

Peep-in' through the knot-hole Of grand-pa's wood-en leg,____

Who'll wind the clock when I am gone?____

Go get the ax, There's a flea in Liz-zie's ear, For a

boy's best friend is his moth-er.____

LITTLE BROWN JUG

Arrangement by Elie Siegmeister

332

2

'Tis you who makes my friends and foes,
'Tis you who makes me wear old clothes,
Here you are so near my nose,
So tip her up and down she goes.

CHORUS: Ha! ha! ha! etc.

3

When I go toiling to my farm
I take little brown jug under my arm
Place him under a shady tree,
Little Brown Jug, 'tis you and me.

CHORUS: Ha! ha! ha! etc.

4

If all the folks in Adam's race
Were gathered together in one place
Then I'd prepare to shed a tear
Before I'd part with you, my dear.

CHORUS: Ha! ha! ha! etc.

5

If I'd a cow that gave such milk,
I'd clothe her in the finest silk,
I'd feed her on the choicest hay,
And milk her forty times a day.

CHORUS: Ha! ha! ha! etc.

6

The rose is red, my nose is, too,
The violet's blue and so are you;
And yet I guess, before I stop
I'd better take another drop.

CHORUS: Ha! ha! ha! etc.

LITTLE BROWN JUG

THE GOLDEN GOBLET of the Gods, the bottomless horn of Norse mythology, the "beaker full of the warm South" spoken of by the poet, the costly wine-glass broken after every drink by the French aristocrat of tradition, can have contained no more ecstatic liquids than were held within the walls of the "little brown jug."

IT'S THE SYME THE WHOLE WORLD OVER

Arrangement by Elie Siegmeister

She was just a parson's daughter,
Pure, unstyned was 'er fyme;
'Till a country squire came courtin'—
And the poor girl lorst 'er nyme.

So she went aw'y to Lunnon,
Just to 'ide 'er guilty shyme.
There she met another squire;
Once agine, she lorst 'er nyme.

Look at 'im with all 'is 'orses,
Drinking champyne in 'is club,
W'ile the wictim of 'is passions
Drinks 'er Guinness in a pub.

Now 'e's in 'is ridin' britches,
'Untin' foxes in the chyse,
W'ile the wictim of 'is folly
Mykes 'er livin' by 'er wice.

So she settled down in Lunnon,
Sinkin' deeper in 'er shyme,
Till she met a lybor leader
And ag'yn she lorst 'er nyme.

Now 'e's in the 'ouse of Commons
Mykin' laws to put down crime,
W'ile the wictim of 'is plysure
Walks the street each night in shyme.

Then there cyme a bloated bishop.
Marriage was the tyle 'e told.
There was no one else to tyke 'er
So she sold 'er soul for gold.

See 'er in 'er 'orse and carriage,
Drivin' d'ily through the park.
Though she's myde a wealthy marriage
Still she 'ides a brykin' 'eart.

In a cottage down in Sussex
Lives 'er payrents old and lyme.
And they drink the wine she sends 'em.
But they never speaks 'er nyme.

In their poor and humble dwellin',
There 'er grievin' payrents live,
Drinkin' champyne as she sends 'em
But they never can forgive.

It's the syme the whole world over,
It's the poor what gets the blyme,
While the rich 'as all the plysures;
Now, a'nt that a blinkin' shyme!

IT'S THE SYME THE WHOLE WORLD OVER

A MEANINGFUL MORSEL for maudlin moralists. Will also do to oil up
your rusty Cockney accent.

THE ELEPHANT AND THE FLEA

Arrangement by Elie Siegmeister

MODERATELY

Way down South where ba - na - nas grow A flea stepped on an
The horse and the flea and the three blind mice Sat on a curb - stone

e - le - phant's toe, The el - e - phant cried with tears in his eyes,
shoot - ing dice. The horse he slipped and fell on the flea,

"Why don't you pick on a fel - ler your size?"
"Whoops" said the flea, "That's a horse on me!"

Chorus

Boom, boom, ain't it great to be cra - zy, Boom, boom, ain't it great to be

bring out left hand

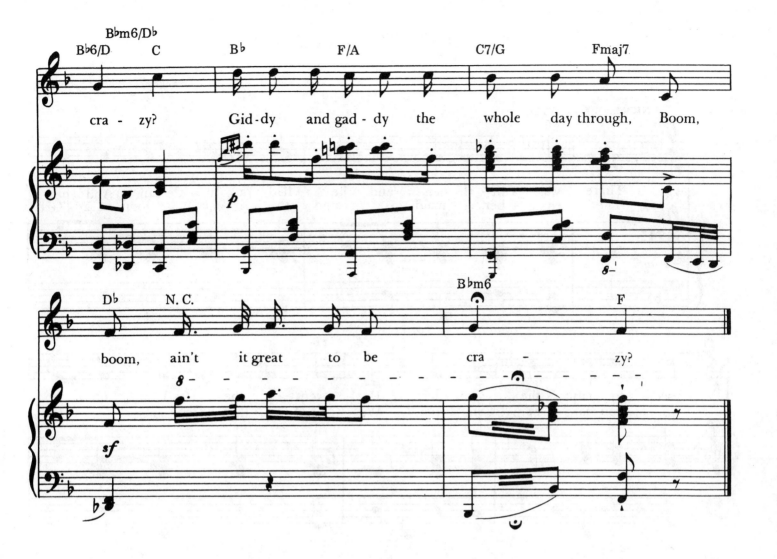

THE ELEPHANT AND THE FLEA

ANIMALS THAT SPEAK and behave as crazily as humans sometimes do are
not, of course, the invention of Walt Disney; they are a good old American tradition, going back to Davy Crockett and beyond. This ode to
cheerful dementia is in the direct line.

NO MORE BOOZE

Arrangement by Elie Siegmeister

NICKELODEON STYLE

There was a lit-tle man and he had a lit-tle can, And he
The cham-ber-maid came to my door, "Get

used to rush the grow-ler; He went to the sa-loon on a
up, you la-zy sin-ner, We need those sheets for

Sun-day aft-er-noon, And you ought to hear the bar-ten-der hol-ler: —
ta-ble-cloths, And it's al-most time for din-ner."

Chorus   DETERMINED

No more booze, no more booze, No more booze on Sun-day;

The Wicked City

[HONKY·TONK SONGS]

THE TURN of the century brought to an end the heroic days of the West. The endless frontier had been closed at last, and with it went the glamour and romance that made Jesse James and Billy the Kid material for newspaper headlines, novels, songs, and the dreams of small boys.

With the frontier days gone, the focus of theatrical, literary and musical attention shifted to the Big Bad City. It was the era of muckraking, suffragette parades, exposés of the big trusts, clean-up campaigns and anti-vice crusades. In the light of the gaslamps, long-sleeved, hour-glass-waisted ladies plied their nefarious trade, while eminent divines thundered against Sin and Corruption. Tammany was in its heyday, and emphatic reformers on soap-boxes cried out for the poor working girl. Temperance advocates wept, because for all their documentary evidence of the evils of alcohol, the law still provided for closing the saloons only on Sunday.

With themes such as these, the popular sheet-music business, which had always traded on sentiment, attained heights hitherto undreamed of. It was the era of soul-rending tragedies, of life-long shame produced by One Moment of Weakness. It was the day when many a throat choked with anguish to the rhythms of "The Fatal Wedding," "The Little Lost Child," "The Picture That Is Turned to the Wall," "The Moth and the Flame," "Just for the Sake of Our Daughter," "Only a Bird in a Gilded Cage," and "Take Back Your Gold." (Those without feeling will, of course, only scoff and sneer.)

It was "After the Ball" that broke all existing records for popular song-hits. Whether it was the Tragedy of the Fatal Misunderstanding, the Pathos of Eternal Regret, or the heroic sweep of the melody that did it, will remain a problem for the sociologist. Suffice it to say that "After the Ball" is the first song that comes to mind, together with "Sidewalks of New York" and "Daisy Bell," when one thinks of the naughty, gay, tearful old days of the horse-car when mother was young.

Meanwhile on the other side of the tracks, quite another type of music was growing up. The city had never been known as the birthplace of folk song, but the mauve decade was brewing a strange new brew. Out of dives, honky-tonks, waterfront emporiums and hop joints that provided an inexpensive if temporary release from the monotony of small town life and from work in mills or sweatshops; through the smell of stale beer and old smoke, came the strains of tunes that were to become rowdy American classics, that were destined to live on when the more made to order contemporary music hall epics of Purple Passion were long forgotten.

Where did the story of Frankie and the Man who Did her Wrong originate? There are many claimants. Some try to identify the original Frankie; others say her name wasn't Frankie at all, but Sadie, Josie, or Lil, and that Johnny's real name was Albert. We are told that he was shot with a forty-four, a Gatling gun, or with just a plain revolver. The song is reputed variously to have come from St. Louis, Cincinnati, the South, the Mountains.

All that we do know is that, together with "Willie the Weeper," "Cocaine Lil," and the "St. James Infirmary—or Gambler's-Blues," it was the start of a new, vigorous strain in native song. While the throats that gargled it out on the back alleys, might never have sung a scale, and the hands that pounded it on tinny pianos never known Czerny, the new "low-down" style was genuine. Its language was stark, colorful, straight from the shoulder. Its tunes were raucous and cheap, but strong. It was this barrel-house and honky-tonk concoction that with various other admixtures was to evolve in two decades through rag-time and jazz to the liveliest, most potent popular dance music Americans had ever made the world trip a foot to.

E. S.

FRANKIE AND JOHNNY

Arrangement by Elie Siegmeister

Fran - kie and John - ny were lo - vers, Oh, Lor - dy, how_ they could love! They swore to be true_ to each oth - er, Just as true as the stars a - bove, He was her man,_____ but he done her wrong. _____

Frankie and Johnny went walking,
Johnny in his brand new suit.
"Oh, good Lord," says Frankie,
"Don't my Johnny look cute."
He was her man, but he done her wrong.

3

Johnny said, "I've got to leave you,
But I won't be very long,
Don't you wait up for me honey,
Nor worry while I'm gone."
He was her man, but he done her wrong.

4

Frankie went down to the corner,
Stopped in to buy her some beer
Says to the fat bar-tender,
"Has my Johnny man been here?"
He was her man, but he done her wrong.

5

"Well I ain't going to tell you no story,
Ain't going to tell you no lie.
Johnny went by, 'bout an hour ago,
With a girl named Nellie Blye,
He was your man, but he's doin' you wrong."

6

Frankie went home in a hurry,
She didn't go there for fun,
She hurried home to get a-hold,
Of Johnny's shootin' gun.
He was her man, but he's doin' her wrong.

7

Frankie took a cab at the corner,
Says "Driver, step on this can."
She was just a desperate woman,
Gettin' two-timed by her man.
He was her man, but he's doin' her wrong.

8

Frankie got out at South Clark Street,
Looked in a window so high
Saw her Johnny man a-lovin' up,
That high brown Nellie Blye.
He was her man, but he's doin' her wrong.

9

Johnny saw Frankie a-comin',
Out the back door he did scoot,
But Frankie took aim with her pistol;
And the gun went "Root a toot-toot!"
He was her man, but he done her wrong.

10

"Oh roll me over so easy,
Roll me over so slow,
Roll me over easy boys,
'Cause my wounds they hurt me so.
I was her man, but I done her wrong."

11

Bring out your long black coffin,
Bring out your funeral clo'es,
Johnny's gone and cashed his checks,
To the grave-yard Johnny goes.
He was her man, but he done her wrong.

12

Drive out your rubber-tired carriage,
Drive out your rubber-tired hack;
There's twelve men going to the grave-yard,
And eleven coming back.
He was her man, but he done her wrong.

13

The sheriff arrested poor Frankie,
Took her to jail that same day
He locked her up in a dungeon cell,
And threw the key away,
She shot her man, though he done her wrong.

FRANKIE AND JOHNNY

THIS MOST FAMOUS of American low-down songs is sung in three hundred different ways throughout the land. Who were these famous lovers, and where was the tragic story enacted? Some say that it happened in real life and that the original Frankie lived in St. Louis. Others say she hailed from Cincinnati, San Francisco, Omaha, Seattle, the mountains. Still others say her name was not Frankie at all, but Sadie, Josie, Lil; and that Johnny once masqueraded as Albert. He is variously reported to have been killed by a forty-four, a Gatling gun, or by just a plain revolver. But whatever the make of the gun, on one thing all are agreed: that it went off blasting, "Root-toot-toot!"

WILLIE THE WEEPER
[COCAINE LIL]

Arrangement by Elie Siegmeister

* *Don't hesitate to add extra notes when needed or switch the tune around as the spirit moves you for the various verses.*

** *Symbols in italics for guitar with capo across 3rd fret*

2

He went to the hop-joint the other night,
When he knew that the lights would all be burning bright,
I guess he smoked a dozen pills or more,
When he woke up he wuz on a foreign shore.

3

Queen o' Bulgaria wuz the first he met;
She called him her darlin' an' her lovin' pet.
She promised him a pretty Ford automobile,
With a diamond headlight an' a silver steerin'-wheel.

4

She had a million cattle, she had a million sheep;
She had a million vessels on the ocean deep;
She had a million dollahs, all in nickels an' dimes;
She knew 'cause she counted them a million times.

5

Willie landed in New York one evenin' late,
He asked his sugar for an after-date.
Willie he got funny, she began to shout:
Bim bam boo!—an' the dope gave out.

WILLIE THE WEEPER

A LOW-DOWN epic of the coke-house. Broadway reincarnated Willie the Weeper as "Minnie the Moocher." After a temporary glory, Minnie died, but Willie still weeps. Floating through an ecstatic fantasy of uninhibited adventures, he "plays poker with presidents, eats nightingale tongues a queen cooks for him . . . he lights his pipe with a hundred dollar bill, has heart affairs with Cleopatra, the Queen of Sheba and movie actresses," said Carl Sandburg.

COCAINE LIL

(To the same tune as "Willie the Weeper")

1

Did you ever hear about Cocaine Lil?
She lived in a cocaine town on a cocaine hill;
She had a cocaine dog and a cocaine cat,
They fought all night with a cocaine rat.

2

Lil went to a snow party one cold night;
The way she sniffed was sure a fright.
There was Hophead Mag with Dopey Slim,
Kankakee Liz with Yen Shee Jim.

3

Along in the morning about half-past three,
They were all lit up like a Christmas tree.
Lil got home and started for bed;
Took another sniff and it knocked her dead.

4

They laid her out in her cocaine clothes.
She wore a snowbird hat with a crimson rose.
On her tombstone you'll find this refrain:
"She died as she lived, sniffing cocaine."

COCAINE LIL

THE WEIRD ONES—Hophead Mag, Dopey Slim, Kankakee Liz, Yen Shee Jim—what a crew!
Big gold chariots on the Milky Way
Snakes and elephants, silver and gray.
No surrealist ever saw 'em worse. Like "Frankie and Johnny," this song is thought to date from the 1910's or 20's.

THE ROVING GAMBLER

Arrangement by Elie Siegmeister

FREE AND EASY

I am a rov-ing gam-bler, I've gam-bled all a-round, Wher-ever I meet with a deck of cards I lie my mon-ey down.

* Hold last time only.

2

I've gambled down in Washington and I've gambled over in Spain;
I am on my way to Georgia to knock down my last game.

3

I had not been in Washington many more weeks than three,
Till I fell in love with a pretty little girl and she fell in love with me.

4

She took me in her parlor, she cooled me with her fan,
She whispered low in her mother's ears, "I love this gambling man!"

5

"O daughter, O dear daughter, how could you treat me so,
To leave your dear old mother and with a gambler go?"

6

O mother, O dear mother, I'll tell you if I can;
If you ever see me coming back again I'll be with the gambling man."

7

"O mother, O dear mother, you know I love you well,
But the love I hold for this gambling man no human tongue can tell.

8

I wouldn't marry a farmer, for he's always in the rain;
The man I want is a gambling man who wears the big gold chain.

9

I wouldn't marry a doctor, he is always gone from home;
All I want is the gambling man, for he won't leave me alone.

10

I wouldn't marry a railroad man, and this is the reason why;
I have never seen a railroad man that wouldn't tell his wife a lie.

11

I hear the train a-coming, she's coming around the curve,
Whistling and a-blowing and straining every nerve.

12

O mother, O dear mother, I'll tell you if I can;
If you ever see me coming back again I'll be with the gambling man."

The Melting-Pot

[SONGS OF REGIONAL GROUPS, IMMIGRANTS]

THE EARLY SETTLERS in this country were Spanish, French, English, Irish, Swedes, Germans and Dutch. On the muddy streets of their primitive villages little boys and girls played games, and danced to songs in many different languages, among them "Malbrough s'en va-t-en Guerre," "Ach, Du Lieber Augustin" and "Rosa, Willen Wy Dansen." After the British had gained mastery of the colonies of most of the other nations, children sang the same melodies, but now "Malbrough" had become "The Bear Went Over the Mountain"; "Augustin" became "Did You Ever See a Lassie?" and "Rosa, Willen Wy Dansen," "Rosa, Let Us Be Dancing."

Today, long after America has attained its own musical maturity, the same process of absorption and adaptation continues, with Neapolitan, Russian and Mexican folk melodies being transformed into popular radio favorites: "The Woodpecker Song," "Two Guitars," and "The Dove." Americans have always taken the cultural treasures brought over by the settlers of every nationality and added them to our national store. The successive waves of immigration which brought to these shores peoples of a score of different races and nationalities contributed greatly to the enrichment of our musical heritage. All the racial strains had their share in the development of our own indigenous music when, at length, it did develop. England and Scotland were responsible for the greatest number of ballads, Africa and Ireland for the largest part of the minstrel songs (to which, however, even distant Poland added her bit *); while in the shaping of rag-time and jazz, Negro, Spanish, Hungarian, Jewish and French Creole influences are said to have had their share. It is significant that out of this

*See "Walk-jaw-bone."

most varied of mixtures has come the most characteristic of all American musical styles.

Musical strains have come to us not only from Europe, but from Spanish America as well. Cubans have brought the Rumba and the Conga (Americanized by Cole Porter in "Begin the Beguine"); South Americans, the Tango; Mexico has contributed such colorful and characteristic songs as "La Cucuracha" and "Cielito Lindo"; while the latest addition is the saucy West Indian style known as "Reggae."

While many of these national strains have become an integral part of the American musical language, others have retained their autonomous character, generally as a result of compact local settlements of fairly isolated language groups. This has been the case with the Slovaks and Poles in the Pittsburgh iron and steel area; with French-Canadians in Maine; with Mexicans in Texas and New Mexico, all of whom have retained their own native folk songs. In some cases these groups have developed a new style, based on a mixture of the traditional idiom with American influences. Such are the songs of New Orleans Creoles; of Jews in the sweatshops of New York and Chicago; of the Pennsylvania Dutch around Bethlehem, and the street cries of Italian peddlers in almost any big city.

In the field of classical music it is to the credit of many foreign-born Americans that they became the most ardent exponents of Americanism in music. Among these were the German, Father Heinrich, who in the 1830's went to Kentucky, lived with the Indians and was the first to write symphonic works with such titles as "Yankee Doodliad," "Pocahontas," and "The Pilgrim Fathers"; Louis Moreau Gottschalk, the son of an English Jew and a Creole mother, who was one of the first to utilize such native Negro dances as "The Banjo," the "Bamboula," and "Le Bananier" in larger works; the Irish-born Victor Herbert; the Hungarian-American, Sigmund Romberg; and the Bohemian-American, Rudolf Friml. And the most beloved of all modern American composers, George Gershwin, was born in Brooklyn, of Russian-Jewish parents.

Thus, reaching deeply into the fertile store of world culture, America has added new riches to that store.

E. S.

SALANGADOU

Arrangement by Elie Siegmeister

* Symbols in italics for guitar with capo across 1st fret

THE NEGRO SLAVES brought to the French settlements in the Mississippi valley spoke a special dialect of their own, termed Creole. After the Louisiana Purchase they continued this patois and sang their characteristic native songs. Creole songs are quite different from those of the English-speaking Negro. They show the French influence, not only in their musical style, but in their frivolous and sarcastic subject matter. Some of them have a very simple folk quality, and convey a note of tenderness. Such is this song of a mother who has lost her little girl, "Salangadou."

RÉMON

Arrangement by Elie Siegmeister

HEARTY, WITH LOTS OF SPIRIT

I heard from Ré - mon, Ré - mon, He said to Si - mon, Si -
Mo par - lé Ré - mon, Ré - mon, Li par - lé Si - mon, Si -

mon, He said to Ti - tine, Ti - tine, that he was un - -hap py. O
mon, Li par - lé Ti - tine, Ti - tine, Li tom - bé dans cha - grin. O

dame Ro - mu - lus, oh,__ Fair dame Ro - mu - lus, oh!__ O
femme Ro - mu - lus oh,__ Belle femme Ro - mu - lus, oh!__ O

dame Ro - mu - lus, oh!__ How could you be cru - el to me?
femme Ro - mu - lus, oh!__ Belle femme qui ca vou - lé mo fai.

352

"SUNG TO a simple dance called the "Coonjai" . . . when the "Coonjai" is danced, the music is furnished by an orchestra of singers, the leader of whom. . . . sustains the solo part, while the others afford him an opportunity, as they shout in chorus, for inventing some neat verse to compliment some lovely danseuse, or celebrate the deeds of some plantation hero. . . . The usual accompaniment, besides that of the singers, is that furnished by a skilful performer on the barrel-head drum, the jaw-bone and key."

Allem, Ware and Garrison:
Slave Songs of the U. S. (1867)

LA CUCARACHA

[THE COCKROACH]

Arrangement by Elie Siegmeister

1. When a fel-low loves a maid-en And that maid-en does-n't love him
2. *Cuan-do u-na quier-e a u-na Y es-ta u-na no lo quier-e*

It's the same as when a bald man
Es lo mis-mo que si un cal-vo

Finds a comb up-on the high-way,
En la cal-le encuentr un pein-e.

Chorus

La cu-cu-ra-cha, la cu-cu-ra-cha

Does n't want to trav-el on, be-cause she has-n't, oh no she
Y a no quier-es ca-men-ar, Por-que no tien-es, por-que le

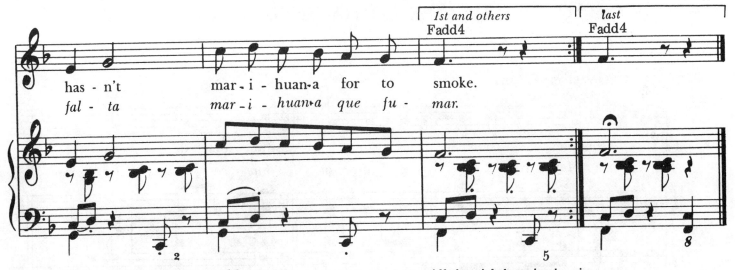

has - n't   mar - i - huan-a   for   to   smoke.

fal - ta   *mar - i - huan-a*   *que*   *fu - mar.*

2

All the maidens they are golden;
All the married girls are silver;
All the widows are of copper,
And old women merely tin.
CHORUS: The cucaracha, *etc.*

3

My neighbor 'cross the highway
Used to be called Doña Clara,
And if she has not expired
Likely that's her name tomorrow.
CHORUS: The cucaracha, *etc.*

4

All the girls up at Las Vegas
Are most awful tall and skinny,
But they're worse for plaintive pleading
Than the souls in purgatory.
CHORUS: The cucaracha, *etc.*

5

All the girls here in the city
Don't know how to give you kisses,
While the ones from Albuquerque
Stretch their necks to avoid misses.
CHORUS: The cucaracha, *etc.*

6

All the girls from Mexico
Are as pretty as a flower
And they talk so very sweetly,
Fill your heart quite up with love.
CHORUS: The cucaracha, *etc.*

7

One thing makes me laugh most hearty—
Pancho Villa with no shirt on.
Now the Carranzistas beat it
Because Villa's men are coming.
CHORUS: The cucaracha, *etc.*

8

Fellow needs an automobile
If he undertakes the journey
To the place to which Zapata
Ordered the famous convention.
CHORUS: The cucaracha, *etc.*

LA CUCARACHA

WHILE OF inderminate origin, the text of this most ingratiating of the Mexican songs, widely known in New Mexico and bordering states, might place it around the time of the Mexican Revolution. While this, however, could be correct for the stanzas mentioning Pancho Villa and his opponent, Venustiano Carranza, the rest of the verse, bearing a more archaic character, points to an earlier origin. It it likewise with the tune—a seeming mixture of old Spanish lute music and the newer vivacity and rhythm of Mexico. *La cucaracha,* though actually the word for cockroach, is a term used to describe a dried-up old maid. At the time of the revolution it was also freely applied to Carranza.

DE MEXICO HA VENIDO

Arrangement by Elie Siegmeister

LIVELY, RHYTHMICAL

From Mex - i - co there's just come a strange new de - cree, That
De Mexi - co ha ve - ni - do un nue - vo des - pa - cho

all the old wo - men mar - ry the young men so free,___ But
Que se cas - en las vie - jas con los mu - cha - chos, Y

all the young men say this will not come to pass, The
los mu cha - chos di - cen que son muy ca - paz, De

spin - sters they can mar - ry old Bar - a - bas. die!
ca - sar - se las vie - jas con Bar - a - bas.

And Barabas he says, "No, it's not on the level—
Let the old women go and marry the devil."
The devil he's not stupid, and straightway does cry,
"Before I'd marry that kind, I'd rather die!"

2

Y Barabas dice que non puede ser
Que se casen los viejas con Lucifer.
Y Lucifer les dice que son muy capaz,
Que se voyan los viejas con los demonios!

DE MEXICO HA VENIDO

THIS TUNE IS Mexican not only in its characteristic folk humor, but in
its peppery tune, which, like many of its kind, depends for its effect on
a subtle interplay of shifting rhythms.

SCHLOF, BOBBELI

Arrangement by Elie Siegmeister

SCHLOF, BOBBELI

THE PENNSYLVANIA DUTCH who settled around Harrisburg, Lancaster, Bethlehem, and Reading from a hundred to two hundred years ago still remember—and sing—the old German love songs, dances, children's songs, and lullabies, in their own special dialect, which is often a mixture of English and German. In parts of eastern Pennsylvania, and in this song, "father" is "dawdi" rather than "Vater"; "mother" is "mommie" rather than "Mutter."

ME JOHNNY MITCHELL MAN

Arrangement by Elie Siegmeister

HEARTY DANCE RHYTHM

VERSE 1. Oh, you know Joe Sil-o-vat-sky, Dat man my brud-der; Last
CHORUS I___ dunt___ 'fraid fer nut-tink, Dat's me nev air shcare.

night he come ter my shan-ty; "John I'm come an' tell you fer, I'm
Com-in' shtrike to-mor-ra night. Dat's de biz-ness, I dun't care,

tell you fer to-mor-ra, Eve-nick dark like night, Lot-sa
Right a-here I'm tell you, Me no shcab-by fella, Me___

min-ers all, beeg an shmal, gon-na have a shtrike.
good un-ion cit-i-zen, me John-ny Mit-chell man.

FINE

Dun't be shcab-by fel-la, John, Dat's I'm tell you right!" I'm say,

"No, sir, Joe come out on shtrike, Me John-ny Mit-chell man!"

2

Vell, me belong fer union,
Me good citizen,
Seven, mebbe 'leven year
I'm vorkin's in beeg, beeg Merica;
I'm vorkin' for de Black Heat'.
Down in Lytle shaft,
In de Pine Hill shaft, Pine Knot shaft,
Un ev'ry place like dat.
Me got lotsa money,
Nine hoondret mebbe ten,
Un shtrike kin come, like son-of-a-gun,
Me Johnny Mitchell man. Vell,
CHORUS: I dun't 'fraid, *etc.*

3

Ah, son-of-a-gun, Mister Truesdale,
Dat's a bugger, Mister Baer,
He dun't vantsa gib it ten per zent,
Cripes a'mighty, dat's no fair.
I'm vorkin' in a gangway,
Vorkin' in a breast,
I'm loadin' coal ev'ry day
By jeez me nevair rest.
Me got lotsa money,
Nine hoondred mebbe ten,
Un shtrike kin come, like son-of-a-gun,
Me Johnny Mitchell man. Vell,
CHORUS: I dun't 'fraid, *etc.*

ME JOHNNY MITCHELL MAN

MUCH OF THE anthracite coal mining in eastern Pennsylvania is done by Americans of Slavic birth or extraction. Their special—and colorful—dialect is rendered in this song. Johnny Mitchell was a union organizer, and after urging his friend, "Don't be shcabby fella, John," the miner boasts, "Me good union citizen—me Johnny Mitchell man."

I CATCHA DA PLENTY OF FEESH

Arrangement by Elie Siegmeister

I sail ov-er the o - cean blue,__ I catch- a da plen-ty of feesh;__ The rain come down like hell.__ And the wind blow through my wheesk.__ O Mar-i - an, my good com-pan, O Vi-va le Gar-i-bal - di! Vi - va, vi - va, vi - va l'I-tal - i - ane!__

THE SPECIAL DIALECT of English formerly spoken by the hundreds of thousands of Italian-born Americans was a familiar one in New York, Chicago, and San Francisco some years ago.

This fisherman's song, heard in San Francisco, expresses the wholesome joy in life that manual laborers can derive from their work.

ON MEESH-E-GAN

New Words and Music adaptation by John A. Lomax and Alan Lomax

Arrangement by Elie Siegmeister

MODERATELY

Frainch-man he don't lak to die in de fall,

When de mairsh she am so full of de game

An' de lee-tle bool - frog he's roll ver-ra fat

An' de lee-tle moosh - rat he's jus' de same.

2

Come, all you great beeg Canada man
Who want fin' work on Meesh-e-gan,
Dere's beeg log drive all troo our lan',
You sure fin' work on Meesh-e-gan.

3

When you come drive de beeg saw log,
You have to jump jus' lak de frog.
De foreman come, he say go sak,
You got in de watair all over your back.

4

P'rhaps you work on drive tree-four day,
You fin' dat drive dat she don' pay,
You go to Sag-e-naw right away,
Wait roun' tree-four day 'fore you get your pay.

5

Mebbe you stay in Sag-e-naw tree-four week,
You get de ague, you feel damn seek,
One ounce quinine, two pound cal-o-mel,
You tak all dose 'fore you got well.

6

Now you all great beeg Canada man
Who want fin' work on Meesh-e-gan,
Dere's great beeg snake all troo our lan'
You sure get bit on Meesh-e-gan.

ON MEESH-E-GAN

IN THE LUMBER-CAMPS of Maine, Minnesota, Michigan, a familiar figure
is the raw-boned French-Canadian lad. His songs are often French, but
this one, in English, relating the hardships of the "beeg log drive" on
"Meesh-e-gan" has a savor all its own.

FINNEGAN'S WAKE

Arrangement by Elie Siegmeister

Tim Fin- ni- gan lived in Walk- er Street, An I- rish gen- tle- man might- y odd; He'd a beau- ti- ful brogue so rich and sweet, And to rise in the world he car- ried the hod. But you see, he'd a sort of tip- pling way, For the love of the liq- uor poor Tim was born; And to

One morning Tim was rather full,
His head felt heavy, which made him shake,
He fell from the ladder and broke his skull,
So they carried him home, himself to wake.
They tied him up in a nice clean sheet,
And laid him out upon the bed,
Wid a gallon of whiskey at his feet,
And a barrel of praties at his head.

CHORUS: With my, etc.

3

His friends assembled at the wake
Miss Finnigan call'd out for the lunch,
First they brought in tay and cake,
Then pipes, tobacco, and whiskey punch;
Biddy O'Brine began to cry,
Such a pretty corpse she never did see,
Arrah Tim Mavourneen why did you die?
"Ah! hould your gab," said Paddy McGree.

CHORUS: With my, etc.

Then Peggy O'Connor tuck up the job,
"Biddy," says she, "you're wrong, I'm sure,"
But Biddy gave her a pelt in the gob,
And we left her sprawling on the flure;
Oh! then the war did soon enrage!
'Twas woman to woman, and man to man,
Shillelagh law did soon engage!
And a row and a ruction soon began.

CHORUS: With my, etc.

5

Then Mickey Mollaney raised his head,
When a gallon of whiskey flew at him,
It missed, an' falling on the bed,
The liquor scatter'd over Tim;
Be-dad he revives, see how he rises,
And Timothy, rising from the bed,
Saying, "Whirl your liquor round like blazes!
Arrah! Gudaguddug, do you think I'm dead?"

CHORUS: With my, etc.

FINNEGAN'S WAKE

IN REVOLUTIONARY TIMES, one American out of every ten was Irish-born, and millions more came over during the great waves of immigration in the mid-nineteenth century. It is not surprising that the rhythm and color of the Irish dance tune, the jig, the ballad, and love song, permeated so deeply into the body of our native song. The flavor of Ireland entered into such early American songs as "Jefferson and Liberty," "Paul Jones' Victory" and "The Hornet and the Peacock," continued in "Old Zip Coon," "Joe Bowers" and "When Johnny Comes Marching Home," and was still strong in the more recent "State of Arkansas" and "The Shoe-maker."

"Finnegan's Wake" (from which the title of James Joyce's famous novel was taken), a familiar vaudeville tune, was widely sung in this country after the 1860's, and is still recalled by some old-timers.

The '10's and '20's

[MODERN BLUES, WANDERING SONGS]

Got nowhar to lay my weary head,
Oh my babe, got nowhar to lay my weary
head.

ABOUT 1910, a new and original type of American song was introduced in New York's Tin Pan Alley: the Blues. Whether it was because the new style corresponded to the need of the moment or because it provided a naïve but simple and direct personal expression in song, the Blues spread rapidly throughout the country. In the troubled years immediately following the first World War, the Blues style was taken abroad, where it immediately proved to be as infectious as in this country.

Soon people were singing the Blues in Paris, London, Rome, Calcutta and Tokyo. In a half dozen different countries, internationally known composers, among them Honegger, Ravel and Stravinsky, eagerly wrote pieces in which they tried to catch the spirit of "Le Blues." In the past half century the blues style has become so much of an international institution, so vital to music publishers, band leaders, record and movie directors that we are likely to forgot how it all began and why.

When asked about the origin of the Blues some years ago, W. C. Handy, acknowledged "grandfather of the Blues," told Dorothy Scarborough:

"Most white people think that the Negro is always cheerful and lively, but he isn't, though he may seem that way when he is most troubled. The Negro knows the Blues as a state of mind, and that's why his music has that name.

"For instance, suppose I am a colored man, and my rent is due. It's twenty dollars, and my landlord has told me that if I don't pay him today he'll put me and my things out on the sidewalk. I haven't got the twenty dollars and I don't know where to get it. . . . I have scraped together ten dollars, but that's positively all I can get and that's not enough . . .

"Now when I know the time has come and I don't get that twenty dollars, what do I do? The white man would go to his landlord, offer him the ten, and maybe get the time extended. But what do I do? I go right out and blow that ten dollars I have and have a gay time. Anybody seeing me would think I was the jolliest darky in town, but it's just because I'm miserable and can't help myself.

"Now if the Negro were making a song about an experience like that, it would be a genuine specimen of Blues." *

Out of the miseries of the most despised class of Southern Negroes: nomadic laborers, street-corner gals, beggars, prisoners chain-gang-bound, came the first melancholy wail of the Blues. They were sung in Georgia, Mississippi, and Texas for at least ten or fifteen years before Handy first thought of writing them down. Said the celebrated Negro musician in 1925:

"Here's a thing called the 'Joe Turner Blues' . . . That is written around an old Negro song I used to hear and play thirty or more years ago. In some sections it was called 'Going Down the River for Long,' but in Tennessee it was always 'Joe Turner.' Joe Turner, the inspiration of the song, . . . was an officer and he used to come to Memphis and get prisoners to carry them to Nashville after a Kangaroo court. When the Negroes said of anyone, 'Joe Turner's been to town,' they

* Dorothy Scarborough: "On the Trail of Negro Folk Songs."

meant the person in question had been carried off handcuffed, to be gone no telling how long." *

Joe Turner had such wide currency all over the South that it has even been suggested that all the early Blues were sung to its tune, with the words being changed to fit the particular mood or situation of the person singing. The characteristic three-line form of the Blues was so simple that it was ideally suited to the constant addition or improvisation of new lyrics, one line being sung twice and then a third added to top them off:

Come wid his fo'ty links of chain— Oh Lawdy!
Come wid his fo'ty links of chain— Oh Lawdy!
Got my man, an' gone.

Thus the same tune—or at least the same musical pattern—could be used for the expression of any one of a dozen different emotions. The fact that the Blues were popularized and are still performed on the radio mainly by deep-throated female "hot" singers has led to the mistaken notion that they are always a woman's cry of longing for her "man." But, as Sterling Brown has pointed out, their subject matter is much broader than this, for there are Blues bemoaning "tornadoes, high water, hard times in farming, or insisting upon the need for travelling, for leaving this cold-hearted town. As well as self-pity, there is stoicism in the Blues." † Sarcastic indifference is not infrequently found, as in the following:

What you gwine to do when dey buhn de bar'l-house down?
What you gwine to do when dey buhn de bar'l-house down?
Gwine move out de piano, an' bar'l-house on de groun'.

When Handy, in 1912, published the first of his famous series, the "Memphis Blues" (which he had written three years before to help win the Memphis mayoralty election for one Mr. Crump) and sold it to a New York publisher for $100, it was the beginning of a

new epoch for Tin Pan Alley. Blues were soon being written by the dozen, and recording companies, recognizing the potent appeal of the new type, began to send apparatus throughout the South to record folk Blues directly from the performance of illiterate rural Negro singers. Not only Memphis and St. Louis, but almost every state in the South and dozens of small towns had their special Blues, as the following list suggests:

Alabama Blues, Mississippi Blues, Lou'siana Low-down Blues, Virginia Blues, New Orleans Hop Scop Blues, Hampton Roads Blues, Shreveport Wiggle, Waco, Texas Blues, Georgia Hunch, New Orleans Wiggle, Selma Bama Blues,* and many others.

For the first time in history, perhaps, a folk style penetrated within a short time of its creation to the sophisticated centers of musical distribution, and was made known throughout the nation to a larger public than would ever have been possible through diffusion by normal methods. Such are the wonders of modern large-scale distribution.

The Blues, however, did not emerge unscathed from this process. The change in environment from the barrel-house, the prison cell, the riverside shack, whence the mournful songs had originally sprung, to the dance floors of elegant hotels or swanky metropolitan night clubs via the studio-suites of Broadway's highest paid arrangers produced a similar change in the physiognomy of the music itself. From the uncouth, rough-throated laments of a simple and unhappy people, they were turned into a languid, sophisticated, elegant entertainment and dance music, as silken as the gowns of the debutantes who danced to its strains on the roof-gardens of expensive hotels. The whole of the former controversy among the advocates of "hot" and "sweet" jazz hinged on the basic change that arose when the primitive folk blues got into the hands of the Tin Pan Alley arrangers. Working on salary for a market, they were more interested in turning out a slick, commercial product with a taste of "blue" quality, but

---

* Scarborough: *Op. cit.*
† Sterling Brown: "Negro Poetry and Drama."

* We are indebted for this list to Odum and Johnson's "Negro Workaday Songs."

shorn of all the roughness that might possibly irritate the ears of paying customers.

Although they both go by the same name, the primitive Blues and the sophisticated commercial product are two quite different kinds of music. As Abbe Niles has pointed out, the original Blues "were woven of the same stuff as . . . the work-songs, love songs, devil songs, the over-and-overs, slow drags, pats and stomps; yes, and decidedly the spirituals." * Winthrop Sargent in his "Jazz: Hot and Hybrid" has shown the essential identity between the musical style of the Negro rural congregations which produced the semi-barbaric "shoutin' spirituals" and that of authentic Blues singers like the late Bessie Smith. Common to both are the characteristic "Blue" intonations, the tendency to "worry" the third and seventh steps of the scale, the alternation between major and minor, the complete rhythmic freedom, the constant renewal of melodic and rhythmic patterns through invention and improvisation.

All these features were turned to account by Negro instrumentalists who played jazz first in the dives of Memphis, New Orleans, and other Southern towns and then in the hotels and night clubs of metropolitan centers. When combined with a high development of instrumental virtuosity by both Negro and white performers, they led to the style that deveolped in the 1930's as "swing." In addition to forming the basis of this "hot" style, the Blues, when played as a slow juicy melody over a throbbing, pulsating background, harmonized by arrangers brought up on Puccini, Rimsky-Korsakov and Debussy, entered into that "sweet" style that became an important segment of our popular music of the time.

In becoming a part of popular entertainment, the Blues acquired many traits of white European musical style not present in the primitive Negro variety. But even the folk variety itself was taken over and widely sung by rural white singers as well. Such are the Blues, "Chilly Winds," "Hungry Ragged Blues," and "Every Night When the Sun Goes In," reorded from the singing of white folk singers in the mountains, many of whom claimed to have composed the Blues themselves. Some of these do have a characteristic mountain quality, while still bearing traces of Negro origin. Thus we see how true music is no respecter of artificial boundaries, but can form a link of sympathy among all down-to-earth Americans.

Although we have discussed them at length, Blues and Jazz were not the only musical developments of the first decades of this century. There were others that reflected the dramatic events of the World War—the hundreds of popular songs ranging from "I Didn't Raise My Boy to Be a Soldier," "Joan of Arc," "Roses of Picardy," "Hello Central, Give Me No Man's Land," to more home-grown songs of the doughboys, such as "Hinky Dinky" with its thousand and one verses that recorded every phase— including the unprintable—of Mr. John Q. American's experience "Over There." There were the songs of wandering hoboes and of the "wild boys" who rode the rods and camped in Hoovervilles looking for work. There were songs of the fat years and the lean, of riding on top of the world and of selling apples. This was the record of the comedy and tragedy, the joy, the hope, the human story of a growing, struggling, forward-moving America.

E. S.

---

* Abbe Niles: Introduction to Handy "Blues."

E. S.

THE BLUES AIN' NOTHIN'

Arrangement by Elie Siegmeister

2

Ah'm goin' down on de levee,
Goin' to take mahself a rockin' chair.
If mah lovin' man don' come,
Ah'll rock away from there.

CHORUS: 'Cause de, etc.

Why did you leave me blue?
Why did you leave me blue?
All ah do is sit
An' cry fo' you,

CHORUS: 'Cause de, etc.

DE BLUES AIN' NOTHIN'

MANY DISSERTATIONS have been written on the origin and meaning of folk-song in general, jazz and the blues in particular. But perhaps the simplest and best explanation is that "De blues ain' nothin' but a good man feelin' blue."

This one was sung at an early date in honky-tonks in the Southwest.

JOE TURNER BLUES

Arrangement by Elie Siegmeister

Dey tell me Joe Turn-er's come and gone _____ Dey
tell me Joe Turn-er's come and gone _____
Got my man an' gone. _____

2

Dey tell me Joe Turner he done come
Dey tell me Joe Turner he done come
Come with fohty links of chain.

Joe Turney, brother of Pete Turney, who was Governor of Tennessee between 1892 and 1896, was in charge of bringing prisoners from Memphis to the Nashville penitentiary. His name (pronounced "Turner" by the Negroes) would bring the blue-est feelings to the sweethearts, mothers, wives of those he came after.

Abbe Niles tells us that "Joe Turner" was known throughout the South before there was any widespread singing of the folk-blues, and that it was sung to different words in various places. In Henderson, Kentucky, it was "Gwine down de river 'fo long." Down in Texas, strangely, it was "Michigan water tastes like sherry wine"; in the Sea Island cotton section of Georgia it was "Gwine down dat long, lonesome road."

"Joe Turner" has been called the grandfather of the Blues.

GAMBLER'S BLUES

[ST. JAMES INFIRMARY BLUES]

Arrangement by Elie Siegmeister

2

On my left stood Joe McKenny,
His eyes bloodshot and red,
He gazed at the crowd around him
And these were the words he said:

3

"As I passed by the old infirmary,
I saw my sweetheart there,
All stretched out on a table,
So pale, so cold, so fair.

4

Went up to see the doctor,
'She's very low,' he said;
Went back to see my woman,
Good God! She's layin' there dead,
Spoken: She's dead!

5

Sixteen coal-black horses,
All hitched to a rubber-tired hack,
Carried seven girls to the graveyard,
And only six of 'em comin' back.

6

O, when I die, just bury me
In a box-back coat and hat,
Put a twenty dollar gold piece on my watch chain
To let the Lord know I'm standing pat.

7

Six crap shooters as pall bearers,
Let a chorus girl sing me a song
With a jazz band on my hearse
To raise hell as we go along.

8

And now you've heard my story,
I'll take another shot of booze;
If anybody happens to ask you,
Then I've got those gambler's blues."

THE GAMBLER'S BLUES
[ST. JAMES INFIRMARY BLUES]

THE MILLIONAIRE GANGSTERS of the roaring twenties found that it was safe to exhibit their wealth only after they were dead. In Chicago, silver coffins were the sign of elegance among the racketeers' elite.

This classic blues starts with drink and a broken heart, and winds up in a grandiose finale. The gambler's vision of his resplendent funeral with its sixteen coal-black horses, its crap-shooting pall-bearers, its hell-raising jazz band, could serve as a model for short-futured gunmen.

PO' BOY

Arrangement by Elie Siegmeister

As I sat down— t' play a game o' coon can, I could— not play— my han'.———— I got to think-in' a - bout— the wo-man I love,— She run a - way— with an - oth - er man.— Run a - way with an - oth - er man,— po' boy, Run a - way with an

oth - er man._____ I got to think-in' a-bout__ the

wo-man I love,__ She run a-way__ with an-oth-er man, po' boy!

(Spoken)

As I went down to the big depot,
The train came a-rumblin' by.
I looked in the window, saw the woman I loved,
And I hung my head and cried.

I hung my head and cried, po' boy,
I hung my head and cried.
I looked in the window, saw the woman I loved,
And I hung my head and cried.

3

I jumped right on the train platform,
I walked right down the aisle.
I pulled out my forty-some odd
And I shot that dark-skinned child.

I shot that dark-skinned child, po' boy,
I shot that dark-skinned child.
I pulled out my forty-some odd
And I shot that dark-skinned child.

They took me down to the big court house;
The judge he looked at me.
I said, "Oh, kind-hearted Judge,
What am it gwine to be?"

What am it gwine to be, po' boy,
What am it gwine to be?
I say, "Oh, kind-hearted Judge,
What am it gwine to be?"

5

The judge he heard the contract read,
The clerk, he took it down.
They handed me over to the contractor,
And now I'm penitentiary-bound.

And now I'm penitentiary-bound, po' boy,
And now I'm penitentiary-bound.
They handed me over to the contractor,
And now I'm penitentiary-bound.

6

The night was cold and stormy,
It sho' did look like rain.
I ain't got a friend in the whole wide world,
Nobody knows my name.

Nobody knows my name, po' boy,
Nobody knows my name.
I ain't got a friend in the whole wide world,
Nobody knows my name.

CHILLY WINDS

Arrangement by Elie Siegmeister

2

O make me a pallet on the floor, darlin' baby,
O make me a pallet on the floor, darlin' babe,
An' I'm goin' to my dark lonesome home.

3

O who'll hoe your corn when I'm gone, darlin' baby,
O who'll hoe your corn when I'm gone, darlin' babe,
An' I'm goin' to my dark lonesome home.

4

I'm goin' if I have to ride a rail, darlin' baby,
I'm goin' if I have to ride a rail, darlin' babe,
An' I'm goin' to my dark lonesome home.

* Symbols in italics for guitar with capo across 1st fret

EVERY NIGHT WHEN THE SUN GOES IN

Arrangement by Elie Siegmeister

Ev-ery night —— when the sun goes in, —— Ev-ery
night when the sun goes in, —— Ev-ery night when the sun goes
in, I hang down my head and mourn-ful cry.

True love, don't weep, true —— love, don't mourn, True love, don't
weep, true —— love, don't mourn, True love, don't weep nor —— mourn for
me, —— I'm go-in' a-way to Mar-ble-town.

2
I wish to the Lord that train would come
I wish to the Lord that train would come
I wish to the Lord that train would come
To take me back where I come from.

3
It's once my apron hung down low,
It's once my apron hung down low,
It's once my apron hung down low,
He'd follow me through both sleet and snow.

4
It's now my apron's to my chin
It's now my apron's to my chin
It's now my apron's to my chin
He'll face my door and won't come in.

From Cecil Sharp's English Folksongs of the Southern Appalachians, published by Oxford University Press.
by Permission of Oxford University Press

HALLELUJAH, I'M A BUM

Arrangement by Elie Siegmeister

Oh, I love my boss and my boss loves me,
And that is the reason that I'm so hungry.

CHORUS: Hallelujah, I'm a bum, etc.

3

Oh, springtime has come; I'm just out of jail,
Without any money, without any bail.

CHORUS: Hallelujah, I'm a bum, etc.

4

I went to a house and I knocked on the door;
A lady came out, says, "You've been here before."

CHORUS: Hallelujah, I'm a bum, etc.

5

I went to a house and I asked for some bread;
A lady came out, says, "The baker is dead."

CHORUS: Hallelujah, I'm a bum, etc.

6

When springtime does come, oh, won't we have fun
We'll throw up our jobs and we'll go on the bum.

CHORUS: Hallelujah, I'm a bum, etc.

HALLELUJAH, I'M A BUM

HARVEST HANDS who followed the sun and the crops around the seasons often found themselves "riding the rods" and wondering where the next job was going to turn up. Also their minds often centered around that engaging question: when does the next meal come along? This song was a familiar one, sung outside the doors of Salvation Army missions for many years.

THE PREACHER AND THE SLAVE

Tune of "In the Sweet Bye and Bye"
Arrangement by Elie Siegmeister

MODERATELY LIVELY

Long-haired preach - ers come out ev' - ry night; And they tell you what's wrong and what's right; But when asked a - bout some - thing to eat They will an - swer with voi - ces so sweet:

Chorus

You will eat by and by In that glor - ious land be - yond the sky Work and pray, live on hay; You'll get pie in the sky when you die.

2

If you fight hard for children and wife,
Try to get something good in this life
You're a sinner and bad man, they tell;
When you die you will sure go to hell.
CHORUS: You will eat, *etc.*

3

Workingmen of all countries, unite!
Side by side we for freedom will fight.
When the world and its wealth we have gained,
To the grafters we'll sing this refrain:
CHORUS: You will eat by and by,
When you've learned how to cook and to fry.
Chop some wood, 'twill do you good,
And you'll eat in the sweet by and by.

THE PREACHER AND THE SLAVE

WHEN JOE HILL was executed in Utah in 1915, men on the road, in
jungles, in jails, and in union halls from California to Alabama to Massachusetts mourned his passing, for his songs were known and sung far
and wide. On the eve of his death, he wrote:

My will is easy to decide,
For there is nothing to divide.

HINKY DINKY

Arrangement by Elie Siegmeister

Oh far - mer have you a daught - er fair, par - lay - voo,__ Oh far - mer have you a daught - er fair, par - lay - voo,__ Oh far - mer have you a daught - er fair Who can wash a sold - ier's un - der - wear? Hin - ky din - ky par - lay - voo.__

2

2

Mademoiselle from Armentières, parlay-voo,
Mademoiselle from Armentières, parlay-voo,
Mademoiselle from Armentières,
She never heard of underwear.
Hinky dinky parlay-voo.

3

The captain's carrying the pack, parlay-voo,
The captain's carrying the pack, parlay-voo,
The captain's carrying the pack
I hope to God it breaks his back.
Hinky dinky parlay-voo.

4

The officers get all the steak, parlay-voo,
The officers get all the steak, parlay-voo,
The officers get all the steak
And all we get is a belly-ache.
Hinky dinky parlay-voo.

5

One night I had "beaucoup" jack, parlay-voo,
One night I had "beaucoup" jack, parlay-voo,
One night I had "beaucoup" jack
Till a Mademoiselle got on my track.
Hinky dinky parlay-voo.

6

The M.P.'s say they won the war, parlay-voo,
The M.P.'s say they won the war, parlay-voo,
The M.P.'s say they won the war
Standing guard at a cafe door.
Hinky dinky parlay-voo.

7

The general got the croix-de-guerre, parlay-voo,
The general got the croix-de-guerre, parlay-voo,
The general got the croix-de-guerre
The son-of-a-gun never was there.
Hinky dinky parlay-voo.

8

The generals stayed behind the line, parlay-voo,
The generals stayed behind the line, parlay-voo,
The generals stayed behind the line
With plenty of women and plenty of wine.
Hinky dinky parlay-voo.

9

From gay Paree we heard guns roar, parlay-voo,
From gay Paree we heard guns roar, parlay-voo,
From gay Paree we heard guns roar,
But all that we learned was "Je t'adore."
Hinky dinky parlay-voo.

10

They say it is a terrible war, parlay-voo,
They say it is a terrible war, parlay-voo,
They say it is a terrible war
But what the hell are we fighting it for?
Hinky dinky parlay-voo.

HINKY DINKY

THE FAVORITE of the first A.E.F. has many verses which are printable,
and many more—alas—which are not!

AH'M BROKE AN' HUNGRY

Words and music by Lawrence Gellert
Arrangement by Elie Siegmeister

AH'M BROKE AN' HUNGRY

THIS NEGRO wandering song, gathered in the deep South, has an elemental directness. It says much with few words. The tune is remarkable for its drifting, shifting quality.

Broadway to Route 66

[SONGS OF THE '30's AND '40's]

AFTER MORE than two hundred years of development, American song is still in the making. Unlike the popular and folk songs of certain other lands whose creative well-springs seem to have gone dry, our songs have come up abundantly as cucumbers in rich soil. This recent music was not full of yearning for the archaic, the faraway, the unobtainable; instead, it reflected daily life: not only the America of romance, day-dreams, boy-meets-girl, but also the land of railroads, airplanes, great roads and dams, dust bowls, people on the move. From Broadway to Route 66 (the road on which the Joads travelled to the Promised Land) a nation kept on singing, singing songs bitter and sweet, lovely and harsh—but singing.

With the triumph of the T.V. and the sound film, the distinction between the music of the city and the country has grown smaller. The old traditions of native country music have been drowned out by the roar of the loud speaker. The music of Broadway and Hollywood has penetrated to the lonely mountain valley, to the horseman on the plains, to the lumberjack deep in the woods. The handiwork of the obscure Negro in the South comes back to him, modified, clothed in elegant costume, amplified a thousandfold.

Jazz and rock, which are so much part of our daily lives that we eat, breathe, work, and go to sleep with them, have many faces. To some critics, they are our country's most distinctive contributions to music; to others an irritation and a bore; to millions of teenagers, an ecstatic ritual; to certain publishers and record companies, the life blood of the music business.

As in earlier decades, American song continued to flourish in the 1930's and 40's in two fruitful areas: city, or theater songs, and country, or folk songs. The period spanning the Great Depression and World War II saw the concern for the "common man" reach its height. Like their fellow artists in other fields—John Steinbeck, Carl Sandburg, and William Faulkner in literature, and Edward Hopper, Reginald Marsh, and Marsden Hartley in painting—the creators of Broadway's musical shows turned to the common people of America as inspiration for some of their finest shows, from which some of the greatest songs emerged.

Many of these reflected a synthesis of three great strands of our music: the popular, the folk, the jazz. A few years before 1930, Jerome Kern started the trend on a high level, with "Can't Help Lovin' That Man" and "Old Man River", from "Show Boat." George Gershwin brought it to a classic high point with "Summertime," "It Ain't Necessarily So," and "Bess You Is My Woman Now," from his magnificient "Porgy and Bess." Burton Lane, Harold Arlen, and Richard Rodgers made distinctive contributions in their songs "How Are Things in Glocca Morra," "The River and Me," and "Oh What A Beautiful Morning" from their respective musicals "Finian's Rainbow," "Bloomer Girl," and "Oklahoma." Marc Blitzstein's "Nickel Under Your Foot" from "The Cradle Will Rock" and Frank Loesser's title song from "Guys and Dolls" celebrated the raffish music of the city streets. All these formed a great literature of American theater song at its height during the FDR period.

While Hollywood, the T.V. and Broadway have overshadowed the unsophisticated rural music of this country, this music by no means vanished. Far from New York, in the sand-dunes of Florida, the coal country of Harlan, Ky., in the dust-bowl of Oklahoma, the traditions of "ballad-makin' " were alive vigorous as ever. Not as pretty, not as sweet, not as flashy as that of Hollywood; no tricky orchestrations, no raspy "belters," no musical stunts. But the body and bone of America were still there. The voice of the mountain still sharp and angular, the spiritual still full-throated, the prairie lullaby soft and tender. And news: of storms, tornadoes, big things coming up; highways, dams, the TVA; escapes from the chain gang; migrations from the dusty country. A people on the move, a march of the Israelites out of Egypt on Route 66. We read of it in Steinbeck's book, saw it in John Ford's movie; and we heard it from the guitar of the "dustiest of the dust-bowlers," Woody Guthrie. Another rusty-voiced Homer, he sang the story of the "Grapes of Wrath" because "the Okies back there haven't got two bucks to buy the book, or even thirty-five cents to see the movie, but the song will get back to them and tell them what Preacher Casey said."

And today, in the new ballads of freedom, in the songs of struggle, defiance and hope, the voice of our people is still heard. Right out of the farms and factories, out of the heart of America it comes, to remind us.

*Our country's strong, our country's young,
And her greatest songs are still unsung.**

* John La Touche in the "Ballad for Americans."

E. S.

UPON DE MOUNTAIN

Arrangement by Elie Siegmeister

A poignant, moving narrative, from the Georgia hills. Guaranteed to "get" you as you sing it over and over again.

SISTERN AND BRETHREN

Arrangement by Elie Siegmeister

SLOWLY, MAJESTICALLY

Sis - tern and breth-ren, stop fool - in' wid pray, Sis - tern and breth - ren, stop fool - in' wid pray, When black face is lift - ed, Lawd turn - in' way.

2
Heart filled wid sadness, head bowed down wid woe,
Heart filled wid sadness, head bowed down wid woe,
In his hour of trouble, where's a black man to go?

3
We're buryin' a brudder dey kill for de crime,
We're buryin' a brudder dey kill for de crime,
Tryin' to keep what was his all de time.

4
When we's tucked him on under what you goin' to do?
When we's tucked him on under what you goin' to do?
Wait till dey arousin' fo' you?

5
Yo head 'taint no apple fo' danglin' from a tree,
Yo head 'taint no apple fo' danglin' from a tree,
Yo' body no carcass fo' barbecuin' on a spree!

SISTERN AND BRETHREN

WALLINGFORD RIEGGER felt that this song "may, in time, take a place
beside "Go Down, Moses." Be that as it may, it is evidence of the fact
that the South is still producing noble and heart-stirring folk music.

393

KU KLUCK KLAN

Words and music by Lawrence Gellert
Arrangement by Elie Siegmeister

MODERATELY LIVELY

It say in de Bi-ble How Lawd he make man, But
Poor man ain' got 'em No blank-ets or rugs; Git

who in de Hell make Ku Kluck Klan? Shaped like a tad-pole,
thank-in' de Lawd he all cov-er wit bugs. But six - foot shoot-er

Smell like a skunk Hide in mid-night sheet Like chintz in a bunk.
Rid in hoss - back Don't wan' him____ a - com-in' 'Roun' mah shack.

Chorus

Ku Kluck Klan,____ Ku Kluck Klan,____ Low-est down creep - er in de lan'.

KU KLUCK KLAN

Some folks may be impressed by the hooded knights who "hide in midnight sheet like chintz in a bunk," but not the Southern share-cropper who sang this song in his tumble-down shack.

From the collection of Lawrence Gellert's Negro Songs of Protest. By permission of Lawrence Gellert.

* Symbols in italics for guitar with capo across 3rd fret

THE T. V. A.

Arrangement by Elie Siegmeister

LIVELY

My name is Wil - liam Ed - wards, I live down Cove Creek way, I'm work ing on a proj ect they call the T. V. A. The bless the T. V. A.

2

The Government began it when I was but a child,
But now they are in earnest and Tennessee's gone wild.

3

Just see them boys a-comin', their tool kits on their arm;
They come from Clinch and Holston, and many a valley farm.

4

All up and down the valley they heard the glad alarm,
"The Government means business"—it's working like a charm.

5

Oh, see them boys a - comin'—their Government they trust;
Just hear their hammers ringin'—they'll build that dam or bust.

6

I meant to marry Sally, but work I could not find;
The T. V. A. was started and surely eased my mind.

7

I'm writing her a letter, these words I'll surely say:
"The Government has saved us, just name our wedding day."

8

We'll build a little cabin, on Cove Creek near her home;
We'll settle down forever and never care to roam.

9

For things are surely movin' down here in Tennessee;
Good times for all the valley, for Sally and for me.

10

Oh, things looked blue and lonely until this come along;
Now hear the crew a-singin' and listen to their song.

11

"The Government employs us, short hours and certain pay;
Oh, things are up and comin', God bless the T.V.A."

THE T. V. A.

ANYTHING NEW, anything big, anything exciting is apt material for
"ballad-makin' ": a fire, a murder, a war, a dam. As this song indicates,
the great construction project brought many a changed outlook on life
to folks "down Cove Creek way."

From Ballad Makin' in the Mountains of Kentucky by Jean Thomas, published by Henry Holt and Company, Inc. Printed by permission. Music arranged for publication by Walter Kob.

I'M GOIN' DOWN THIS ROAD FEELIN BAD

Arrangement by Elie Siegmeister

MODERATELY EASILY

I'm a-goin' down this road feel-in' bad, _____ I'm a-goin' down this road feel-in' bad, _____ I'm a-goin' down this road feel-in' bad, yes Lord-y, And _____ I ain't gon-na be treat-ed this ____ a-way. _____

Yes, they fed me on cornbread and beans,
Yes, they fed me on cornbread and beans,
They fed me on cornbread and beans, yes Lordy,
And I ain't a-gonna be treated this a-way.

3

Got me way down in jail on my knees,
Got me way down in jail on my knees,
Got me way down in jail on my knees, yes Lordy,
And I ain't a-gonna be treated this a-way.

4

Takes a ten dollah shoe to fit my feet,
Takes a ten dollah shoe to fit my feet,
Takes a ten dollah shoe to fit my feet, yes Lordy,
And I ain't a-gonna be treated this a-way.

5

I'm a-goin' down where the climate suits my clothes,
I'm a-goin' down where the climate suits my clothes,
I'm a-goin' down where the climate suits my clothes,
And I ain't a-gonna be treated this a-way.

I'M GOIN' DOWN THIS ROAD FEELIN' BAD

WOODY GUTHRIE, one of the many Okie balladeers who sang this song, told us: "I don't know nothing about music. Never could read or write it. But somehow or other, when the black old dust hit our country, I was among the first to blow. When it cleared off again, I woke up with a guitar in one hand and a road map in the other one. Went as far as the map said, and the cops said it was California."

A song that was well-known along U.S. Route 66, it was sung by the character, Eddie, in the motion picture of "Grapes of Wrath."

Guthrie toured the entire country making up and singing songs such as this, in union halls, hotels and meeting halls.

TOM JOAD

Words by Woody Guthrie
Arrangement by Elie Siegmeister

2

Tom Joad he caught a truck-driving man
And there he caught him a ride;
He said, "I just got out of McAlester Pen
On a charge called 'Homicide'—poor boy,
On a charge called 'Homicide.' "

3

That truck rolled away in a big cloud of dust,
Tommy turned his face toward home,
He met Preacher Casey and they had a little drink
But he found that his family they had gone, Tom
He found that his family they had gone.

4

He found his mother's old fashioned shoe,
He found his daddy's hat,
He found little Muley, and little Muley said,
"They been tractored out by Cats, Tom,
They been tractored out by Cats."

5

Tom Joad went down to the Neighbor's farm,
There he found his Family;
They packed their duds, and loaded in a car,
His mother said, "We got to git away, Tom,"
His mother said, "We got to git away."

6

The twelve of the Joads made a mighty heavy load,
And Grandpa Joad did cry,
As he took up a handful of land in his hand,
Said, "I'm stickin' with the farm till I die!
I'm stickin' with the farm till I die."

7

They fed him shortribs, coffee, and soothing syrup,
And Grandpa Joad did die—
They buried Grandpa Joad by the side of the road;
Grandma on the California side,
Grandma on the California side.

8

They stood on a mountain and they looked toward the West
And it looked like the Promised Land,
A bright green valley with a river running through,
There was work for every single hand, they thought,
There was work for every single hand.

9

The Joads rolled into a Jungle Camp,
And there Ma cooked a stew,
And the hungry little kids of the Jungle Camp
Said, "We'd like to have some, too, Miss,
We'd like to have some, too."

A Deputy Sheriff cut loose at a man,
He shot a woman in the back;
Before he could take his aim again,
It was Preacher Casey dropped him in his tracks, Boy,
Preacher Casey dropped him in his tracks.

They handcuffed Casey and they took him to jail,
And then he got away,
He met Tom Joad by the old River Bridge,
And these few words he did say, Preacher Casey,
It was these few words he did say:

12

"Well, I preached for the Lord for a mighty long time,
I preached about the rich and the poor;
Us workin' folks has got to get together,
'Cause we ain't got a chance anymore, Boys,
We ain't got a chance anymore."

13

The Deputies come, and Tom and Casey run
To a place where the water run down;
There a Vigilante thug hit Casey with a club,
And he laid Preacher Casey on the ground, Boy,
He laid Preacher Casey on the ground.

14

Tom Joad he grabbed that Deputy's club,
He brought it down on his head,
Tom Joad took flight in that dark, rainy night,
A Deputy and a Preacher layin' dead, two men,
A Deputy and a Preacher layin' dead.

15

Tom Joad ran back to where his Mother was asleep,
He woke her up out of bed,
He kissed "goodbye" to the mother that he loved,
And he said what Preacher Casey said, Tom Joad,
He said what Preacher Casey said:

16

"Everybody must be just One Big Soul
It looks that way to me;
Wherever you look in the day or night,
That's where I'm a-goin' to be, Ma,
That's where I'm goin' to be.

17

Wherever Little Children are hungry and cry,
Wherever people ain't free—
Wherever men are a-fightin' for their rights,
That's where I'm a-goin' to be, Ma,
That's where I'm a-goin' to be."

TOM JOAD

FEW COULD TELL the story of "Grapes of Wrath" more compactly and
with greater force than the simple ballad, "Tom Joad" by Woody
Guthrie.

A NEW WIND A-BLOWIN'

Words by Langston Hughes
Music by Elie Siegmeister

* Symbols in italics for guitar with capo across 1st fret

402

THE TRADITION of ballad-making, singing of real things as they are actually happening, is still part of our land and people. While reading proof on the second edition, I received some lines from Langston Hughes—lines which seemed to sum up the feelings of most Americans during World War II. What law says that you cannot compose a ballad even while reading proof? So that people might sing of our struggle, of the freedom we have, and the greater freedom to come, I made the Negro poet's words into this ballad for the time.   E. S.

About the authors...

Elie Siegmeister

Elie Siegmeister is one of America's foremost composers, whose music is known throughout the world. His thirty-five orchestral works have been performed by leading orchestras and conductors and his operas have been presented in both the United States and abroad. He has composed music for Broadway, Hollywood film, and the ballet in addition to numerous works for the concert hall.

This versatile man is a widely-known author, conductor, educator and pioneer in the American folk music renaissance. In 1939, he founded the American Ballad Singers, with whom he toured the United States for many years, bringing the treasures of our folk-song heritage to national attention.

Born in 1909, he studied at Columbia University, with Nadia Boulanger in Paris, and at Juilliard Graduate School. Mr. Siegmeister joined the faculty at Hofstra in 1949, later to become the composer-in-residence, and, finally, Professor Emeritus in 1976. The recipient of numerous awards, he is also a founder of the American Composers Alliance, the Kennedy Center's National Black Music Competition, and he is a member of the Board of Directors of ASCAP.

He has several published books in addition to A TREASURY OF AMERICAN SONG, including the richly endowed collection of essays, THE NEW MUSIC LOVER'S HANDBOOK (newly revised edition, 1986).

About the authors...

Olin Downes

Olin Downes (1886-1955) was renowned as the music critic of the New York Times for thirty-two years. After his early musical training, at the age of twenty, he began his career as a critic on the Boston Globe, where he remained for eighteen years. Called to the New York Times in 1924, he soon established himself as a diligent music critic with eclectic tastes, lucid style and firm, incisive judgment.

Over the years, he was a popular lecturer at Chautauqua, the Berkshire Festival, the Brooklyn Academy of Music, and Boston and Harvard Universities. He also was a commentator for Sunday broadcasts of the New York Philharmonic Symphony Orchestra. The author of many articles, he contributed to a wide variety of magazines, both popular and technical.

Downes' keen interest in folk music made him an ideal collaborator on this renowned collection. He was "...refreshed and impressed anew with the richness of this stuff (folk music) and its endless potentialities for development."

In addition to A TREASURY OF AMERICAN SONG, his published works include: THE LURE OF MUSIC (1918), SYMPHONIC MASTERPIECES (1935), and SONGS OF RUSSIA (edited).

Index